D0712231

LONELY AT THE TOP

THE HIGH COST OF MEN'S SUCCESS

THOMAS JOINER

palgrave
macmillan

To the Order of Saint Walpurga

LONELY AT THE TOP
Copyright © Thomas Joiner, 2011
All rights reserved.

First published in 2011 by PALGRAVE MACMILLAN® in the United
States—a division of St. Martin's Press LLC, 175 Fifth Avenue, New York,
NY 10010.

Where this book is distributed in the United Kingdom, Europe, and the
rest of the world, this is by Palgrave Macmillan, a division of Macmillan
Publishers Limited, registered in England, company number 785998, of
Houndmills, Basingstoke, Hampshire RG21 6XS.

Palgrave Macmillan is the global academic imprint of the above companies
and has companies and representatives throughout the world.

Palgrave® and Macmillan® are registered trademarks in the United States,
the United Kingdom, Europe and other countries.

ISBN: 978-0-230-10443-3

Library of Congress Cataloging-in-Publication Data

Joiner, Thomas E.
    Lonely at the top : the high cost of men's success / Thomas Joiner.
        p.   cm.
    Includes bibliographical references and index.
    ISBN 978-0-230-10443-3 (hardback)
    1. Success—Psychological aspects.   2. Depression, Mental—Social
aspects.   3. Masculinity—Social aspects.   I. Title.
BF637.S8J624   2011
155.3'32—dc22

                                                        2011009532

A catalogue record of the book is available from the British Library.

Design by Letra Libre

First edition: November 2011

10 9 8 7 6 5 4 3 2 1

Printed in the United States of America.

CONTENTS

ACKNOWLEDGMENTS

I am tempted to note the good luck that I have a lot of friends—from my Atlanta childhood, to Walpurgians, to FSU Psychology, and beyond—but, as I assert in this book, it is not luck. On the contrary, it is active work—work that I relish, am grateful for, and find vitally sustaining.

Speaking of work and gratitude, FSU Psychology is a juggernaut with which I am very proud to be associated. Should you find the claim of "juggernaut" dubious, check the data, by which I do not mean the ditzy reputational rankings of various magazines, but rather, the numbers on grants, citations, and publications assembled by the National Research Council. A major reason for this success is our remarkable group of PhD students, past and present, among whom mine are, as of this writing, Timmons, Anestis, Bender, Selby, Fink, Smith, Ribeiro, Bodell, Hames, and Silva, and this is not to mention the many PhD alumni of my group, nor (I hope) dozens of future students.

We have assembled an impressive group of professors at FSU Psychology, the breadth and depth of whose work serve as a daily inspiration to me. The ideas in this book benefited in particular from the work and thought of Roy Baumeister, who at work is just across the hall, and who at home is just down the street.

My wife, Graciela, and my sons, Malachi and Zekey, not only appear in these pages, but they give me continued reasons to strive even as they keep me connected.

I am grateful to Jen Hames for diligent editorial assistance. Agent Anna Ghosh's insight and ideas substantially improved this book, as did editor Luba Ostashevsky's thoughtful guidance.

SECTION I

THE PROBLEM

1

THE LONELY SEX

HAVING NO ONE STARTS OUT
AS HAVING EVERYTHING

As the October sun rose in the Oakland-Berkeley Hills in 1991, the firemen were vigilant, as ever, but they felt confident that they had the previous day's blaze under good control. Nevertheless, they understood well that seemingly dormant fires can roar back to life, particularly under conditions of high winds, high temperatures, and active hotspots. As the firemen tended hotspots and sweated into their gear in temperatures in the nineties, the wind swirled. A single glowing ember took flight on the wind and drifted innocently enough outside the original fire zone. The ember floated along and landed in a tree.

Within seconds, the scene turned chaotic and lethal. The tree exploded into flames that spread rapidly; the resulting fire was out of control, and the firemen's task changed from fighting the original fire's dwindling hotspots to fighting for their own survival. Twenty-five people would lose their lives in the fire, including a firefighter and a police officer.

Others, too, experienced the dramatic shift from everyday activities to a life-or-death battle. The fire's scope included homes within minutes; at its most ferocious, it was igniting one home every eleven seconds, forcing homeowners to flee for their lives. In the desperate few moments on their way out of their homes—homes they were unlikely to see again, homes that, in many cases, contained extremely valuable things like artwork, rare books, gold, and jewelry, not to mention stores of cash, and, in at least one case, the sole copy of an author's book in progress—these people were faced with choices. One choice can hardly even be called that: of course people saved—or at least attempted to save—loved ones and pets. But beyond each other and pets, what to salvage on the way out the door?

Few if any grabbed art or jewelry, but many people salvaged photographs, pictures of people they loved.

Were the story to end there, some would view it as sweet, others as trite; either way, a basic if incomplete truth is revealed: we need each other. We primates are gregarious, and embedded within our cells and souls is a pressing need to belong and connect. This happened in the hills above Oakland as people reached past jewelry and money to desperately latch onto photos of friends and family. Ending the story there would also produce a homily: gather others around you and you will flourish.

It is not quite so simple. If it were, there would not be millions and millions of lonely people; there would not be a million people worldwide who die every year by suicide; and there would be no need for this book.

Much of human nature can be understood in the context of the truth that we need each other. Much but not all. In the weeks and months following the fire in the hills above Oakland, the same people who had reflexively spurned material things in favor of mere images of those they loved turned on each other and no longer spurned material things.

In his 2000 book, *Almost Home,* David Kirp quotes one of the people whose home was destroyed: "Just when the fire experience is encouraging you to detach from worldly possessions, purify your intentions, and all that, the realpolitik of your insurance policy rises up to inflame pride, greed, guilt, and every other unenlightened emotion you can think of."[1] A major part of the homeowner's advice did not involve Zen: "Fight for your price."

In the fire's aftermath, very close-knit neighborhood groups developed to support and advocate for one another. But, as David Kirp stated, "Once in receipt of their insurance settlements, most residents stopped participating in the neighborhood associations. Some householders who had been leaders in their insurance groups cut their own backroom deals, agreeing not to reveal the terms of their settlement to anyone else in their own group."[2]

The book quoted another resident whose home was destroyed and then rebuilt. Referring to his new home, the resident said, "It was God who gave us a magnificent 360-degree view."[3] The logic implicit in this statement is that God decreed that the fire should occur, destroy many homes, injure dozens of people, and take the lives of twenty-five. The statement also omits the fact that the rebuilt house has window views engineered to angle upward, thus avoiding the view of the fire's aftermath and also of others' homes—a kind of purposeful isolation through architecture.

The fire in the hills above Oakland and Berkeley produced a desperate but also sweet moment, an encouraging pulling together over several weeks, and a dispiriting and drawn-out ordeal of greed, pettiness, and conflict thereafter. This provides a fuller picture of human nature than the image of the fleeing homeowners neglecting valuables in favor of pictures. They did do that, but they also turned on each other. This picture applies to people generally—to men and women alike. But in the struggle to contend with these conflicting aspects of human nature, and to form sustaining and satisfying bonds despite conflict, greed, and the like, one sex does relatively well, and the other is the lonely sex.

SQUARELY IN MY MID-FORTIES, I found myself just the other day flipping back and forth between TV channels alone; as I roamed around the channels, the one that advertises local houses for sale came up, and I wondered, should we get a bigger house? We can do it financially, why not? And then I asked myself why, and the reason scared and shamed me—a bigger house would allow more distance between me and my wife and sons (who, in my partial defense, were yelling right outside the door). My thought was to use money to buy more distance between me and my own flesh and blood.

Such thoughts did not plague my youth. Boys are not much lonelier than girls; men are a lot lonelier than women.

The purpose of this book is to explain this fundamental truth, to explore why and how men do not start out as, but increasingly become, the lonely sex; to show why and how men become lonely with age; to draw out the consequences—catastrophic consequences in some cases—of accelerating male loneliness; and to pose feasible solutions.

If ending up lonely were a race, it would start out as a fair one, with males and females evenly matched, more or less. In true Pyrrhic fashion, men go on to "win" the loneliness race; to the victor go the spoils of alcohol problems, depression, divorce, and even death. "Oh, lonely death on lonely life."[4] This book will argue that these words, uttered by Melville's Captain Ahab in *Moby-Dick,* capture a particularly male sentiment.

I AM ASKING YOU to ponder loneliness, a request that, upon initial reflection, may seem unnecessary. Much as everyone knows what suffocation is, everyone knows what loneliness is. Is there then really any need to ponder it? In one sense, probably not: it is true that everyone has an instinctive sense of loneliness. How could it be otherwise in a species as gregarious as we are? Moreover, as we will see later in the book, there are schools of thought that tend to overthink loneliness, viewing it, implausibly, and even dangerously in my opinion, as a romantic opportunity for things like "self-discovery" (itself something I view with suspicion, as it is often a rationalization for solipsism and neighboring narcissistic absorptions).

Nevertheless, accurate and useful definition benefits from consideration of both parsimony and nuance. A parsimonious explanation of loneliness along the lines of "feeling alone" will not do; not only is it tautological, it leaves too much out. A detailed understanding of loneliness—its component parts and its relationship to things like health—is something I will develop throughout the book, but an initial definition to consider is "immutuality," which is the opposite of the meeting of minds and the opposite of fellow feeling. Loneliness is, rather, the disconnection of minds, an unpeopled feeling. This can happen in a crowd, or in deep isolation, and as we will see, it can happen gradually, under the radar of awareness, especially in men, who, as a group, are prone to the dulling over time of their loneliness sensors.

MEN MAKE A LOT of money and have all the accompanying privileges and power. This has been so for millennia. Men are overrepresented in each of the following categories, just to choose a few: those earning over $100,000 per year; Fortune 500 company CEOs; and US presidents, state governors, and senators. To my knowledge, surveys that rank countries on various indices of equality have always returned the same result: the number of countries in which women enjoy superior status over men? Zero.

A vibrant and vigorous group men should be, one would assume. But one would be wrong. For each of the twelve leading causes of death, mortality is higher for men than for women. A 2007 report stated, "Males experience higher mortality rates than females at all stages of life from conception to old age."[5] For every 100 girls, 125 boys are conceived. The mortality sex difference begins even before birth—for every 100 girls, only 105 boys are born, down from the 125 conceived. Around 20 percent of males don't even make it to birth. And for those who do make it, very low birth weight and failure to thrive syndromes are more prevalent than they are for girls.

It is noteworthy, I think, that for the age range in which reproduction was common in ancestral times (and now in much of the world), from early adolescence into the twenties, men outnumber women (despite the fact that the mortality difference has already started to take its toll on male babies and boys). This truth is not about women dying young through, for example, childbirth. Rather, it is about male vulnerability and risk-taking over the long-term. This means a kind of "musical chairs" situation for men in competition with each other for women—a deadly serious competition (sometimes literally) given what is at stake—with the numbers requiring male losers, and allowing for scenarios in which there are no female losers.

By mid-thirties, women outnumber men. This trend is especially pronounced in the wake of catastrophic wars like World War II, in which casualties were overwhelmingly male. In 1960, fifteen years after the war ended, there were 126 German women for every 100 German men. By age one hundred, there are four times more women than men. Of the ten people who have been comprehensively documented to have lived more than 115 years, all but one are women. An incident occurred in late November 2010 that illustrates the link between female gender and reaching 100 years of age. A greeter at Walmart was shoved to the ground by a shopper; the greeter had asked for the shopper's receipt as the latter exited the store, and, instead of the receipt, received a shove. The greeter was one hundred years old. The article's headline did not reveal the gender of the centenarian greeter, and, based on the fact that there was a physical altercation, one might have guessed that the greeter was a man. But even stronger odds attach to the fact that, given that someone is a centenarian, it is overwhelmingly likely that the person is a woman, as indeed, the Walmart greeter was (she was bruised but otherwise unhurt, and intended to return Walmart greeting the next day). In an October 20, 2010, piece in the *New York Times,* it was documented that the number of centenarians has increased almost three-fold since 1990. The number in 2009 was 96,548, according to the Census Bureau. Of these, only approximately 19,000 are men.

Men are thus more numerous at ages where male abundance benefits women (reproductive musical chairs). In a sense, men lose. This same pattern is observable across much of the animal kingdom. In bees and ants, for instance, swarms of males compete to inseminate a few females; copulation literally kills the males; and after all is said and done, the females are left to continue the species. The fate of male ants and bees illustrates that nature views males as, in a sense, relatively expendable. The individual male bee is not particularly important; he is just one of a swarm.

That the bell continues to toll for men throughout his lifespan is apparent in examples in which men die prematurely, either because of versions of expendability or because of surprising physical vulnerability. Consider the plight of the Donner Party. In the winter of 1846–47, the group was trapped by snows high in the Sierra Nevada, and some members of the party resorted to cannibalism to survive. As a rule, the men died first and the children next, with far more boys than girls dying. A disproportionate number of women and girls survived. What applied among the Donner Party was true on the *Titanic* as well, though the process was very different. Men gave up seats in lifeboats to women, despite the fact that in many cases seats were going to women whom the men did not even know. We will see this tendency to help strangers again later in the book; it is a tendency that, perhaps surprisingly, characterizes men more than women. Even large differences in socioeconomic class did not undo this pattern on the doomed ship. The poorest women had about a 50 percent chance of survival, compared to a corresponding rate of about one in three for the richest of the men (this, of course, is not to mention the poorest men, most of whom died). And, what applied on the *Titanic* and in the Donner Party applies in the emergency room as well: among severely injured people who go into shock, women are approximately 14 percent more likely to survive than men, even given identical levels of trauma. It also applies among convicted murderers, 10 percent of whom are female, and less than 1 percent of whom are executed. But of the many hundreds of people who have been put to death in the United States for murder since executions were resumed in 1976, how many have been female? Twelve. Not twelve percent, but twelve total out of well over 1,200 executed people (it is also true that men are more likely than women to commit aggravated crimes and to have a history of past criminality). These grim tales all tell a common story of male mortality.

This is particularly so for *lonely* men. Researchers reported in 1996 that among men over fifty, mortality remains fairly low for well-connected men. The lonely ones, by contrast, are more brittle. They can weather one major life event, but if they experience two or more, their mortality rate increases noticeably.[6] Loneliness in men truly is a life-and-death matter, and solutions to this problem—the focus of the last part of the book—are thus literally life saving.

The following conditions kill men either more often or earlier (or both) than they do women: coronary artery disease, stroke, chronic obstructive pulmonary disease, flu and pneumonia, diabetes, HIV, motor vehicle crashes, homicide, suicide, trauma, and liver disease. The incidence of cancer is about 50 percent higher in men than in women, including lung, colorectal, pharynx, stomach, pancreas, and bladder cancers, as well as non-Hodgkin's lymphoma and leukemia.[7] This is why a 2010 entry from *Harvard Men's Health Watch* was entitled "Men—The (Medically) Weaker Sex."[8] Workplace accidents kill men far more than they do women; over 90 percent of all workplace deaths are of men. In the 1991 Oakland-Berkeley firestorm described at the beginning of the book, two people were killed on the job: a fire chief and a police officer, both men. One may respond that this pattern simply has to do with the kinds of work men and women traditionally do, but that evades the essential question of why these differences exist in the first place.

Male mortality has always been thus in the workplace: in hunter-gatherer societies, perhaps the most dangerous and lethal of activities was hunting big game. In his book *Catching Fire*, Richard Wrangham commented, "Hunting large game was a predominantly masculine activity in 99.3 percent of recent societies."[9] Male mortality comes up in a staggeringly diverse array of contexts. A 2009 article wrote of mortality in general in Russia, and how it has fluctuated considerably over the decades, but of late the figures have been quite worrisome: life expectancy was lower in Russia in 2006 than it was in 1964. Predictably, this is especially so for men, as the article notes, "The situation for Russian males has been particularly woeful."[10] In his book *Postwar*, Tony Judt notes, "fertility rates in Communist states tailed off rather sooner than in the West, and from the mid-sixties [fertility rates] were more than matched by steadily worsening death rates (especially among men)."[11]

Male zygotes, male babies, boys, and men thus run a kind of obstacle course, with obstacles including reproductive musical chairs, as well as obstacles ranging from miscarriage to accidents, cancer, suicide, and many other causes of mortality, too. This is true in general, but for some causes of death, it is particularly true. Which cause of death stands out as affecting men far more than women? Given their privileged financial and societal status, perhaps it has something to do with the dark side of wealth and power, such as the cardiac or stroke-related consequences of influential but stressful jobs, or a taste for expensive but unhealthy foods?

No, it is suicide.

In 2005, 32,637 Americans died by suicide. Of those, 25,907—approximately 80 percent—were men.[12] This is a vast overrepresentation, on a par with men's overrepresentation in high income brackets and professional positions of power and status. Much attention is focused, rightly, on men's disproportionate share of wealth and power; too little attention is spent on men's disproportionate share of misery, one index of which is high suicide rates.

Shouldn't power and success prevent suicide, and shouldn't the powerful and the suicidal be mutually exclusive groups? The answer is obviously "no," judging from the overrepresentation of men among suicide decedents. So then the question becomes *Why?* Why would the same group of people be overrepresented in highly paid and powerful positions and in suicide decedents?

My answer, in a word, is loneliness.

LEST DEATH STRIKE YOU as an extravagant claim to lay at the doorstep of loneliness, let's consider male suicide in more detail. Men, especially *older* men, kill themselves at rates that dwarf rates of other groups. This has been true for at least as long as reliable statistics on suicide have been kept, and probably for far longer than that.

Suicide is also affecting our men and women in uniform, a tragedy I see close up as director of the Military Suicide Research Consortium, in which the Department of Defense has invested many millions of dollars. To our knowledge, for the first and only time in human history, a country at war—the United States—lost more of its service members in a month to suicide than to combat (this occurred in early 2009). This is a very worrisome fact, and the military and our Consortium are determined to do something to improve the situation. We are in the early stages of our work, but our working hypothesis is that the factors that cause suicidal behavior in the military are similar to those that cause suicidal behavior in the general population (for example, feeling alienated, whether in general or from one's unit). Of course, our military is mostly male, and suicide decedents within the military are overwhelmingly male. A recent report noted that suicide rates worsened in the first decade or so of the twenty-first century, particularly among men in mid-life. The report stated, "Our analysis of suicide rates among the middle-aged for the period 1979–2005 showed a substantial increase in suicides by men aged 50–59 years."[13]

Findings such as these link death by suicide not only to the male gender—consistent with a theme of this book—but also to the combination of male gender and aging—doubly consistent with this book's thesis. One of the strongest contributors to death by suicide—according to some researchers, the single strongest contributor of any variable ranging from genes and molecules to society and culture—is loneliness.

Men's main problem is not self-loathing, stupidity, greed, or any of the legions of other things they're accused of. The problem, instead, is loneliness; as they age, they gradually lose contacts with friends and family, and, here's the important part, they don't replenish them. Women do not suffer these losses as much, because they tend not to develop the attitudes (explained in later chapters) that underlie accelerating male loneliness across the lifespan, attitudes like extreme independence from others.

If this is so, men at age fifty should be demonstrably less happy than men at age twenty. This trend is evident in a diverse array of sources, not just the scholarly literature. For example, *Esquire* magazine's "Survey of American Men" (October 2010) found that 61 percent of twenty-year-olds reported that they were generally happy, as compared to 49 percent of fifty-year-olds. In the same survey, when asked to rate the level of fun in their lives "right now" on a scale from 1 (no fun) to 5 (lots of fun), 69 percent of fifty-year-old men chose a value between 1 and 3, as compared to 52 percent of twenty-year-old men. In reply to the statement "today is the best time in the history of the country to be a man," 17 percent of fifty-year-old men strongly disagreed, whereas only 10 percent of twenty-year-old men reacted similarly. And, to the degree that optimism about the country's future implies happiness and well-being, consider the two groups' answers to the following question: "Do you believe the United States will be as strong in 2050 as it is to-day?" Thirty-one percent of twenty-year-olds responded with an optimistic yes, whereas only 18 percent of their fifty-year-old counterparts did. The survey did not include women, but, as the pages that follow will show, the fifty-year-old women very likely would have expressed more optimism about the country's future as compared to their male counterparts.

As they age, men tend to drift off and wither, and as they do, they avoid healthy fixes. A 2008 study found that men, far more so than women, had trouble trusting and reaching out for help from others, including from health care professionals.[14] A postmortem report on a suicide decedent, a man in his sixties, read, "He did not have friends. . . . He did not feel comfortable with other men. . . . He did not trust doctors and would not seek help even though he was aware that he needed help."[15]

As people age, they are more likely than younger adults to report discontinuation of mental health treatment due to perceptions of stigma, and this is particularly so for males—a difference that starts early. Boys demonstrate greater perceptions of stigma related to mental health services than do girls.

Instead of attending to their health, men resort to fixes that feel like solutions in the short term, but in the long term are mere "Band-Aid" answers that only exacerbate the problem of male loneliness. These ersatz solutions include things like extramarital sex, divorce, alcohol, guns, NASCAR, and golf—a seemingly random list that, as we will see later in this book, is not random at all.

Relatedly, men's "don't tread on me" reliance on themselves and their bodies, perhaps a viable strategy for the thirty-year-old man, becomes somewhat less so for the fifty-year-old man, and even less so for the sixty-five-year-old man. Needless to say, the bodies of men and women alike are affected by aging, but women, on average, weather age better than men. I have attended every single one of my high school reunions (our thirtieth is in 2013) and this phenomenon is quite apparent there. There are women in our class who are even more physically attractive in their forties than they were in high school; a similar claim can be made about not one single man in our class.

To take another example of the differential effects of aging on the bodies of men and women, imagine a man and a woman of the same age, who from age thirty to age fifty gain 50 percent of their age-thirty body weight; the woman who weighed 100 pounds at age thirty weighs 150 pounds at age fifty, and the man who weighed 200 pounds at age thirty weighs 300 pounds at age fifty. On their surface, these weights reveal a potential relative problem for men—most people asked to imagine a 300-pound man and a 150-pound woman would think the latter healthier, probably rightly so, even though weight gain in this example was proportionately equal.

But there is an additional, deeper problem: women's weight gain tends to be distributed peripherally, to their hips and thighs, whereas men's weight gain tends to be distributed centrally, to their stomachs and waistlines. Women's waistlines thicken after menopause, but so do men's more so than women's. Although women are usually displeased with increased size of hips and thighs, there is evidence that, all things considered, it is a healthier pattern of weight gain than central distribution.

Some of this evidence comes from research on waist-to-hip ratio (WHR). To measure the WHR, you simply obtain an accurate measure of your waist's circumference (for most people, the measuring tape should go an inch or so below the navel), and of your hip's circumference (measured approximately at the buttocks' largest protrusion), and divide the first number by the last number. Interestingly, beauty pageant winners, as well as centerfolds, have been shown to have very low WHRs. This was true in the 1980s, when overall thin shape was fashionable, and in the 1950s, when a fuller overall shape was in fashion. Even as fashion in body shape changed from full to very thin, the WHR remained constant—Jane Russell, Marilyn Monroe, Farrah Fawcett, and Cindy Crawford differ considerably from each other regarding overall body shape, but have very similar WHRs.

In both sexes, higher waist-to-hip ratio has been correlated with an array of health problems. But, as with loneliness, men experience more of the problem and thus suffer more of its sequellae.

A related problem in men is evident in people's comfort in their own skin. As my colleagues and I recently showed, just as women's intense focus on and discontent with their bodies start to fade in their forties (as compared to their twenties and thirties), men's focus shows the exact opposite trend—high satisfaction in their twenties and thirties, and increasing discomfort and dissatisfaction in their forties and beyond.[16] Tellingly, the reason that women become increasingly comfortable with their bodies is that they start to deprioritize them.[17] It's not that they no longer care how they look; rather, it's that their care for their loved ones, especially but not limited to children, and for careers makes most other things somewhat trivial in comparison. By contrast, at the very time of life that men's bodies start to desert them—late forties and beyond—is the very time that their loneliness is accelerating. A poll in *Men's Health* magazine revealed that almost half of the men in the sample would rather "lose an arm" than permanently gain one hundred pounds.[18] The survey did not include women; had they been asked, many probably would have responded similarly. This underscores a point to be taken up in this book's final chapter: many of the processes described in the book happen for men and women alike; but for men, these processes are more fraught and thus pernicious, as we will see.

The trick is to transition from "don't tread on me" attitudes to "I want to give and receive connection and help to and from those I love." This transition vexes men much more than it does women, in part because women, on average, are not encouraged in extreme "don't tread on me" stances, and thus do not have as much of a transition to make.

Economic downturns like the one that began in 2008 tend to make a bad state of affairs even worse for men. When there is a bad storm—whether a thunderstorm or economic storm—shelter is essential. A crucial bulwark against economic strife is connection to others—it softens the blow, sustains us, and has pragmatic functions like access to advice, material support, and job opportunities from family and friends. Relationships constitute shelter from economic storms . . . *genuine* and *sustained* relationships, that is, not superficial, one-dimensional ones. There is at least some evidence that economic stress induces men to resort to quick-fix distractions, including sexual dalliances. It is probably not a coincidence, in this light, that the breast size of centerfold models in *Playboy* and *Penthouse* increases by 3 percent during recessions.[19]

Past economic recessions have taken more of a toll on younger workers than on older ones, which stands to reason, in that the polished skills and overall experience of older workers protected them. But this recent recession has been different: jobless rates for people over the age of fifty-five have not reached such high levels since the Great Depression.[20] Moreover, of people over fifty-five, men are more affected than women in the current economic downturn. An economist with the North Carolina Security Commission stated, "People losing jobs are increasingly male and increasingly older." This is largely because the recession is disproportionately hitting sectors in construction, manufacturing, and finance, areas in which men are overrepresented. The Georgia labor commissioner, highlighting the novelty of a recession that hits men in general, and older men in particular, noted that two-thirds of those seeking job training during this downturn are male, the exact opposite pattern observed pre-recession. The commissioner stated, "This is a masculine recession." The processes outlined in this book are, recession or not, most acute and pernicious in older men; a recession that hits this same group the hardest is worrying.

The most pernicious economic downturns, not surprisingly, are those that cause a lot of job loss and home loss. A 2010 headline read, "Gender Pay Gap Smallest on Record."[21] Good news. But the headline continued, "Men's Jobs Affected Most in Recession." Not such good news: the idea was to narrow the gender pay gap by increasing women's salaries, not by decreasing men's. In general, the recession did not see it this way. The article also affirms a point of departure for the current book: it states, "men have retained their lead in alcoholism, suicide, homelessness, violence, and criminality."

A recent study conducted by faculty at the Florida State University College of Business examined the impact of the recent recession on men's and women's attitudes about balancing careers and interpersonal life.

Over 1,100 full-time workers were surveyed. Perhaps understandably, the authors wanted to find some optimistic trends in the results, and so, for example, one finding was summarized as "48 percent reported that the recession increased their *appreciation of family*" [emphasis theirs]. This means, however, that for more than half of the sample, appreciation of family was *not* increased. Similarly, a key result was that "49 percent admitted that the recession helped them recognize the value of *people over things*" [emphasis again theirs]; we will encounter the people-versus-things distinction again later. Here, too, alas, more than half of the sample's appreciation of people over things was not enhanced. A third result—and here the gloom is a little harder to conceal—was that "23 percent indicated that the recession increased awareness of an *over-commitment to work* at the expense of family and recreation." Here again, the italics are theirs; in each of the three instances I have included, a phrase is italicized, apparently as a way to show that some good has come out of this recession; that some people at least have increased their awareness of things like valuing family and others over work and the dangers of over-commitment to work. And it is true that some people's awareness of these things has increased, according to the study's results. It is just that it is somewhat underwhelming how few people's awareness has been changed; were a recession going to achieve such a change, one would think it would be a recession like this one, which in some people's reckoning is second in severity only to the Great Depression. The streak of above–9 percent jobless rate in this current downturn is clearly the worst since World War II. (Let's do keep things in perspective, however. A recent article pointed out, "We've had 40 of these recessions since 1800, and even a half-dozen as bad as this one. We should have acquired in two centuries a cautious faith in the trend, which is up and up and up since 1800 by about 2,000 percent per person, conservatively measured."[22])

In keeping with the more somber appraisal of the FSU College of Business study's results, it was reported that "more than 70 percent of employees acknowledged that most days at work 'seem like they will never end.'" One participant in the study, a forty-eight-year-old manager of a production facility who was laid off by a longtime employer, stated, "I broke my back for this company, missed my kids growing up, and for what? Nothing!" The person who said this, consistent with this book's overarching theme, was male. In fact, a main conclusion of the study was that men and women differ substantially in their recession-related worries. Men were focused on the workplace, concerned about things like job insecurity and competitiveness and even hostility in work settings. Notice the absence in men's concerns of other people (except others as competitive or hostile). Women, by contrast, voiced worry about conflicts between work and family life and were bothered by the toll that increased job obligations took on the family.

Most, if not all recessions produce these kinds of concerns. Not all downturns, however, lead to individual catastrophes like increased suicide. But hard times that steal homes and careers always spur increases in suicides, and those decedents will disproportionately be men.[23] In 2008 and 2009, there were several prominent economy-related suicides reported in the news, all of whom were men over fifty (for example, Bernie Madoff investor René-Thierry Magon de la Villehuchet). Systematic data on the yearly suicide rates in recent years are not yet available, but there are other signs that this recession is taking a grave toll. A 2010 article quotes a clinical psychologist talking about her practice, "I'm finding myself overwhelmed with people who want to be seen because they're anxious and depressed over the economy."[24] I know from firsthand experience that a very common complaint of mental health practitioners is that they do not have enough business; to find them saying they have too much is thus notable indeed.

Therefore, in times of hardship, the problem of male loneliness may become even more prevalent—and thus of even more urgent concern to men and to the people around them—and solutions even more needed as well. Further still, the problem is likely to linger: in the Great Depression, the peak in suicides did not occur until a full year after the peak unemployment rate of 25 percent was reached.

The problem could be even longer lived. There are changes in population personality trends that may exacerbate economic trends. University of Michigan researchers reported in 2010 that college students' empathy had decreased by 40 percent over the last twenty years or so. A twenty-year-old in 2010 is, on average, less concerned about others and more selfish than was a twenty-year-old in 1990. Empathy's flipside—self-centeredness—has spiked. I was mindful of this at a recent FSU football game when, during a TV timeout, the Jumbotron showed an ad from a local dentist. The gimmick of the ad was the "smilecam"—a camera trained on some individuals in the crowd, and the public address system intoned, "If you're captured on camera, smile and show us the star you *really* are."

The implication is that everyone is inherently special, not by virtue of effort or by dint of achievement, but by being selected more or less at random by a camera operator. And not just unique—itself a dubious claim but at least a coherent and defensible one—but a star. Moreover, the ad deals with the obvious fact that, in actuality, very few of the selected people will be "stars" in any genuine sense of the word, by emphasizing the word "really," which implies that a person's star quality is present, just as yet unrecognized—a perspective very much in harmony with the premise and indeed the occasional outcome of shows like *American Idol*. That the pabulum of the "smilecam" ad raises hardly an eyebrow from anyone in the crowd reflects the real possibility that we have entered into a true age of narcissism. Had the ad run as recently as thirty-five years ago, I think it would have elicited at least snickers from at least some of the crowd, but in 2010, it seems quite natural to assert that everyone is—or at least deserves to be ("entitled to be" would actually be the more apt phrasing)—a star. Had Lewis Carroll been at the game, he would have snickered, and would have been reminded, as was I, of one of his lines in *Alice in Wonderland*: "Everybody has won, and all must have prizes." An age of narcissism is worrying because it could usher in an age of even more loneliness.

Tony Judt might have snickered along with Carroll. In his book *The Memory Chalet*, he wrote, "Why should everything be about 'me'? Are my fixations of significance to the Republic? Do my particular needs by definition speak to broader concerns? What on earth does it mean that 'the personal is political'?"[25] It should be noted that, at the time of writing these words, the author was suffering from amyotrophic lateral sclerosis, which he knew would soon take his life; he thus had reason for self-fixations, and, to his credit, he understood that even dying does not really justify them.

Once you start looking for the attitude that "everyone is a star" in advertising and the media, it turns up everywhere. An ad encouraging people to buy NFL jerseys and to personalize them with a name or nick-name printed on the back assures the audience, "No one is as special as you." Really? How about the guys who wear those jerseys for real, the world's most elite athletes? They seem pretty special.

NPR ran a segment on the demise of humanities offerings in many universities.[26] A student affected by these cuts complained, "My dreams mean more than anything in the world." This statement was given with-out consideration of the larger effects of the cuts—for instance, faculty and staff who were fired because of them—and was given unselfcon-sciously. And the statement was given without qualification; it was not that the student's dreams meant something, nor that they meant quite a lot to her, but rather that they meant "more than anything in the world." Is it old fogey-ism on my part to assert that this statement would never have been uttered even by college students of the "selfish eighties," not to mention by those of previous generations? Research studies empirically documenting a rise in self-centeredness suggest that the answer to this question is "no."

Men who are currently in their twenties are therefore more likely than ever to be self-focused and thus to neglect the hard work of cul-tivating and maintaining friendships. As with men before them, this is an approach to life that, while perhaps tenable for a few years, is not sustainable over the long term and may end disastrously.

In arguing that men have it bad, especially in economic hard times, and regardless of the times, increasingly as they age, am I being too easy on men? I am, after all, one of them, and so could be accused of bias. But I do not think I am being easy on men at all, for three rea-sons—reasons that the rest of the book draws out. First, I think the cold, hard numbers bear out my thesis. Second, it should be recalled, I am not exactly extolling men's virtues here; rather, I am delineating weaknesses, the very existence of which I believe are underappreciated, and the causes of which, to my knowledge, have not been pondered at all, at least not in the way proposed here. Third, my explanation incorporates—indeed, starts from—the proposition that men are, in a sense, spoiled. The assertions that men have it very hard, and that boys and young men had it easy are thus, to my way of thinking, not contradictory. On the contrary, they are each true facts that tell a story of male development across the lifespan, one that starts out with advantages. These advantages, however, develop into liabilities, much as a trust fund is an advantage that can develop into a liability should its holder find the need for job skills never obtained.

Women's satisfaction with themselves accelerates with age, largely as a function of increasing satisfaction with major life roles like, for example, being a mother. Men, too, can reap the benefits of roles like fatherhood, but on average, they do so less often and less successfully than their female counterparts. This leaves many men lonely, socially unresourceful, and desperate for real connections, wisps of which they get from a drink, from the links, or from the roar of a gun or a car.

Why does this process happen to men? When you're seven, or twelve, or seventeen, or twenty-two, friendships are virtually unavoidable. In his memoir *Dry*, Augusten Burroughs describes making a new friend as an adult in rehab, "It's the kind of friendship that's easy to make when you're six or seven. You let a kid have your swing and suddenly he's your best friend. Suddenly, you don't care that you hate math because you can hate it together. And after school you want to play together. You never question it. You never say to yourself, *Am I spending too much time with him? Am I sending the wrong signal?*"[27] That rehab made this happen in adulthood shows both the hope and the challenge of solving the problem of men's accelerating loneliness. The hope is that under the right conditions, the new and instant friendships of childhood can find their way into adulthood; the challenge, of course—and it's a very considerable one—is to arrange and engineer the right conditions. Not everyone goes to rehab.

When you're a child or an adolescent, friendships are ready-made—and this is true for virtually everyone, men included. This is why boys are not much lonelier than girls. The routine of school (class, recess, lunch, etc.), day after day, with kids of the same age, *forces* children to socialize. As my two sons went through elementary school, every year would bring at least one new best friend. When they were in the early grades, I used to amaze and amuse them by saying, "Ok wait, as you know, I have ESP, and I'm getting a signal . . . this new friend, it's coming to me, it's coming to me, he is in your class, isn't he?!!" The son in question would respond accordingly, "Whoa, Dad, how'd you know that?" "Wait, wait, I think there's more, yes, it's coming to me, it's coming to me, his desk is near yours, isn't it?!!" By third grade, they had figured out that my trick of using the rule of simple proximity translated into my "ESP."

It is true that some kids socialize more than others, but that is not the point. The point is that, as at no other time of life, socializing and forming friendships are *institutionalized* by school, with effects (more or less) on everyone, boys and girls alike. Put differently, the rule of proximity affects everyone in those settings (indeed, as I will argue later in the book, it affects everyone, period, *as long as* it is given the chance to work). In elementary-school classrooms across America, it is difficult to find a friendless child, even among the shy or troubled. Alas, this doesn't last forever—it amounts to a kind of social trust fund that will run out soon enough—and half the population knows this. The other half—men—seem not to absorb this lesson.

If what I am arguing here is true, there should be persuasive studies that: (1) document a difference between men and women in loneliness, with the men being more lonely at some point after childhood; and (2) pinpoint the initial emergence of this gender difference somewhere around the teens, or at the latest, the twenties. In fact, this very pattern of findings has been obtained; several studies have found the expected gender effect, and have identified adolescence as the time of its emergence.[28] One of these studies was a meta-analysis—a quantitative pooling of the results of past individual studies—that found that the association in adolescence between male gender and loneliness was large and very robust, clearly emerging in the majority of studies reviewed.

This set of studies is intriguing not only because it produces results corroborative of the precise predictions derived from my "lonely sex" thesis, but also because they were obtained even despite the male tendency to deny or to be oblivious about things like loneliness. In fact, there is empirical evidence that admitting to loneliness is more stigmatizing for men than for women.[29] Therefore, the male gender effect on loneliness, characterized as "strong" in the literature, may be stronger still once this issue of male obliviousness is factored in. This obliviousness—the state of being alone but unaware—is essential to understanding male loneliness because it is one of three prominent forms of male loneliness, the others being "lonely in a crowd" and "truly lonely."

"Alone but oblivious" affects men, particularly in the early stages of their trajectory toward loneliness, before it is so obvious that everyone, even men, notices it. "Lonely in a crowd"—feeling alone when not being alone—is vexing because of the disharmony between actual and felt aloneness, and because it can be deceiving, in that others assume, wrongly and occasionally catastrophically, that a person does not feel lonely because he is with others. A large proportion of suicide deaths are of this character: men who, on the inside, feel desperately alone, even though others are there with them who are expressing love and support. The men tell no one, and they stun everyone with their deaths, which come from out of the blue to everyone except the men themselves, now deceased. Of course, people can be "truly alone"— both desperately lonely and actually alone, and a fair number of suicide deaths have this signature as well.

The life and death of the novelist Jack London illustrates two of these three conditions. In his teens and twenties, London was a gregarious, adventurous young man, who, for instance, spent months at sea on seal-hunting ships, a setting in which friends are, to a degree, ready-made. Proximity is in abundance on such ships. However, the literature of loneliness in adolescence suggests that loneliness was likely starting to emerge for London; in his twenties he may well have started to become "alone but oblivious." The arc of his life can be discerned from chapter titles in a biography of the author: early chapter titles are "Superman" and "Howling at the Moon"—which could also serve as apt descriptors for London's fiction and which, tellingly, fit the "alone but oblivious" theme in that they connote strength but do not refer to other people.[30] A final chapter, documenting London's lonely decline and suicide, is entitled "The Noseless One." By then, he was no longer oblivious to his loneliness, he was truly lonely. London's shipmates would have scoffed—as London himself would have when he was twenty—at the notion that he would kill himself, friendless, within twenty-five years or so. It would have seemed preposterous to these vibrant and adventurous young men, and yet it did indeed happen. Year by year, friends fell away and were not replaced. Hardly anyone was there to care for London when youth and vigor faded, and when he needed friends the most.

Men, on average, fail to make the crucial transition from the institutionalized, ready-made friendships of childhood to the earned, worked-for friendships of adulthood. That they fail to do this is reflected in their suicide rates, their divorce rates, and, well, their friendlessness. Why they fail involves several interrelated processes.

Men seem to be under the impression that friendships will always be provided for them, with little effort, just as they were in the halcyon days of third grade. This, in a very real sense, spoils them, a phenomenon facilitated by their being spoiled in other ways by preferentially available opportunities and treatment. Like all meaningful relationships, friendships require work to initiate and maintain. Except under grade-school conditions, a passive, spoiled approach will eventually and steadily result in the loss of friends. This is a gradual process because men can coast for a while on friendships made in adolescence and in places like college. Jack London at age thirty-five was probably still unaware of the disastrous end in store for him within a mere fifteen years. By the end, he recognized the catastrophe, but by then it was too late. This anecdote is generalizable: by their fifties, the erosion in men's social circles is often so clear that even they themselves recognize it, but upon inspection, it can be seen even earlier, in the late twenties and thirties. It's a little like hair loss in that way.

I was discussing this idea with a female colleague and was pleased that she was nodding in agreement. I anticipated that she would think of examples of men she knows who fit this narrative closely, for they are legion. She went in a different direction, but still corroborated my general thesis, saying, "I think you're on to something with this. Girls would *never* think that friendships don't take work; it's all so *effort-ful* for girls. You have to know about the various cliques, and who fits into each and how, and who is whose friend." I got tired just from trying to imagine it, never mind live it. But girls do live it—as we will see, research supports precisely what my colleague was claiming—and, while living it imposes a kind of cost, the cost ends up being a very wise investment in the future. Eric Wilson, the author of a memoir on depression, wrote, "Mature people, a minority . . . know it's really our imperfections that make us human—and get down to the rewarding work of creating a *human* connection, one that muddles communally through the contingencies of life."[31] This author packed a lot of wisdom into this one sentence: with words like "work" and "muddles" he conveys the "lunch pail" aspect of relationship maintenance; with words like "communally" and "rewarding," he captures the vital reasons for putting in the work.

He might have added that this "mature minority" is disproportionately female. Women not only know *that* one has to expend effort to initiate and maintain friendships, they know *how*—both forms of knowledge represent advantages women enjoy over men, advantages that were hard-won in the crucible of female childhood and adolescence, which forces relating, discourages extreme forms of independence, and rewards focus on relationships and not just on money and status.

In addition to becoming spoiled, there is a second and related reason why men stumble in the transition from the easy friendships of childhood to the hard-won friendships of adulthood. In their twenties and thirties, men seem to focus, naturally enough, on money and status, and they do so through the lens of jobs and careers. To be sure, women do this, too, but as a rule only men seem to focus on money and status to the exclusion of maintaining friendships and seeking new ones. A focus on money and status can erode relationships because, as in any situation, the more attention one pays to a certain thing (e.g., wealth), the less attention there is available to allocate to other things (e.g., new friends). Moreover, in his 2002 book *The High Price of Materialism*, psychologist Tim Kasser persuasively shows that a focus on the accumulation of wealth and material goods has multiple negative effects, including less overall happiness and, key to my argument, less intimacy in and satisfaction with relationships. This untoward effect of materialism operates across the age and income spectra. Thus, in early adulthood, men, more than women, face a dilemma—a dilemma about which they are not very aware for the next twenty years: namely, they believe that their focus on money and status will buy them a happy future—a belief fueled by a materialist culture—when in actuality, it is setting them up for the hard fall of lonely years in their forties and beyond. A lucky few can get by on the friendships they made back in the day. But many can't, and over time, men drift away from friendships and simultaneously earn money and status. This leaves them puzzled indeed—they spent years achieving money and status, finally got it, and yet they feel lonely and empty. Lonely at the top. It wasn't supposed to be like that. The trouble for the lonely sex is that it *is* like that.

I want to describe accelerating male loneliness, to trace its origins, map out its consequences, and propose solutions. The book's approach includes cutting-edge scientific research—my own as well as other scientists' work—but also emphasizes anecdotes and case studies to enliven and humanize the scientific material. Finally, the book's approach is personal as well, because I myself am an aging man, but especially because I believe the process I will describe in the book killed my dad, who died by suicide at age fifty-six.

I recall standing in my parents' bedroom as a five-year-old boy, as my dad was getting ready to go to work one day. My dad ran a successful business with—and was very good friends with—a famous athlete. He was focused on wealth and status, and had already achieved them, but really the only person you could call a best friend in his life was his business partner, and even that, in retrospect, was a shallow friendship. I suddenly got very worried for my dad—and for us—and asked, "Dad, what would happen if you and him weren't friends anymore?" He chuckled, and with a tone that was full of confidence and was also dismissive (not in a mean way but in a "it's no problem" way), he answered me with his own question, "You worried about that?" Twenty years later, when they weren't friends or business partners anymore, my dad killed himself.

This is not a story about how I was a prescient five-year-old. Rather, it is an "out of the mouths of babes" tale about a child who had just started kindergarten, dreaded the first day, and couldn't wait to go back the second day because of all the friends magically convened there, and who could see what a thirty-five-year-old man could not: that my dad's growing friendlessness was a problem, if not at that moment, then eventually.

And he could see what a five-year-old could not: Why should he worry, he had enough money, seemingly endless professional prospects, a beautiful young wife, and two healthy children? The five-year-old's retort of "yeah but no friends" can be answered, "I don't need friends, I have you and your sister and your mom and I have money and a bright future." It's a good answer—an answer, as I will demonstrate, that is relatively unique to men—and yet it's a tragically poor answer, too, because he did need friends after his children left home, his marriage became distant, and his prospects dried up. The five-year-old wins this debate, but it is certainly not a win—my dad is dead.

That a child sees what a man cannot illustrates something fundamental about the problem. Men wear blinders of a sort, blinders that are relatively unique to them. What are the origins, characteristics, and consequences of these blinders? Are there remedies for them?

THE NATURE OF LONELINESS AND ITS WOEFUL CONSEQUENCES

What is loneliness, and why and how does it mar and kill?

My own research on loneliness has developed and used the following definition: "the experience of solitude, disconnection, and lack of closeness; a lack of social contact relative to what is desired."[32] A crucial point, then, is that loneliness is an internal *emotional* experience, but an aspect of it, a lack of social contact—is objective and *social*. There are two aspects, and usually these two work hand in glove. If one reports that, objectively speaking, one enjoys a large number of social contacts, then one usually also reports feeling emotionally connected, subjectively satisfied—in a phrase, not lonely. But these two aspects are not always in harmony, as the phrases "alone in a crowd" and "oblivious but alone" suggest.

This distinction between internal emotional experience—the perception of loneliness—and external objective social connections is not merely academic. A classic finding from research on social support shows that, with regard to predicting an array of mental and physical health indicators, *perceived* social support can matter as much as or more than the objective number of supportive friends.[33] A person with two friends who feels very supported may well have better outcomes than a person with ten friends who does not experience that support. A person who is supported and looked up to can nevertheless experience profound loneliness, as is sometimes seen in suicide notes. The following are examples from Edwin Shneidman's 1996 book *The Suicidal Mind*—in each case, despite the expressed sense of loneliness, the person was not objectively alone: "If I haven't the love I want so bad, there is nothing left"; "I really thought that you and little Joe were going to come back into my life but you didn't"; "I just cannot live without you. I might as well be dead. . . . I have this empty feeling inside me that is killing me. . . . When you left me I died inside."[34] Marie Osmond's son Mike told his mother on the day before his death by suicide that he was "miserable and without friends." In fact, the first known suicide note, written in Egypt and dated to approximately 2000 BC, read, "I am laden with misery, and lack a trusty friend."[35]

If the emotional, internal experience of loneliness is meaningfully distinguishable from the social, external referent, the distinction should be apparent in anecdotal and empirical reports alike, and in fictional accounts as well. As an example of the latter, the show *The Kids in the Hall* presented a sketch in which an unkempt man, dressed in pajamas and a bathrobe, explains to the camera that he is lonely. This premise is, in itself, not particularly funny, a relevant fact because *The Kids in the Hall* is a sketch comedy show. Two details add the color and humor: the man's tone is oddly upbeat and carefree; his foot is propped up in front of him, and his toe is badly injured, cartoonishly made up to be huge and discolored. The loner explains to the audience that he should probably see a doctor about his toe but has no friends to encourage him to do so, and at any rate, he is not too worried, the toe's continuing discoloration, inflammation, and healing is entertainment. What is the matter with the guy in the sketch? There are a few things, but a really odd thing, and the thing that creates most of the sketch's tension and humor, is the discordance between the man's social and emotional loneliness. That is, he *is* lonely, but he doesn't seem to *feel* lonely. It is as if he is lacking or is oblivious to an internal sensor, signaling to him that there is a problem. Problems with this internal loneliness sensor will prove essential to understanding escalating male loneliness across the lifespan. The philosopher Kierkegaard wrote, "What characterizes despair is just this—that it is ignorant of being despair."[36] This is quite inaccurate about many forms of despair, but correct about "alone but oblivious" versions of loneliness.

"Alone but oblivious" is, in a sense, the flip side of the "lonely in a crowd" scenario. Emotional loneliness and objective social connections can become disharmonized in two ways: "lonely in a crowd" and "alone but oblivious," the latter like the character in the sketch. Both occur, and as we shall see, "alone but oblivious" begins relatively early (it characterized my dad at age thirty-five) and can continue for decades, whereas "lonely in a crowd" tends to characterize older men more than younger men (like my dad in the days and weeks before his death by suicide—he was not alone, far from it, but he felt that he was). This brings us to an important point: in the end stages of the life development process I am describing, men vacillate between "alone but oblivious" and "lonely in a crowd." In catastrophic cases like those involving suicide, the final hours and minutes involve very painful awareness of "lonely in a crowd" feelings . . . or they can involve "truly lonely" feelings because it is, alas and of course, the case that people can feel lonely precisely because they truly are bereft.

Sketch comedy and anecdotal examples are one thing, but the distinction between social and emotional loneliness has been validated in scientific research as well. In my own work, I have used a statistical sorting technique that sorts like with like.

My research on loneliness has shown that emotional facets of loneliness sort with each other and social facets sort with each other, but that the emotional and social facets are discernible from one another. This suggests, of course, that it is possible to experience the one and not the other.

For many painful experiences, as long as you are going to experience the one, it is good *not* to experience the other—for instance a cut, but not an infection. But what if the one is a sensor for the other, as I believe emotional loneliness is for social loneliness? As an analogy, consider your car's gas tank and its sensor, the gas gauge. It is possible to experience the problem of an empty tank, together with a gauge that says "full." Here, it is *not* good to experience the one and not the other—you will run out of gas and will be surprised at the fact. As long as you are going to have the problem of the empty gas tank, you also want the "problem" of the gauge's empty reading, so that you are signaled to fix the source issue. A working sensor, of course, is not a problem at all, but rather the signal toward a solution.

A similar point, incidentally, has been made regarding tolerance to alcohol—a factor, as we will see, involved in men's trouble with loneliness (and a possible solution of sorts, too). In a bout of drinking, the problem of too much alcohol can be curbed in response to the signal of drunkenness. For a person whose "alcohol sensor" is working well, one or a few too many will activate the sensor ("I'm too drunk"), which in turn signals the solution (stop drinking). By contrast, the braggart who boasts of high alcohol tolerance is actually saying that his sensor is broken, that he no longer has a signal for when he's had too much and is thus doing himself physical harm by continued drinking.

In the same way, in the *Kids in the Hall* sketch, the loner's loneliness sensor is broken; he no longer has a signal for when he's too lonely and is thus doing himself harm by continued isolation. Here, comedy imitates life, because men are more prone to problematic loneliness sensors than are women. For men, it is not exactly that the sensor is broken. Rather, it is that they have stopped attending to the sensor; it is working, but they don't track it, with consequences analogous to those resulting from your not looking at your working gas gauge. One of my friends ran out of gas recently because he literally could not see the gas gauge—he had leaned a business card in the little slot near where his gas gauge was. He remembered to call his business associate, but he forgot to fill his gas tank.

My friend was focused on business to the exclusion of something that ended up being important, an anecdote that I believe captures a very general process. Men, especially in early adulthood, don't look at the loneliness sensor because they are distracted by other things—status and money, for example—things that men, more than women, think are important (and that indeed *are* important); the trouble with men is, in part, that they sacrifice the importance of friendship and connection on the altar of status and money. Women do this, too; men just do it more.

The sensor problem just described is "alone but oblivious," a result of disharmony between emotional and social loneliness. George Orwell said, "To see what is in front of one's nose needs a constant struggle."[37] Orwell meant it in general, but regarding interpersonal connection, obliviousness is an experience that is common to the lonely sex in the twenties and thirties, but that can continue for decades thereafter. The other form of disharmony is "alone in a crowd," also a result of lack of coordination between emotional and social loneliness, and an experience common to the lonely sex in the fifties and beyond (though at this stage of life there tends to be a back-and-forth vacillation between the "lonely in a crowd" and the "alone but oblivious" states, and in some cases the state of being truly alone). These forms of loneliness are, roughly speaking, equally common.

I regularly serve as an expert witness in legal cases involving death by suicide. The usual scenario is that someone has died by suicide, and someone else, or some agency, is getting sued because of it. Often the family of the decedent is suing a hospital or doctor, claiming (sometimes quite rightly, sometimes not) that more should have been done to prevent their loved one's death. Not surprisingly, in virtually every case in which I've bee involved, the decedent was a man, age forty or older. And in every case, the man had become alienated and angry in the months leading up to his death, often pushing away friends and family who sensed something was amiss and tried to intervene. These men were all very lonely, but if asked, I doubt that they would have acknowledged the fact of their loneliness, a fact that everyone else found glaringly obvious—they were alone but oblivious to their condition. More precisely, they would not have acknowledged it until their final minutes, hours, or days, when they were consumed with feelings of "lonely in a crowd" or were truly lonely. By then, it was too late.

I have asserted that emotional loneliness is social loneliness's sensor or gauge, and that men's attention to this gauge is diverted. If these assertions are true, then at least two things should follow: (1) social loneliness should be, in a sense, more fundamental than emotional loneliness—the thing that is "sensed" (social loneliness, or actual gasoline level) should be more fundamental than the thing that is the sensor (emotional loneliness, or the gas gauge); and (2) the connection between social and emotional loneliness should be closer for women than it is for men—if men have lost track of their sensor, the relation between the sensor (emotional loneliness) and the fundamental thing it's sensing (social loneliness) should be attenuated for men in contrast to women.

This is exactly what my research on loneliness has uncovered. Profound problems should be more associated with social loneliness (the thing "sensed") than with emotional loneliness (the sensor). Indeed they are. My colleagues and I showed that lacking friends was more predictive than emotional loneliness of the onset of major depressive disorder. It was also more predictive of the profound social impairment that can accompany the condition.[38]

I have trouble recalling older men from my more than twenty years of clinical experience. It is not a problem with my memory. Rather, it is a reflection of this book's thesis: men tend not to reach out to others, including mental health professionals. One of the few older men whom I can recall from my clinical practice suffered from a profound form of major depressive disorder. His depression was so intense and long-standing that it rendered him virtually motionless. Getting to therapy—walking from his house to the car and from the car to the therapy office—was as grueling to him as a marathon would be to others, maybe even more so. Once in the therapy room, talking was an ordeal, to the extent that early sessions with him consisted of about 90 percent silence. Past treatments had not worked, including several inpatient psychiatric admissions, antidepressant medicines, and electroconvulsive therapy. What did ultimately work was a relentless focus in therapy on very gradually reconnecting him to others, first a family member, then other relatives, then former friends. Watching videotape of the man at the beginning of treatment and then six months later reminds one of Oliver Sacks's *Awakenings,* the movie version of which starred Robert De Niro as one of several catatonic patients who were transformed by treatment, in those cases by a medicine called L-DOPA. The depressed, nearly catatonic man from my practice was transformed, too, not in his case by medicines, but by a rigorous program of loneliness reduction.

In addition to the finding that lacking friends is, in a sense, more fundamental than emotional loneliness (e.g., more predictive of major depressive disorder), my research has also affirmed the attenuated connection in men between their social and their emotional loneliness. In the research mentioned earlier, which sorts like with like, one can derive an estimate of the strength of association between two categories; for instance, between lacking friends and emotional loneliness. When this is done on loneliness data from a mixed sample of men and women, you see a strong association between lacking friends and emotional loneliness. When all is well, one signals the presence of the other; there is a harmony between the two. When the analysis is repeated among women only, the result is the same with the relationship even clearer. But when the analysis is repeated among men only, the result is different: the connection between lacking friends and emotional loneliness is weaker.[39] The connection between lacking friends and emotional loneliness is attenuated in men, but it is not broken altogether—a fact that will be relevant in generating solutions to this problem. To put the impaired but not broken loneliness sensor of men in context, it is interesting to consider syndromes that do involve a fully broken sensor. One set of such conditions is autism spectrum disorders.

There is a range of conditions in the autism spectrum. The clearest and most severe autistic disorder involves serious communication problems; repetitive, stereotyped behaviors; and marked impairment in social interaction. The condition can involve extreme sensitivity or aversion to physical touch, which, as we will see later, can in a milder form characterize men—and, interestingly enough, autism spectrum disorders are more common in males than females. Impaired social interaction in autism can be very profound, including no sharing of interest or enjoyment with others, and an absence of social and emotional reciprocity—put differently, a broken loneliness sensor.

There is thus a continuum from fully functional loneliness sensors to the fully faulty ones seen in some people with autism; most people are located near the "fully functional" part of the continuum, but men, on average, are located nearer to the midpoint of this continuum, with neither fully faulty nor fully functional loneliness sensors.

Autism spectrum disorders are not the only examples found in nature of the connection between lacking friends and emotional loneliness in men. Nor is it the only example of a problematic instance of a natural phenomenon being out of tune with its own signal. Consider pain in this light. There are individuals, though they are quite rare, who are unable to feel pain. These people might be viewed as fortunate. Perhaps, but only for the duration of their short lives. Such people usually die quite early, because things like infections, joint problems, and appendicitis go unnoticed. For the person with appendicitis, the signal to go to the hospital—that is, pain—is helpful indeed. A different set of people, those with syringomyelia, are unable to feel pain in specific body areas, especially the hands. A smoker with this condition may not notice that a burned-down cigarette is causing severe finger burns. This smoker is cut off from the usually helpful signal of pain.[40] My own theoretical work on suicidal behavior, described in the books *Why People Die by Suicide* and *Myths about Suicide*, have made a similar point. People are designed such that any injury, including self-injury, should set off warning signs and alarm bells. Those who die by suicide have learned a kind of fearlessness of pain, injury, and the like; that is, they have dulled their sensors.

People with autism, syringomyelia, or severe suicidality have permanently dulled sensors. Sensors can be temporarily dulled—numbed might be the better word—in the laboratory as well. Interestingly, in the best characterized paradigm, the numbing agent is not pharmacological, but interpersonal—social exclusion itself temporarily makes people emotionally numb, men and women alike. In these studies, participants

fill out a brief personality questionnaire that they believe will be interpreted by the experimenter.[41] Participants do indeed receive an interpretation, but unbeknownst to them, they are randomly assigned to one
of three feedback conditions, regardless of their answers to the personality questionnaire. In the "future belonging condition," participants
are given the following feedback: "You're the type who has rewarding
relationships throughout life. You're likely to have a long and stable
marriage and have friendships that will last into your later years. The
odds are that you'll always have friends and people who care about
you." This is the group you hope to end up in if you are a participant in
one of these experiments.

In contrast, participants in the "future alone" condition heard the
following feedback: "You're the type who will end up alone later in life.
You may have friends and relationships now, but by your mid-20s most
of these will have drifted away. You may even marry or have several
marriages, but these are likely to be short-lived and not continue into
your 30s. Relationships don't last, and when you're past the age where
people are constantly forming new relationships, the odds are you'll end
up being alone more and more." I know, ouch. But more on this in a
moment, and a quick disclaimer: these studies are carefully scrutinized
and approved by university institutional review boards. Also, notice
how this feedback mirrors the thesis of this book: that men lose connection as they age.

The third group constitutes a control condition, the "misfortune
control condition," and is included so that any effects of social exclusion can be specifically attributed to it and not to the receipt of negative
feedback in general. Participants in this third condition heard the following interpretation of their test results: "You're likely to be accident
prone later in life—you might break an arm or a leg a few times, or
maybe be injured in car accidents. Even if you haven't been accident
prone before, these things will show up later in life, and the odds are
you will have a lot of accidents."

People in the "future belonging" and even in the "misfortune control" groups are more or less unfazed by the procedure. But a host of
negative consequences have been demonstrated for those in the "future

alone" condition: in the laboratory, they engage in more aggressive behavior, less helpful behavior toward others, more self-defeating behavior (e.g., excessive risk-taking, procrastination), and less intelligent thought and logical reasoning. One thing "future alone" participants tend *not* to display, very surprisingly, is negative mood or distress. Instead, their mood state is best characterized as "numb."

Consider the implications, then, of repeated, real-life social exclusion and loneliness: a dulled, numbed sensor, combined with things like excessive risk-taking, anger, and aggression, and a lack of awareness of the consequences (due to the dulled sensor). If this sounds like a description of a typical man to you, you are not alone. A 2008 article stated, "A lot of men have terrible tempers, and what's more, they think it's normal."[42] If you experience a lot of loneliness—as I believe men, in particular, do—your sensor will be out of tune, and you will be more likely to engage in behaviors such as aggression, anger, and excessive risk-taking that may leave you more lonely still, further numbing your sensor, leading to still more negative consequences, and so on and so forth—a negative spiral that can end very badly indeed.

There may be a silver lining, of sorts, to anger, because it is an emotion that involves engagement. Yes, its valence is negative, but its motivation is toward engagement and approach, as opposed to withdrawal and isolation. Men need more of the approach motivation, but not more—preferably less—of the negative valence of anger. Realistic ways to achieve this are a main focus of the last half of the book.

To summarize, loneliness is the experience of unwanted solitude and disconnection; it has two facets—social and emotional loneliness. Social loneliness involves the actual lack of friends and connections to family; it is the more basic facet of loneliness. Emotional loneliness—the internal perception of loneliness—is a sensor for the first facet. In men, the close connection between the emotional sensor and actually lacking friends is, relative to that in women, awry, with potentially severe negative consequences.

This is my answer to the question "What is loneliness?" But what of the other question posed above: Does loneliness mar and kill, and if so, how and why? Loneliness ranks high among the categories of human misery. William James thought a neighboring experience—being ignored—might even be at the very pinnacle of human suffering. In his seminal 1890 book *The Principles of Psychology,* he wrote, "No more fiendish punishment could be devised, were such a thing physically possible, than that one should be turned loose in society and remain absolutely unnoticed by all the members thereof. If no one turned around when we entered, answered when we spoke, or minded what we did, but if every person we met 'cut us dead,' and acted as if we were nonexistent things, a kind of rage and impotent despair would before long well up in us, from which the cruelest bodily torture would be a relief."[43] (It is interesting to note that people sometimes do torture themselves to gain relief from loneliness. A main motivation in patients who engage in nonsuicidal self-injury (not intended to result in death)—cutting is the most common form—is to gain relief from negative and painful emotional states like loneliness. In a sense, the self-injury "works" in that it releases natural painkillers and also distracts the individual from emotional pain. A main goal in the psychotherapy of this condition is to replace self-injury with more adaptive forms of mood regulation.)

A recent study demonstrates the cruelty of being ignored.[44] The researchers were interested in a phenomenon they called "clique isolation," and whether it would increase loneliness and thereby increase depression. They studied over three hundred children and asked each to provide the names of four friends. From the children's lists, a computer algorithm identified cliques—clusters of friends who listed each other as friends—and also identified those children who were not included in any cliques and thus experienced "clique isolation." As expected, the team found that clique isolation was a strong predictor of loneliness, which was, in turn, a significant contributor to the development of depression.

Loneliness leads to depression even among astronauts. In his book *Dragonfly,* Bryan Burrough documents the plight of an astronaut visiting the Russian space station Mir. The astronaut's world was peopled by four men—two cosmonauts who were on board with him, his "ops lead" (the main mission control person on the ground assigned to him), and his flight surgeon. Relationships with the latter two had deteriorated before the astronaut was in space, which, along with his struggles learning Russian, interfered with his forming of close bonds with the two cosmonauts on board. He was isolated, became increasingly withdrawn, and grew lonely and thus depressed. In a reference to a cardinal symptom of depression—anhedonia or the loss of the capacity for pleasure and enjoyment—he recalls thinking, "you love space, you've always enjoyed space. Why don't you love space now?"[45] A different astronaut also profiled in the book represented the "alone but oblivious" type; he alienated the two cosmonauts on board as well as everyone on the ground. At one point, he refused all voice communications with the ground, insisting that all connections be electronic. Had someone asked if he felt lonely, he very likely would have said "no"—alone, but oblivious.

Loneliness researchers have characterized it as an "inner worm that gnaws at the heart."[46] They probably did not mean that literally, but subsequent research affirms that they might just as well have. That loneliness is associated with harm and death has been documented in a dizzyingly diverse array of problems. Loneliness is as strong a risk factor for illness and death as smoking, obesity, and high blood pressure.[47] Lonely women have more difficult labor during pregnancies, experience more postpartum depression, and have babies with lower Apgar scores (a test designed to quickly evaluate a newborn's physical condition after delivery) and lower birth weight, all as compared to non-lonely women—although loneliness and its various roots are less common in women, when they do occur, they are pernicious.[48]

Lonely adults find sleep less restorative than do others, even when sleeping the same duration.[49] Shy people are more vulnerable to major depressive disorder than others, and loneliness has been shown to be the reason.[50] Loneliness is associated with decreased functioning of the immune system, and urinary levels of stress hormones are higher in lonely people.[51] Married people—who probably have, on average, lower loneliness levels than others—survive cancer better than single individuals.[52] Loneliness increases the risk of dying from heart disease, cancer, and stroke.[53] Loneliness is a strong predictor of suicidal behavior; this is true among children,[54] adolescents,[55] and adults[56] alike. Decelerating use of interpersonal language in poetry is more characteristic of poets who kill themselves than of other poets; that is to say, lonely poets are more likely to kill themselves than less lonely poets.[57] That loneliness is a powerful risk factor for suicidal behavior was an important point in John Sym's *Lifes Preservative against Self-Killing*, published almost 400 years ago.[58] A full reckoning of the steep costs of loneliness is needed before we are positioned to consider workable solutions to the problem, which is the focus of the last part of the book.

The costs of loneliness are steep indeed: it may also deteriorate the brain. In a study reported on in 2008, researchers assessed social connectedness and cognitive functioning in over 16,500 US adults age fifty and older.[59] A list of ten words was presented to participants, and recall was tested immediately; it was tested again after five minutes had elapsed (thus making twenty the highest number of words participants could recall). The total number of words remembered served as the index of cognitive functioning, and social connection was measured as a composite of contact with spouse, family, and neighbors, as well as volunteer activities. Overall, at the outset of the study when the average age was approximately sixty-five, participants remembered around eleven words total. Six years later, the average total had dropped a bit, to ten words total. More to the present point, however, the researchers concluded, "Memory among the least [socially] integrated declined at twice the rate as among the most integrated."[60]

A severe and acute form of loneliness—bereavement—may change the functioning of the heart. Researchers at the University of Sydney studied approximately eighty people who had recently lost a loved one, as well as a similar number who had not, and found that periods of very rapid heartbeats were more common in the bereaved group.[61] Overall, the average heart rate was approximately seventy-five beats per minute in the bereaved participants, as compared to approximately seventy-one beats per minute in the control participants. These changes in heart rhythm, by themselves, are not necessarily reason for concern, but, in interaction with pre-existing vulnerability, they can increase the risk of problems. In fact, it is known that the months following the death of a loved one represent a time of heightened vulnerability for heart attacks and strokes.

A BBC News item from 2009 opened, "Fresh evidence adds weight to suggestions that loneliness makes cancer both more likely and deadly."[62] A recent meta-analysis (a study of studies) makes the predictive relationship of loneliness to death in general very clear.[63] To quote the researchers, "Data across 308,849 individuals, followed for an average of 7.5 years, indicate that individuals with adequate social relationships have a 50% greater likelihood of survival compared to those with poor or insufficient social relationships. The magnitude of this effect is comparable with quitting smoking and it exceeds many well-known risk factors for mortality (e.g., obesity, physical inactivity)."

Loneliness thus kills and mars indeed. But how does it do so, how does a social thing get "under the skin" and, crucial in the present context, why are men so prone to become victims of loneliness the killer? With regard to how it kills, at least three kinds of mechanisms are at work, one interpersonal, one psychological, and one cellular/genetic.

The interpersonal mechanism is not hard to fathom, and has already been foreshadowed by the loner in the *Kids in the Hall* sketch: lonely people experience fewer opportunities for others to provide them with help and advice ("you better get that toe checked out"). The psychological mechanism, too, has been foreshadowed, in this case by the "future alone" studies, in which participants manipulated to experience loneliness displayed characteristics like excessive risk-taking and procrastination. It is not difficult to imagine how excessive risk-taking and procrastination ("I'll get my toe checked out next week") might erode health.

A related psychological mechanism is that being connected to others makes us feel more capable in general, and in particular, more efficacious in handling hardship—a "strength in numbers" effect. A study demonstrating this fact fitted undergraduates with backpacks that were quite heavy. The students were led to the base of a steep hill, and then asked to estimate how steep the hill was. Same heavy backpack, same hill for everyone, but steepness estimates ranged considerably. What accounted for this range?

A major factor was having a friend nearby. Those who were alone when they made their judgments of the hill's slope saw the hill as a difficult challenge, whereas those who stood next to friends when making their estimates viewed the hill as less daunting. Among those who were with friends, the longer the friends had known each other, the less troubling a challenge they viewed the hill. Same hill for everyone, with the same objective steepness—but it appeared easier to those who were with friends.

In addition to interpersonal and psychological mechanisms of the impact of loneliness on health, a very intriguing cellular mechanism for the effects of loneliness involves the length of telomeres. Telomeres are the protective coating on the tips of chromosomes, somewhat similar to the plastic sheath at the end of a shoelace that keeps the lace from fraying. Just as when an aglet weakens or breaks, a shoelace frays, so when a telomere shortens, a chromosome frays. You don't want your chromosomes fraying; if they do, the business of duplicating the chromosome and all of its crucial information cannot proceed fully, because the "frayed" information is lost. When it comes to DNA, information loss is not a good thing and can result in many problems including, for example, cancer.

Crucial to loneliness and in particular to accelerating male loneliness across the lifespan, it has been shown that social stress shortens telomeres,[64] a finding that has been positively characterized, accurately I think, as "a leap across a vast interdisciplinary canyon."[65] And it has been shown, in turn, that telomere shortening is predictive of mortality.[66] Telomere shortening occurs in men and women alike in response to social stress, but as we have seen already, men suffer from a pernicious form of social stress—loneliness—as compared to women.

Cancer researchers have done work on mice showing that social isolation can affect the expression of genes involved in the development of cancer. A 2009 project involved mice who were all genetically predisposed to cancer, and all similarly so.[67] Some mice were in a usual lab environment, which includes normal patterns of social interaction between the animals; other mice were in an unfavorable social environment, characterized by social isolation. Despite the fact that both groups of mice were genetically and thus biologically quite similar to one another, there was a marked difference between them in a highly biologically relevant outcome: the socially isolated group developed significantly more tumors than did the normally interacting group. One of the researchers involved in the study remarked that "the social environment may in fact alter the biology of cell growth." The effects of the social environment were literally "getting under the skin" of these mice, here, in the production of cancer. Needless to say, this study is more relevant to mice than to humans, but the reason studies like this are done is to shed light on disease in humans through animal models of the illness in question.

Perhaps all of this concern about loneliness and its aftermath is alarmist. What if, for example, men and women are getting less lonely over time? After all, social media really did not exist ten years ago, and now they do, so loneliness may have decreased, at least in well-connected sectors of society. Even if this were true, I would stand by the assertions that loneliness is a more vexed issue for men than for women, a problem that is exacerbated by aging; and that those who are affected by loneliness experience a host of untoward health consequences as a result.

But it is not even true that loneliness is decreasing, far from it. An October 2010 article described a survey conducted by *AARP: The Magazine;* the article's lead was "Americans are getting lonelier by the day," and it asserted that "chronic loneliness is rising at staggering rates for Americans."[68] The survey, conducted on over 3,000 people age forty-five and older, revealed that 35 percent of the sample was chronically lonely, whereas, ten years earlier, a similar survey had returned a figure of 20 percent. The article concluded, "the percentage of people who are lonely in their 50s nearly doubled in the past 10 years and increased almost 50% among those in their 60s." This trend may occur into the future for quite a while; a study from Loughborough University in England found that approximately 1 in 5 students reported chronic loneliness. Twenty percent may not sound especially high, but it should be recalled that these are young people immersed in a social environment of rampant opportunities for connection, and still 1 in 5 report not just that they are lonely, but chronically so. And 1 in 5 may be an underestimate. A recent project surveyed 320 US institutions and found that more than half of students reported significant feelings of loneliness.[69] A headline stemming from a BBC survey affirms this perspective: "Facebook generation is loneliest." The Australian Unity Wellbeing Index revealed that more than 30 percent of Australians reported loneliness as a substantial problem, with men more affected by the problem than women.

Even as loneliness is shortening the list of people one can count on for solace and support, it is shortening one's telomeres; even as loneliness deprives the flow of healthful information from friend to friend, it disrupts the flow of information—DNA in this case—from parent cell to daughter cell. Loneliness exerts this effect on anyone who experiences it; the more loneliness, the more the damage and disruption. Men suffer more from loneliness, and as we have seen, this is due in part to their having lost track of their loneliness sensor.

Was their sensor damaged to begin with, or did it develop malfunctions over time?

I think it's mostly the latter, that it malfunctions over time. My sons both seem to have fully functioning sensors. I did too when I was their age. I remember throwing a crying fit at age seven, not because I was prone to such fits, not because I had been excluded by a friend, and not because I wasn't with a friend (I was at the time), but because I imagined the possibility of social exclusion by a friend—a functioning sensor indeed. But that was then. Men's loneliness sensor gets dulled, making them the lonely sex, with untoward results for them as well as for those who know and love them.

ARE THERE SOLUTIONS to this problem? Group therapy where older men sit around and cry or draw with each other? As a man in his forties from Georgia who has been to NASCAR, the Indy 500, and the Super Bowl, who likes alcohol a lot more than guns (but understands the latter's attraction), and who played golf as a kid, may play it again, and in the meantime watches it on TV, I'm quite sure the answer to group therapy is "no." This book's final section proposes solutions for the lonely sex, but only those that are realistic given the very real constraints that male identity exerts on participation in things like group therapy. In my opinion, a fatal flaw of past work on men's problems is that solutions are posed that could work, in principle, for the average person, but do not work, in practice, for actual men. This flaw in past work has been compounded by the error of misunderstanding the problem for which solutions are needed—in many quarters, men are accused of all sorts of things, when the core problem is really that they reap the harvest of late-life loneliness from the seeds of early neglect of cultivating lasting friendships. My goal in this book is to deliver on the promise of explicating this core dilemma; to show the way out of this lonely morass via solutions men will find credible and viable.

I can spot ersatz solutions because I am a relatively hard-drinking sports fan from Georgia—a son of the American South, where suspicion is high, rightly I believe, about ornate solutions that seem unnatural. But just as urging men to go to group therapy is doomed as a solution, so is going too far in the other direction. A recent article stated, "'retrosexual' has all but replaced 'metrosexual' in the lifestyle sections of national magazines, which are full of stories about affluent urbanites wearing hunting garb, buying designer axes, and writing about the art of manliness on blogs with names like (ahem) the 'Art of Manliness.'"[70] I won't be recommending that men convene in the woods to get in touch with their primitive sides (though, as we will see, reconnecting to nature itself—as opposed to attempting to reconnect with man's primitive nature—is one component of a viable solution to male loneliness). The intermediate area between overly "soft" solutions like group therapy and "hard" ones like living by one's wits in the woods is thus the goal. It should be noted, however, that one of these extremes is probably more mistaken than the other; going too "soft" is probably less effective than going too "hard." There is a reason, after all, that the term "retrosexual" exists. And, just from my own store of personal experiences, I can think of ones that were both fairly "retrosexual" and also memorable and facilitative of bonding with my friends—for instance, Viking night in college, when we dressed in hides, ate full roasted chickens with our hands off of bare tables, and drank mead. I can remember no such bonding experiences that are more in the direction of group therapy. This is not to say that I recommend juvenile, liquor-fueled dress-up experiences as a solution to male loneliness, nor do I argue that group therapy is always or even usually useless; the point, rather, is that there is a sweet spot, and, on the continuum from a caricature version of group therapy all the way on up to Viking night, erring in the direction of the latter is probably best.

Not only am I a child of the American South, a professor, a clinical psychologist, and a survivor of Viking night, I am also the son of my father. My dad had close friendships in early adulthood, but they faded or failed for whatever reason. I have godparents; they were close friends of my dad's and I can still recall the excitement he showed when our families socialized. Tellingly, he lost touch with them, to the extent that I had not seen them in the ten years or so before his death by suicide (his death occurred twenty years ago as I write), and I cannot recall their names. My dad had friends, and the problem is not precisely that he lost them (though that is part of it); the precise problem is that he did not replenish them—and I believe it killed him, or more accurately, led him to kill himself. His autopsy report should read "Male, age fifty-six, cause of suicide: friendlessness."

This was not the case for another man I knew who lived well into his eighties and died from natural causes. This guy John was a hard-living, son-of-a-bitch type, but very likable. At his memorial service, I was surprised to learn of a habit of his—he called at least one friend a day just to talk for a few minutes. Through the years he had some male friends who found these calls a little pointless. Well, as someone noted at the memorial service, they all died long before John did. He worked at initiating new friendships and maintaining old friendships, and it sustained him. As the book's concluding section will show, solutions for the lonely sex are not very complex; they can be as simple—and thus as credible and as viable—as calling one person per day.

LONELINESS IS A VICIOUS KILLER. It preferentially stalks men. Like the victims of many killers, the victims of loneliness don't realize the danger until it's too late.

Men are coddled and spoiled in many ways, but it is not all wine and roses. When it comes to death, illness, and injury, men take it on the chin, and women are left, relatively speaking, unscathed; less affected, that is, by illness, injury, and early mortality.

The power, success, and money of men belie their frailty, a frailty that I believe derives from escalating loneliness. The trouble starts when friends are no longer served up on a platter. Women seem to cope with this transition better than most men, in part because their "loneliness sensors" are much more attuned than those of men. Men, as a rule, focus laser-like on money and status, achieve them, and end up feeling empty and lonely because all the while they neglected friendships. The origins, characteristics, and consequences of this problem—and remedies for it, both adaptive and less so—represent this book's principal concern. We start the story in the next section on the problem's origins, which are fuelled by a spoiled mindset and attitudes like "don't tread on me," a hallowed saying of American independence, but, as we shall see, a problematic one.

SECTION II

THE CAUSES AND THE CONSEQUENCES

2
CAUSES
BECOMING SPOILED

In a fit of over-ambition or perhaps just plain idiocy, I asked my fourteen-year-old son some questions about differences between boys and girls on how spoiled they are. The answers were not only monosyllabic and monotonic, but bereft of helpful information—answers like "no" and "they're the same." Of course his answers were like that. What was I thinking?

I don't have a daughter, but many of my friends do (and I have two younger sisters), and it is my distinct impression that, had I asked a fourteen-year-old girl the same questions, I might not necessarily (though possibly) have gotten more accurate answers, but I am certain I would have gotten *more* answers. I recently visited one of my old friends who now has a teenage daughter, and I found the sheer volume of talk that occurred between her and her parents absolutely staggering. Not annoying or otherwise unpleasant (though my friend assures me that this occurs, too), but simply so voluminous as to bring to mind comparisons between dripping faucets (my son) and rivers (my friend's daughter). It wasn't small talk, either; the torrent occurred regardless of topic, including the very ones that send my son into total silence, like the topic of boyfriends and girlfriends, for instance.

Herein, at least anecdotally, lies a gender difference—amount of talking. It is a difference to which I will return shortly, and reflects differences that are deeper and not quite so obvious. But, first, another anecdote related to my son's laconic nature: I find it quite normal and at times he is wise, humorous, considered, and perceptive (and yes, at times, very annoying). By stark contrast, my wife finds it absolutely maddening. This has many consequences, including my wife's evident and escalating frustration, my son's bewilderment and, on occasion, irritability about why she wants to know so much, and frequent conversations about adopting baby girls (yes, plural), one of whom would be named Sofia, from Mexico (my wife's *patria*) or some other country like Guatemala. I have never initiated one of these conversations.

Male concision meets female verbosity—or is it male brusqueness or even defensiveness? A difference between males and females, then, involves the simple quantity of words uttered. Women talk a lot, and lest you attribute this statement to my being male and thus biased or to my naively buying into stereotypes, don't just take it from me. Take it from researchers from the Netherlands, who studied teens' secret keeping from parents.[1]

Over three hundred adolescents were included in the study— approximately equal numbers of boys and girls—and they were assessed once a year from around age thirteen to around age sixteen. As the study progressed, boys' secret keeping clearly outpaced that of their female counterparts. Intriguingly, in boys, the extent of secret keeping was not particularly strongly associated with problematic relationships with their parents, suggesting that for boys, secret keeping (at least from parents) is more or less par for the course. And for girls? Recall, overall they tended to be less secretive—that is, to talk more—with their parents, but, for those girls who were secret keepers, relationships with parents tended to be rocky. The study suggests that boys' reticence with parents not only is salient, but accelerates during adolescence and is the norm; this pattern matches exactly the anecdotal example of my son as compared to my friend's daughter.

Perhaps all this is simply specific to the Dutch, or to the matter of keeping secrets from parents, but the evidence suggests otherwise. For example, a study on kids from the United States, Argentina, and Italy found that, compared to boys, girls were more responsive to their mothers, and more willing to involve mothers in their own activities.[2]

A very different kind of research converges on the very same conclusion. Kids, needless to say, develop various interests ranging from trucks to friends to dolls to sports to books, but a few kids develop interests that are extremely intense. For instance, consider the following description of a young boy's interest, taken from a research article on the phenomenon of intense interests in childhood: "Early in [his] second year, an interest emerged for brooms and sweeping floors. It soon expanded to encompass cleaning brushes and then generalized to all sorts of other brushes—hairbrushes, paintbrushes, toothbrushes, and so on. His parents indulged his passion to the extent that there were eventually toothbrushes in every room of the house so he would never have to be without one."[3] This is an intense interest indeed, very nearly an obsession, and is also in regard to something that most other people find mundane and uninteresting. Not just that, the interest is completely unpeopled, an important point to which I will soon return.

This article makes two key points. First, the development of extremely intense interests in childhood is far more common in boys than in girls. Second, here is a list of the most common categories of interests developed by children in the study: vehicles, trains, machines, balls/spherical things, and dinosaurs. Twenty-eight of the children in the study had developed one of these five categories of intense interest; all but one were boys. A commonality among these five categories is that they do not involve people at all. In categories that are less impersonal (e.g., babies, live animals), the gender difference is less pronounced.

Thus far, we have seen phenomena in boys like secret keeping, reticence, and interest in things that do not involve people. These are some of the seeds that lead boys more than girls to develop a spoiled attitude. If you can sit back and be silent—that is, not work very hard socially—and yet, you are nevertheless responded to, you might absorb the message that relationship cultivation and maintenance work is unnecessary, that you are to the social manor born. Put differently, you might become interpersonally spoiled.

IN AN TALK ENTITLED "A Tale of Two Hormones," the speaker stated (after classifying herself as "the renegade du jour"), "Wherever you go, you will see females far less likely than males to see what is so fascinating about ohms, carburetors, and quarks."[4] In the same remarks, she summarized data on mathematically gifted girls and boys—the top 1 percent in math ability among US tenth graders. The boys' top interests, not surprisingly given their math interests, were things like math and science; the girls' top interests, and keep in mind they were every bit as mathematically talented as the boys, included literature, art, and social services. Even among uniquely capable math whizzes, the girls' main interests are peopled, the boys' are not.

This distinction has been coined the "people versus things" dichotomy, and it is apparent not just in high schoolers, but even in babies. Four-month-old baby girls enjoy looking at facial expressions more than do their boy counterparts, who preferentially attend to things like shapes, patterns, and blinking lights—here again, an unpeopled domain. At age two, boys' speech is more likely to be about the unpeopled terrain of cars and trains, whereas that of girls is more likely to contain references to people. These kinds of differences are even apparent in chimpanzees' attitudes toward sticks. In a recent study published in *Current Biology,* the only stick-related activity in which females engage more than males is cradling and carrying a stick as if it were a baby chimp.[5] Female chimps invest sticks with a human-like quality; male chimps do not.

Make no mistake, hormones like testosterone matter for males and females alike. To take one of many possible examples, researchers took testosterone levels from University of Chicago business school students. Those with higher testosterone levels, male and female alike, were more willing to choose high-risk, high-reward career trajectories like investment banking. Here, a "male" hormone is associated with a focus on money and status, another process covered in a later chapter that is a source for accelerating male loneliness across the lifespan.

Imagine you are in a psychology experiment that a lab technician tells you is about "the relationship between chemicals in the body and psychology." You fill out some questionnaires, provide a saliva sample in a small cup, and then the tech tells you that the rest of the study will be conducted in a small office down the hall. Unbeknownst to you, the experimenters have arranged for an actor—the term researchers often use is "confederate"—to walk toward you and bump into you, not in a way that will cause injury or pain, but in a way that is rude. Would you react with some form of aggression, at least verbal aggression? The saliva in the cup can, to a degree, foretell the answer to this question: when researchers conduct this kind of study, testosterone levels in the saliva sample predict whether or not the bumped-into person will react aggressively

My overall argument, it should be noted, is not that all or even most men's worlds are completely unpeopled (though it is my argument that, given that an individual is asocial, odds are high that that individual is male). In this context, consider the following anecdote, versions of which I myself have witnessed many times.[6] The setting is an academic conference, and into a crowded room walks the editor of the field's main journal. The editor is, by virtue of the position, powerful, and therefore many people would like an audience; a kind of entourage forms in the editor's wake, hardly an unpeopled existence, but also one for which the editor is doing little interpersonal work.

Note that thus far, I have not mentioned whether the editor is a man or a woman; at this point in the story, it does not matter.

The scene now shifts to the same conference, two years later, after the editor has stepped down. To quote psychologist Roy Baumeister, writing about male editors, "Once they stop being editors . . . these same guys wander alone through the social hours, drink in hand, hoping to latch on to somebody else's conversational group."[7] Putting aside my personal angst as a current journal editor, I think the last part of this story would be different if the editor were female. After stepping down, her entourage, like her male counterpart's, would be gone. But would she be as lonely at the cocktail party? No, because, if she is similar to the average woman, her world is peopled beyond her position as editor due to ongoing interpersonal effort;

his is peopled—again if he is similar to the average man—largely as a function of his position as editor, not because of interpersonal effort. When the position is gone, so are the people.

The hormones alluded to in the "A Tale of Two Hormones" talk are, to put it simply (if somewhat inaccurately) the "male and female hormones" testosterone and estrogen, respectively. The moniker "male and female" is inaccurate because both substances reside in the bodies of both men and women, but it is nonetheless useful because testosterone and estrogen are so essential to male and female development, respectively. There is indeed little doubt that their levels, both in utero and beyond, influence behavior and attitude, at least to some degree. Of course they also influence the body itself. In addition to the quite obvious areas of influence such as sexual characteristics, I will focus instead on a more subtle and surprising one—finger length.

Why do we place our wedding bands on the fourth digit, the "ring finger?" "Because it's the ring finger" is not a satisfactory answer; a moment's reflection on times when our ancestors did not wear rings or anything else will show it was necessarily not always thus.

An intriguing possible factor is that the fourth digit is particularly sensitive to the presence, prenatally, of testosterone. It is, of all the five digits, the most "sexed"—at least if by "sexed" it is meant influenced by sex hormones. More specifically, research suggests that prenatal testosterone promotes the growth of the fourth digit, whereas prenatal estrogen increases the length of the second digit (pointer finger). This means, then, that ratio of the lengths of the second to the fourth fingers will be lower in men than in women. That is, men, on average, will have relatively shorter second digits and relatively longer fourth digits, making their ratio lower (the bigger number being in the denominator). For women, on average, the opposite will be the case. This ratio is well established before birth, and fixed by age two and has been shown to be a valid indicator of the prenatal hormonal environment. It works the same way, incidentally, in baboons, mice, and other species, too.

Most people, upon learning of this interesting fact about nature, begin to examine their own ring fingers and pointer fingers, trying to judge their relative lengths. Eyeballing does not work well in this regard, however, because the differences come down to millimeters and also because the two fingers are placed differently on the hand; examine your palm, and notice that the ring finger is situated at a lower relative position than the pointer finger.

Now turn your hand over, because there is one way to get some sense of this phenomenon just by eyeballing. Examine the hair pattern across your fingers. This works for men and women both—though women are certainly less hairy than men, women do have some hair on their hands and (the backs of) their fingers. For many people, the ring finger will be relatively hairier than the other fingers, and this has to do with that digit's sensitivity to testosterone (this works in both genders, though it's often clearer in men simply because of an increased hairiness overall). Furthermore, for many people, the pointer finger will be relatively more hairless than the other fingers, due to this digit's sensitivity to estrogen. (For more fun with your various digits, the same pattern, at least with regard to digit length, occurs in the toes, but in reverse: men's second toe tends to be longer than women's; men's fourth toe tends to be shorter than womens').

A uterine environment that is relatively high in testosterone and relatively low in estrogen tends to produce not just longer ring fingers and shorter pointer fingers, and not just hairier ring fingers and less hairy pointer fingers, but also the following things: relatively high mental rotation ability; relatively low verbal fluency; physical strength; speed; athletic ability; and autism spectrum disorders.

These characteristics are all relatively more common in men than in women. Moreover, with one exception, none of these traits is very peopled. The one exception, of course, is verbal fluency but this exception corroborates the larger point, because this ability—which is peopled in the sense that to be verbal means interacting with others—is somewhat higher, on average, in women. A female friend of mine who is a successful novelist told me that she is suspicious of this latter fact. She is, quite demonstrably, above average in verbal fluency, and, she claimed, she strives to keep her life as unpeopled as she can. Her doubts were allayed somewhat, however, when I reminded her that she spends hours every day writing stories about people.

Extremely intense interests can characterize autism, a syndrome alluded to in chapter 1 and mentioned again just above. A keen fascination with the way machines work or with train schedules and the like is not uncommon in autism—a condition that is more likely to strike boys than girls. I have already noted that baby boys tend to look at geometric shapes and other unpeopled things more than do baby girls. Of interest in this context, a 2011 paper reported a study of around one hundred toddlers who watched a one-minute movie.[8] On half the screen, moving geometric images were displayed; on the other half of the screen, children were displayed engaging in activities like dancing or doing yoga. The research team was interested in how long the toddlers fixated their eyes on the two different halves of the screen, and whether this fixation duration might be able to predict autism spectrum problems. In a fascinating result, 100 percent of the toddlers who fixated on the geometric patterns for 70 percent of the time were independently classified as having autism spectrum symptoms (and most of them were boys).

Children with extremely intense interests, as is true of many people with autism spectrum disorders, are interested in the relatively clear-cut mechanics of how things work. So, to a somewhat lesser degree, are people who display the personality characteristic of *instrumentality*. This trait, which involves attitudes of assertion, focusing on the bottom line, not caring how you get there as long as you get there, and being a "go-getter," is already reliably evident in children by age three or so, as is the fact that significantly more boys than girls show this personality characteristic and is largely due to genes and other elements of biology. (Incidentally, it is an interesting fact that, among boys, first-borns tend to be more instrumental than later-borns—a finding to which I will return in the final chapter.)

Instrumentality is a spur to becoming spoiled. The trait encourages ignoring relationships in favor of things and outcomes; it facilitates the taking for granted of relationships that characterizes men more than women; and it is thus a main source for male loneliness and all the woe that comes with it.

One of my favorite if well-worn American colloquialisms is "you can't get there from here." The phrase's meaning is primarily that there is no direct route from A to B (perhaps because of natural rural barriers like mountains and rivers); the only possible way is indirect. First, go from A to C, and only then can you go directly to B, from C. The saying is likely frustrating, if not impenetrable, to those with instrumental personality characteristics, who are in a hurry to "get there," and who do not care how they "get there" as long as they do. The sentiment underneath the saying implies that instrumentality does not always work, that there are times when it pays to slow down, focus at least as much on process as on outcome, and put off ultimate goals for smaller ones. The phrase's denotation does not include "stop and smell the roses" advice, but its connotation can be expanded to include it.

Instrumentality, however, clearly has some advantages. For instance, it is a protective factor against depression (although, as we have seen and will explore in more detail, it can also forestall problems that come crashing down on men in later life). Instrumentality is involved in one of the clearest gender differences in all of psychology, namely, that approximately twice as many women as men are affected by major depressive disorder (the same is not true, intriguingly, about bipolar disorder, with which men and women are afflicted about equally). The depression gender difference is an interesting fact in its own right, and is also notable because it is one of the relatively few exceptions to the "men take it on the chin" rule of health described earlier. As has already been documented, men experience more and earlier health problems than do women, and much of this is attributable to loneliness. Depression is an exception to this rule.

Reams of evidence support the perspective that women experience more depression than men, but that certainly does not stop people from doubting the fact. The doubts usually run along one of two lines of thought, both mistaken. One is that the gender difference in depression is not genuine, but rather is an example of bias against women. This assertion implies that having depression is a flaw or weakness, a view that colludes with prejudice against those with mental disorders. This is a prejudice that I think is as appalling as any other, and one ultimate goal of my scientific work is to reduce it. In this same vein, at a workshop I gave on depression, I heard someone exclaim: "Of course the people who do this research must be all men!" This is one of those statements that is impressive in its mistakenness. For not only does the statement implicitly endorse prejudice against those with mental disorders, it is factually wrong, as the most prominent researchers on the topic are women.

The other line of thought that questions the depression gender difference accuses researchers not of bias, but of a lack of imagination. More specifically, the usual criticisms are things like "well, of course researchers find that more women than men are depressed, because men won't admit their depression, or won't seek treatment for their depression, or they express their depression in other ways like drinking or anger." It is a relief that these criticisms are at least plausible, because indeed, as compared to women, men drink more, tend to be more stoic about health problems of all kinds, and tend not to seek help. This is the approach taken in *I Don't Want to Talk about It,* a 1997 book on men and depression by Terrence Real.[9] An essential point of the book is that men are out of touch with their feelings and that this has caused a "silent epidemic" of depression in men. There are, in my opinion, two major problems here: (1) There is very scant empirical evidence of a "silent epidemic" of depression in men or anyone else (there is an epidemic of sorts, but it is not silent at all, and it affects women decidedly more than it does men); and (2) Telling men to get in touch with their feelings is, I believe based on personal and clinical experience, doomed to fail because most men will not buy this, because the ones who do are not representative of most men, and because, even for those who do, the essential problem is not really being out of touch with feelings but rather being out of touch with friends.

Ideas like this—for example that men really are as depressed as women but just won't talk about it as much as women will—are viable, and it was important for researchers to address them and rule them out. The bottom line is that time after time, these criticisms have been addressed, and they simply do not explain the gender difference in depression. Differences in traits like instrumentality represent a better explanation.

As another example, consider the idea that men simply express their depression through alcoholism—after all, it is true that more men than women have alcohol problems. So, imagine a study in which all the men and women are matched for drinking level—that is, men are selected for participation who drink, let's say, seven alcoholic drinks per week, and similarly, women are selected who drink seven alcoholic drinks per week. Any differences between the men and women are not likely due to alcohol, because the men and women drink the same amount of alcohol. And what do you find in a study like this? The same old result—for every one man who experiences major depression, two women do. This same gender difference occurs in various socioeconomic and ethnic groups.

Not only is this gender difference one of the better replicated findings in all of psychopathology research, it also occurs cross-culturally. In country after country, despite considerable cultural and other differences, the same depression ratio of two women to one man usually turns up.

An important source for the gender difference in depression is the personality trait of instrumentality. This characteristic protects people from the development of depression. That's the good news about it. The dark side of instrumentality, however, harks back to the "people-versus-things" dichotomy. Instrumentality discourages an emphasis on people qua people and instead facilitates a focus on things, how things work, and also on people as means to ends. Put differently, it encourages an interpersonally spoiled attitude.

The bargain here has Faustian elements for men and women alike. Women have it harder than men—about twice as hard judging by prevalence rates—when it comes to depression, one of the relatively few health conditions to take a higher toll on women than men (though there are others, of course, including complications arising from pregnancy and childbirth). Some of this hardship derives from relatively lower levels of instrumentality in women. On the other hand, this cost in depression vulnerability, and the low instrumentality that underlies it, pays some dividends, because low instrumentality tends to promote a mindset of relatedness and expressivity. This mindset, in turn, decreases women's rates of loneliness over the lifespan, and thereby saves them from the grave consequences, documented above, left in loneliness's wake.

More depression vulnerability in exchange for lower loneliness—a deal that nature conspires to offer women. More loneliness but, via high instrumentality, less depression risk—the corresponding deal most men see. Of course experiencing neither loneliness nor depression would be optimal, but it is illuminating to ask which is the more grievous.

It is a measure of the perniciousness of loneliness that I believe that the better deal is depression risk in exchange for less loneliness. This is saying a lot, because major depressive disorder is a bane indeed. It is a relatively common condition that is probably on the rise, it lingers in quite chronic fashion, it is exceedingly painful and incapacitating, and it can be fatal (the usual mechanism of death being suicide).

Nevertheless, loneliness is a scourge that may outpace even all of this. As we have seen, it is a significant drain on physical health, not to mention mental health, and is a major killer. It causes and exacerbates an array of physical and mental maladies, including depression. The key, however, to fully appreciating loneliness's devastation is to ponder its prevalence. A diverse set of studies converges on the conclusion that serious, chronic loneliness affects at least 1 in 5 people (some studies return rates as high as 1 in 3). Recall, in this context, the study from England in which 1 in 5 college students reported *chronic* loneliness, and this among young people privileged enough to attend a university (and to thereby enjoy all the social connectedness that universities provide). Given the argument presented in this book, as well as empirical findings from various quarters, the 1 in 5 rate could easily turn into 1 in 4 or even 1 in 3 as this cohort ages.

"Epidemic" is probably an exaggeration, though others have made the claim. Some have characterized our time as the lonely century. A May 25, 2010, article in the *Times* of London carried the headline "Britain in Grip of Epidemic of Loneliness."

Given all this, and given that loneliness disproportionately affects men, and that such conditions are more lethal in men than women (as reflected, for example, in the 4-to-1 male-to-female suicide rate—and this despite the 2-to-1 female-to-male depression rate), there is a case to be made that loneliness rivals or even exceeds depression as a contributor to human misery. Patch Adams thinks so. The colorful physician, who was portrayed by Robin Williams in the film *Patch Adams,* recently stated, "Depression is a symptom of loneliness. It is not a disease. Loneliness is the disease."[10] The doctor could perhaps benefit from revisiting some facts (depression is not only a disease, but a very malignant one at that), but his remarks do underscore the truth that loneliness is vicious.

Instrumentality, despite its role as a depression buffer, thus represents a net loss for men. It is a characteristic that helps get things done, and our culture needs that, without a doubt. But it is also a temperamental substrate on which are built things like "spoiled" and "don't tread on me" attitudes. These, too, have their allure, but in the end, there's a "fool's gold" quality to them. They look valuable indeed, only to prove at a later time not merely worthless but also a squandering of all that time spent time gazing at the shine of status and money, and distracted thereby from building relationships that would be sustaining over a lifetime.

It is possible to navigate between the Scylla of hyper-instrumentality and its attendant loneliness and the Charybdis of forsaking instrumentality and its attendant paths to status and money. Routes to a middle way are needed; money and status are essential, but in addition to—not at the cost of—relationship initiation and cultivation. In the *Odyssey,* Odysseus managed to make it through the literal Scylla and Charybdis— sea monsters on either side of a narrow ocean pass—and tellingly, it cost him. His strategy was to err toward Scylla, who likely would pluck off and devour a few of his crew, and to avoid Charybdis, who tended to devour ships whole.

Odysseus made it, but lost six men to Scylla. Analogously, if less dramatically, a main thesis of this book is that men can make it through narrow passes, too, passes that are constituted by tensions between things like status, money, love, friendships, and loneliness. To make it though, an Odyssean approach is needed, not in the sense of being heroic (though it can have those elements), but in the sense of forethought and of a willingness to sacrifice now for the future and for the greater good. Odysseus was an epic hero and a mythical one; the final section of the book examines ways through narrow passes that do not require a mythical hero, but that do require foresight and work.

WE HAVE FOUND THAT, overall, boys are more secretive with their parents than are girls, a secrecy that accelerates over the course of adolescence, and boys are less responsive to and inclusive of their mothers in comparison with girls. Studies show that, should a child develop an extremely intense interest, that child is very likely to be male and that interest is highly likely *not* to involve other people. Boys are more instrumental than girls; and, numerous findings, including those involving mathematically gifted boys and girls and prenatal hormones, point to the generally unpeopled nature of boys' worlds. All of these findings are consistent with the claim of a substantial gender difference in relating to other people, what might be termed "interpersonal orientation." Boys' interpersonal orientation is more distant, independent, secretive . . . and spoiled.

And they literally talk less. In one representative study, researchers were interested not just in gender differences in amount of talking but also in personality differences.[11] In fact, they had some sense that personality factors like expressiveness, openness, and agreeableness would exert strong influences on speech frequency, and perhaps would represent stronger influences than would gender. This is a plausible enough expectation—it stands to reason that a trait like expressiveness would affect speech frequency powerfully, whether the speaker was female or male. And indeed, agreeableness, openness, and expressiveness were each associated with speech frequency. But gender overshadowed them as a predictor; females used substantially more speech than did males, virtually regardless of personality factors.

This result is consistent with the argument I am building here that there are basic social differences between men and women that begin unfolding over time early in development. But even more than that, it is, upon reflection, an incredible result. To get a clear sense of this, think of all the men you know. Some are highly gregarious, some very reserved, and many are somewhere in between the two extremes. Now, do the same mental exercise regarding all the women you know. The overall pattern will probably be similar, although perhaps it will be harder to think of examples of extremely reserved women (as it should be, given my overall thesis). Focus on the considerable amount of variation on sociality *within* each gender. What accounts for most of this variation are the personality factors mentioned above, traits like expressivity, openness, and agreeableness. The fact that, when the genders are combined into one group, gender rises to the top as a predictor of speech frequency, even beyond a personality characteristic like expressivity, shows its fundamental importance. Speech frequency is of obvious importance to interpersonal exchange; indeed, it can be viewed as its currency.

It also represents a kind of defense of my approach in this book; as I will discuss in the final chapter, it can be problematic to categorize with regard to something like gender. Of course not all men become lonely; of course some women do. But, as this study on speech frequency demonstrates, there is validity in the approach, too, because gender is such a fundamental determinant of social behavior in general, and accelerating loneliness in particular.

Expressivity is an interesting difference between men and women in its own right, but I think it also emphasizes differences that are even more profound. Talking to friends is not usually a frivolous and mindless activity. It requires effort and at least some skill. Anything that requires effort and skill improves very noticeably over the course of time with use and practice. My FSU colleague Anders Ericsson studies expertise, and he and his colleagues have shown that the development of world-class expertise in pursuits like chess, music, and various sports requires approximately ten thousand hours of what they term "deliberate practice."[12] Deliberate practice involves focused exertion, not just mindless repetition; it also involves coaching.

When it comes to deliberate, focused effort in the social domain, research from the world over shows that girls and women win out over boys and men. For example, a study comparing friendship behaviors and patterns in the United States and Russia revealed several cross-cultural differences—the aim of the study—but in so doing, found the cross-cultural similarity that women's friendships involved a lot more conversation and were more intimate than men's friendships.[13] This pattern is reminiscent of that in the study on personality alluded to above, in which researchers expected personality to drive differences in speech frequency, but in the end, gender did. In the United States–Russia cross-cultural study, researchers expected cultural differences to explain differences in friendship parameters, and they did to a degree, but in the end, gender was the more powerful explicator. Talk can be viewed as tiny stitches in a social fabric; the more stitches, the more varied and durable the fabric.

Girls also get more "social coaching" than boys do. They get it from each other in the course of conversations, but they get it from older girls and women, too.

This latter point was corroborated by a group of researchers who interviewed approximately four hundred youth, once a year, from the sixth through the tenth grades.[14] The interviews were focused on friendship networks. A major finding from the interviews was that, over time, girls' friendship networks diversified significantly more than the boys' friendship networks did. By "diversified," I mean that the girls gained more male friends than the boys did female friends, and that the girls gained more friends of various ages as compared to the boys (including older ages, which is where "social coaching" can come in), as well as more friends from non-school environments than did the boys. Diversification is not necessarily an unalloyed good, but in agriculture and finance as in social networks, it is a generally good thing because it mitigates risk. If something is askew at school, for instance, those who have both school-based and non-school friends are better off than those with only school-based friends.

This same study produced an additional finding of relevance to my thesis that girls early on form a kind of interpersonal hardiness that boys do not. Specifically, boys were, relative to girls, interpersonally unhelpful to others (to boys and girls alike). In this study, youth in the sixth through tenth grades have already absorbed a lesson: if you need to reach out for support and succor, reach out to girls. This lesson means rich interpersonal connectedness for girls, who can reach out to *and* help each other, and can help boys. And it means relative interpersonal deprivation for boys, who tend to neither reach out to nor help other boys, and whom girls find unhelpful. In this matrix, boys have just one avenue of connectedness (i.e., girls help them), whereas girls have three (i.e., girls help each other and they also help boys). This finding on girl helpfulness is corroborated by an independent line of research on sisterly help: multiple studies have found that women and men alike are less likely to endorse statements like "I am unhappy" and "I have no one to turn to" if they have sisters; the same effect does not hold, however, regarding having brothers.[15] Interestingly, as we will see, there is a form of helping in which boys and men exceed girls and women: helping strangers. But when it comes to interpersonal succor within friendships and family relationships, both genders understand that odds of substantial help are higher if one turns to females rather than to males.

Selfishness is a conduit for spoiled attitudes and behaviors, and it is more a male than a female problem. Because of their instrumentality and higher activity level, together with their laconic and secretive natures, boys elicit responses from others without much effort. The lesson learned is that interpersonal responsiveness will simply take care of itself. There is some truth to this lesson for boys and men, but there is danger, too: letting relationship skills atrophy and thus letting relationships themselves lapse can mean demoralizing loneliness over time. At least in some cases, the consequences of this loneliness are devastating, even fatal.

Of course, girls can be very spoiled, too, but the typical nature of what they are spoiled about differs from that of boys. The stereotypical spoiled girl pouts and throws temper tantrums. But notice the interpersonal nature of both of these behaviors—few people pout or throw tantrums alone. Both are interpersonally engaged and engaging behaviors. Thus, even in the display of spoiled attitudes and behaviors, the boys' display is insular, inward-turning, and relatively unpeopled, whereas the girls' display is fundamentally interpersonal.

BOYS BECOME SPOILED THROUGH the processes described thus far in this chapter, but there is reason to think there are some differences from the outset, too. We have already considered, for example, prenatal hormones. Consider further in this regard the phenomenon of the familiar stranger. Psychologist Stanley Milgram—whom we shall encounter again in later chapters—produced a film called *The City and the Self* in 1972 that focused on the familiar stranger: the person we would recognize anywhere because we see the individual every day at, say, the train station, and yet to whom we have never spoken. The film's narration states, "if we were to meet one of these strangers far from the station, say, when we were abroad, we would stop, shake hands, and acknowledge for the first time that we know each other. But not here." Notice that the familiar stranger phenomenon requires that people continue to remain strangers despite repeated encounters, without one or the other reaching out and breaking the silence between them.

Like many of the processes elucidated in this book, the familiar stranger phenomenon is by no means exclusively male, but rather, tends to occur somewhat more frequently in males than females. Women, more so than men, break the silence necessary for the phenomenon to continue. A fictional example occurred on the TV show *Seinfeld*, in which Elaine wins Jerry's admiration by confronting a familiar stranger who lives in her apartment complex. Here, as often in real life, it is the female who breaks the seal. Male examples—real ones, and ones in which the seal is left untouched—abound. My sons treat kids in their carpool as familiar strangers, a fact that absolutely befuddles my wife, whose attempts to stir conversation among the carpool crowd are valiant but, at least so far, in vain. I predict continuing frustration for my wife in carpool culture, in part because I easily recognize my sons' silence from my own carpool experiences from decades ago.

And even before that—and this is relevant to how a spoiled attitude in boys can begin early on—a neighborhood kid who became one of my best friends was, for about two years, a familiar stranger. It is worth noticing how peculiar this is: Two kids, the same age and the same gender, who saw one another at least weekly from ages five to seven, and whose houses were on the same street, exchanged not one word. Both of us embodied the spoiled attitude of "I needn't make an effort toward friendship." A frog changed all that. My younger sister and I were hanging around this creek that ran through our neighborhood, and I spotted an enormous frog. My sister, in my probably inaccurate estimation, was inadequate as a frog-catching partner. So I yelled to her to go get my future friend, who I had seen riding his bike up the street. She did, and we became good friends then and there. We had known of each other for, at the time, almost one-third of our lives, did not say as much as a word to one another that entire time, and quickly became fast friends because of a frog. This is a story of pitfall and promise both—there is the initial reticence, a considerable obstacle that men in their forties and fifties and beyond suffer from acutely—but then how severe a barrier can it be if it is solved, at least in one case, by the discovery of a frog in a creek?

The narration of the film mentioned above closes with this: "How can we come closer, without the fire, without the flood, without the storm?" Or without the frog? In clinical settings, I have noticed a tendency in some patients to behave suboptimally or even disastrously . . . unless there is an emergency, in which case they snap to and are alert and helpful. Every example of this in my own professional experience has been a male, and every one has had a severe case of attention deficit hyperactivity disorder (ADHD). Things were usually too mundane to engage their scattered attention, but an emergency focused their attention, serving, for a time, as their Ritalin (a psychostimulant medicine that can be helpful to those with ADHD).

This effect harkens back to this book's opening passage, in which the emergency of a wildfire focused people's priorities on their loved ones above all else. A writer focusing on reactions to disasters stated, "Disaster doesn't sort us out by preferences; it drags us into emergencies that require we act, and act altruistically, bravely, and with initiative in order to survive or save the neighbors, no matter how we vote or what we do for a living."[16] The dilemma is the same one posed by the film's narration just alluded to: waiting for a disaster to come along and solve loneliness is not workable. Waiting for a frog to come along—or the many variants of frog finding—may be, however; this topic is the focus of the last section of the book.

Absent emergency, many boys and men are in a set routine of stony disengagement. From many different sources, it is plain that various aspects of male personality are less malleable, or plastic, than aspects of female personality. Male birds as well as the males of many other species, more so than females, display rigidity in behavioral patterns;[17] that is to say, they lack personality plasticity. Roy Baumeister, a psychologist, has made a similar point about humans, focusing on sexual behavior, in a paper titled, in part, "Female Erotic Plasticity."[18] This term tends to confuse people—it has nothing to do with plastic objects, or with flexibility during sex, but it has everything to do with flexibility in attitudes about sex. Across a staggering and very diverse array of studies and observations, the paper demonstrated that, as compared to women, men show a distinct lack of malleability in sexual preferences and behaviors. It is vanishingly rare, for instance, for a man to genuinely endorse heterosexuality as his exclusive preference at one stage in life, change his preference to homosexuality in another phase of life, and then revert to heterosexuality still later. By contrast, patterns like this are more common in women.

Behavioral and attitudinal plasticity is more a female than a male trait, to women's general benefit. To be sure, single-mindedness can have its payoffs; virtually any story of epic adventure (like the early days of the US space program for instance) will attest to this—stories, not coincidentally, that are disproportionately peopled with men. But single-mindedness is not a particularly great mode for relationship maintenance, which requires attention and response to ever-changing dynamics. To maintain a friendship with a person who, for example, simultaneously has achieved a great professional feat and whose spouse is leaving requires flexible and nuanced attunement, rather than relentless single-minded focus.

"THE BRAINS OF GREGARIOUS LOCUSTS are 30 percent larger than those of solitarious locusts of the same species."[19] In addition to providing, with the word "solitarious," a new (if perhaps dubious) way to say "lonely," this result leads one to ponder brain size in humans. This is an erratic field—to put it kindly—ranging from sophisticated fMRI studies relating carefully measured brain size or brain region size to a number of correlates like memory, vision, and the like, to studies that seem like caricatures (only they were meant to be serious) on brain size, occasionally measured by calipers, and its correlations to things like IQ and race.

I myself ventured into this latter field, if it can be called that, showing the deep inanity of the view that races differ in IQ because they differ in brain size. (I did this, satisfyingly enough, using the very same data sets, publically available, from which proponents of this vapid line of thought reached opposite conclusions.)

It would be almost as mistaken to attribute gender differences in IQ—or in "solitariousness"—to brain size. Regarding IQ, there are no differences in overall IQ between men and women to begin with. But there are slight brain size differences, even adjusting for overall body size, with women having slightly smaller brains. On first reading, this might raise the ire of some, who might think I am denigrating women. But think it through. On the contrary, the fact that women have slightly smaller brains but have the same intelligence leads to the conclusion that women's brains are more efficient.

Women are more efficient and effective socializers, too (perhaps in general, but certainly in one-on-one intimate forms of relating, like close friendships). To see this, consider "the Dunbar number." This number, which anthropologist Robin Dunbar set at 150, is the maximum number of significant social ties a human can maintain.[20] One basis for this claim is that socializing is relatively complex and thus makes significant demands on cognitive resources; such resources, of course, are not infinite, and thus there must be an upper limit. The Dunbar number was derived from things like the average size of hunter-gatherer groups and villages during the course of human evolution, as well as from grouping structures in non-human primates. Others have argued that the Dunbar number should be higher, probably about twice as high, and Dunbar himself noted that the number could be as high as 230.[21] There appears to be wide consensus that the number is 300 or less, which brings us back around to the efficient and effective socializing of women, underlain by attitudes about relationships that are anything but spoiled. If one assumes that there is a limit and that face-to-face contacts are, on average, deeper and more meaningful than contacts on Facebook (though the latter have their charms), the proportion of "actual" to "virtual" friends would be an index of the efficiency and effectiveness of socializing. And, in fact, the ratio of "actual" to "virtual" friends tends to be higher for women than it is for men.

Victorian English thinker John Ruskin believed in female superiority, citing among other things, women's better organizational skills. Before readers become Ruskin fans, it should be noted that he used this view to opine that it is better and more efficient when women manage households.[22] John Stuart Mill objected, writing that "There is no other situation in life in which it is the established order, and is considered quite natural and suitable, that the better should obey the worse."[23] Notice here that Mill is objecting to Ruskin's rationale for women's managing households, not to Ruskin's assertion that women are more organized than men. Put differently, they both agree with the conclusion that women are more efficient.

Efficient brains are essential for complex social life. On a recent radio show, it was argued that one possible reason our species has survived and Neanderthals did not involves our socially complex brains.[24] In *Catching Fire,* Richard Wrangham writes, "Primates with bigger brains or more neocortex live in larger groups, have a greater number of close social relationships, and use coalitions more effectively than those with smaller brains."[25] That women are the more effective socializers among humans, and that this is so despite their having smaller brains than their male counterparts, indicates more efficiency in the female brain.

Women's greater effectiveness is multi-determined, but an important point of this chapter is that one source of their success is the lack of a spoiled attitude when it comes to finding and keeping friends. One can see the long-maintained, worked-for social networks in the remarks of a centenarian (female, as 80 percent of them are) interviewed in October 2010.[26] When asked about her secrets for longevity, the woman replied, "I am blessed and I've worked on it. You've got to work, be cheerful and look for something fun to do. It's a whole attitude." The rest of the article makes plain the kind of work and the kind of attitude that is being referred to: the work of socializing, reaching out to family, making new friends and keeping them. The article states, "Like many if not most other centenarians, according to the findings of the New England Centenarian Study at Boston University, [the one highlighted in the article] is an extrovert who has many friends . . . and strong ties to family and community. She continues to enjoy her youthful passions for the theater and opera. A study of centenarians in Sardinia found that they tend to be physically active, have extensive social networks and maintain strong ties with family and friends."

WE HAVE ALREADY SEEN that some important gender differences in sociality emerge even before birth, riding on the back of hormonal differences involving substances like testosterone. One would expect, then, that related differences would be apparent just before and just after birth. For example, one would expect that boys might be more active in utero than are girls, that this difference would persist after birth, and that the difference would mean that, as babies, boys are more demanding than are girls. And there is evidence that all of this is true, though the differences do not become obvious until a few weeks after birth. A recent book notes, "Boy babies are more trouble. They scream and cry more often than girl babies, and louder too."[27] Male babies are more generally active than female babies, a difference that is quite clear by one year of age, and that tends to accelerate thereafter. Researchers in England instructed 208 schoolchildren to attach pedometers to their waists for four days (two days during the week, and two days during a weekend). Weekends were clearly a time of rest; average steps per day during the weekend averaged around ten thousand, as compared to nearly fourteen thousand during an average weekday. More to the present point, boys took approximately five hundred more steps per day than did girls.

Because they are more difficult and active, baby boys demand more attention than do baby girls; with few exceptions, the demands of babies tend to be met. Taken together, this means that from a very early age, the stage is set for a spoiled, even self-centered attitude. It should be the case, then, that self-centeredness in boys should exceed that in girls, and that this difference persists into adulthood.

Here, too, the evidence is overwhelming. In a study of approximately 3,500 people, researchers reported that males were more narcissistic than females.[28] This, by itself, is an unsurprising finding that simply repeats results from past research, but what was interesting in this particular study was that the pattern tended to hold across the life-span (participants ranged in age from eight to eighty-three) and around the world (participants were included from all continents except Antarctica). An earlier study examined "positive illusions"—the tendency to see oneself in a more favorable light than others do, or than is warranted by the facts.[29] Illusions about physical attractiveness and intelligence were evaluated, and, in both cases, males were more likely to hold positive illusions than were females. Moreover, this gender difference was largely attributable to the fact that males reported more narcissism than females.

When narcissism and related traits like lack of caring are extreme, they can be considered mental disorders. More specifically, the two most "selfish" mental disorders are narcissistic personality disorder and antisocial personality disorder. The former condition is characterized by a sense of grandiose entitlement and uniqueness, and the latter by irresponsible, lawless, and out-of-control behaviors and attitudes. Both conditions share the same core features of callous, uncaring, and narcissistic behavior. Substantially more men than women are assigned the diagnoses. In fact, when I think back over the hundreds of patients in mental health settings I have encountered over the years, it takes effort to bring to mind women with these diagnoses (though, with effort, I can think of some); the same exercise regarding men requires virtually no mental exertion at all.

This difference between men and women runs deep. If there were any subgroup in which one might expect women to rival men on narcissism and neighboring traits like callousness, that group would probably be violent offenders. But even when male and female offenders are matched for arrest history, men score higher on ratings of callousness than do women. A 2009 report found that boys were more callous than girls, a pattern that was consistent even among children who were three or four years old.[30]

From many different perspectives, then, men are on average more self-centered than are women. Men are the lonely sex in part because they are the self-centered and spoiled sex.

Much more so than women, men seem to be under the impression that friendships will always be provided for them, just as they were in grade school. They can become spoiled about relationships, a phenomenon facilitated by their being spoiled in other ways by preferentially available opportunities and treatment. There is one school, however, where men, relatively speaking, do not receive preferential admission— the school of hard knocks, which teaches that you have to work hard for everything, including friends, and that you need friends for help during inevitable hardships.

An advertisement for an erectile dysfunction drug advises "you didn't get to where you are by having things handed to you" (and it is remarkable, by the way, how unintentionally funny the lines from some commercials are when written out). "Where you are" is not intended to mean suffering from erectile dysfunction, but rather, a respectable station in life. The idea behind the phrase is smart, because it encourages men to take responsibility for their health problems—something, as we have seen, they are not particularly good at. But the phrase is also somewhat untrue; men, when compared to women, *have* had things handed to them.

The comedian Louis C.K. made a similar point, with a different frame of reference.[31] He was reflecting on the differences between gay and straight men, with his usual approach of saying things that some people find uncomfortable but with an undertone that is very sympathetic and disarming. He said, "Gay men are put through sort of a crucible. . . . They have to go through something to be who they are. They get beat up, they get ostracized. . . . If they survive it, they come out very confident people, they come out having been tested. . . . Heterosexual men have never been put through that test. Nobody says, 'Oh my God you like *women*?' You don't have to defend it for your whole life. So we're not so sure of who we are. . . . We're a mess." The comedian is making the same point about heterosexual men that I am making about men generally: relatively speaking, they have it easy, they aren't tested in the school of hard knocks, and then when something does eventually test them, it shows. "A high station in life is earned by the gallantry with which appalling experiences are survived with grace." It is no co-incidence, in my view, that this sentiment would be voiced by someone who has been tested in the way that Louis C.K. meant; in this case, the person was the playwright Tennessee Williams.

I believe H. L. Mencken had a similar idea in mind, here about women, when he wrote "in women, once they get beyond adolescence, there is always a saving touch of irony; the life they lead infallibly makes cynics of them."[32]

This viewpoint suggests that "whatever does not kill us makes us stronger." That is true, up to a point. Researchers reported on people's reactions to recent negative life events.[33] More specifically, they were interested in the possibility that some people may grow or even thrive in reaction to challenge. Indeed, some people did, whereas others did not. What differentiated the groups was past experience with adversity. Unsurprisingly, those with very difficult pasts were further worn down by recent challenge. Intriguingly, those with little past adversity also reacted to recent difficulties by becoming more demoralized by them. Only those in the middle, with some prior experiences with adversity but not too many, weathered recent challenge well. Just as muscles can be strained to a breaking point and can also atrophy with disuse but do well with moderate exercise, the psychological capacity to handle life stress can be overwhelmed by too much previous adversity, can be underdeveloped by too little, or can be optimized with moderate past challenge.

One overarching thesis of this book is that men and women are not equally represented in the Goldilocksian groups of too little challenge, too much, and just right. In particular, too many men are in the "too lit-tle challenge" group, leaving more men than women socially atrophied.

Like all meaningful relationships, friendships require work to ini-tiate and maintain. Except under grade-school conditions, a passive, spoiled approach will eventually and steadily result in the loss of friends. This is a slow process because men can coast for a while on friendships made in adolescence and places like college. The gradual nature of this loss makes it hard to detect. By their fifties, the erosion in many men's social networks is clear, and it can be seen even earlier, in their late twenties and thirties.

That the process has gradual qualities makes it insidious. It is not that men really want to become or be spoiled (though they do reap attendant, if not lasting, rewards) and it is certainly not that they intend to be bereft in middle age and beyond. It is rather that something is slowly occurring outside of their awareness, something that, despite its slow rate, will accrue day after day for years until it becomes an overwhelming force. It should not be doubted that very slow things can have awesome power, as people whose villages have been slowly but utterly destroyed by glaciers, creeping along inches or at most feet per day, can attest.

The writer Haruki Murakami described this process well in his memoir *What I Talk about When I Talk about Running.* "In certain areas of my life, I actively seek out solitude. Especially for someone in my line of work, solitude is, more or less, an inevitable circumstance."[34] Notice that, to this point in the author's remarks, his words could be read as praise, albeit somewhat muted, of the virtues and benefits of being alone. Had he stopped here, he would have been a member of a camp that is impressed with solitude, viewing it as essential to psychological well-being, even more so than is interpersonal connection. As will become clear throughout this book, I think writers and thinkers in this camp have profoundly misunderstood human nature. But Murakami does not make this same mistake; he continues, "Sometimes, however, this sense of isolation, like acid spilling out of a bottle, can unconsciously eat away at a person's heart and dissolve it. You could see it, too, as a kind of double-edged sword. It protects me, but at the same time steadily cuts away at me from the inside."[35]

This is a nuanced understanding of the allure and the ultimate danger of certain forms of solitude. As I write this sentence, I am alone, though I would never have thought of the fact had I not been writing about loneliness. It would not have occurred to me to think that I am alone, because I don't feel alone. For one thing, I am surrounded by things that are symbols of my connections to others, including a photo of my wife positioned right next to the computer screen. For another (though I urge my PhD students never to do this), I am occasionally checking my email and Facebook account to take mini-breaks from writing; I am electronically far from alone. Were I to take a run through the woods later today, I would be quite alone but the thought "I am very alone" would not bubble up into my awareness, for many reasons, including that I would be thinking about my sons, wife, friends, and family.

These activities involve solitude but are not isolating; they are not essentially about keeping others out. They are not a protective sword. Men, more than women, cut at themselves, beneath their own awareness, by keeping others at bay. Becoming spoiled in youth is an initial stage of this unfortunate tendency, which can metastasize later in life into processes involving "don't-tread-on-me" attitudes, fixation on money and status to the exclusion of most other things including relationships, and feeling "lonely at the top"—processes, respectively, that are the focus of chapters following this one.

A woman in her late forties who wrote in to a magazine advice column seems to agree that men are spoiled.[36] The column's header reads "Are Men Spoiled Rotten?" The reader stated, "My theory is that men of my generation have just had everything given to them. They grew up with at-home moms who took care of them. They came of sexual age before AIDS, when women were becoming independent, sex wasn't evil anymore and being unmarried but living together was OK, so they didn't need to commit. They got good jobs, they had independence plus relationships."

The column's reader is noticing in American men something that the writer Theodore Dalrymple noticed in a quite different context. He writes of young Muslims in arranged marriages, "the young women in these circumstances are superior in every way to their male contemporaries, despite their disadvantages (one is tempted to say because of, rather than despite, them). They are better-spoken, appear vastly more intelligent, and are as charming as the males are charmless, having been born and raised without that sense of entitlement which only a corresponding sense of *noblesse oblige* can render tolerable, and which is entirely absent in this case."[37]

I think the temptation to say "because of" the women's disadvantages, as opposed to "despite" them, is one that he is right to give in to. Skills do not sharpen, immune systems do not thrive, muscles do not grow, and bones do not harden, in the absence of challenge. This principle can apply even to rather disastrous challenges, like the devastation wrought by wars. For example, the catastrophic effects of World War II on Europe are beyond dispute; even so, the war caused many industries to flourish. To take just one example of pre- to post-war impact on industry and the economy, "The UK, the USSR, France, Italy, and Germany (as well as Japan and the USA) *all* emerged with a larger stock of machine tools than they started off with."[38] This same effect on many different sectors of industry laid the foundation, in part, for the boom of the 1950s.

Was it worth it? Hardly. Similarly, some of the disadvantages experienced by women in general—and certainly by the young Muslim just described—are unfair to be sure, and it is not my claim that subjugation or mistreatment is the path to virtue. Nevertheless, genuine strength—physically, psychologically, and as I emphasize throughout this book, socially—is not possible without challenge, and severe challenge can serve even if unjust.

And what of the thought that *noblesse oblige* can temper entitlement? It seems to me quite true that naked entitlement, in the absence of some redeeming and compensatory feature, is hard to bear. I am a university professor, which I view as quite sacred work—a view that does not dim my awareness that many people forsake the work's sacred quality and instead exploit it in the service of base motivations. I therefore do not lack for contact with people who think very well of themselves indeed. How tolerable they are depends completely on whether or not their self-congratulatory stance is widely shared by others, whether it is based on actual achievement and accomplishment, year in and year out. If it is, then their self-view, though an occasional irritant, becomes mostly a quirk of theirs, one that can even be endearing and seems understandable given their prodigious accomplishments. But if their high opinion of themselves is not widely shared—if it is unaccompanied by substantial achievements—woe to the entire social surround. The person him- or herself is not popular, to put it mildly, and may eventually be fired, the usual stated cause for which is poor performance in teaching (which requires earning students' respect, at least to a degree), and an additional cause of which, even if sometimes unstated, is the wake of annoyed and often offended colleagues left in the person's trail.

Such individuals represent a particular example of a broader cultural problem: the elevation of self-esteem over the accomplishments that lead to self-respect. An author wrote of his experiences teaching in public schools that, partly in the service of students' self-esteem, they "were passed from grade to grade and eventually into a world that would be all too happy to teach them, as they drifted churlishly from disappointment to disaster, what the school should have been teaching them all along: that even in America *failure is a part of life.*"[39] It is to the author's credit that he wrote that at all, but particularly so that he wrote it in 1968, long before others began to sound this same note.

More than forty years later, I pointed out to one of my sons the objectively true fact that his grades were relatively "lackluster." He responded that "that kind of undermining won't help." I thought of saying "an eleven-year-old child who uses the word 'undermining' is capable of better grades," but instead I said, "I'm not undermining you, I'm asking you to meet a standard. There's a difference." I was discouraged that his initial line of thought went toward "undermining," but buoyed by the fact that he seemed to absorb my reply about meeting a standard.

I have had many conversations with parents who have had similar interactions with their twenty-first-century offspring. A potential culprit for this problem is the cultural notion that everyone deserves good self-esteem. In a comprehensive review of the literature on self-esteem and its effects, psychologists searched in vain for evidence that increased self-esteem leads to things like better grades and better behavior. On the contrary, their clearest finding was on the dark side of self-esteem:

specifically, too much self-esteem was associated with aggression and violence.[40]

Compatible with these conclusions, Theodore Dalrymple writes in his book *Second Opinion*, "Self-esteem is odious, where it exists, for example, among most criminals, and anyone who even thinks about his self-esteem has sunk into a swamp of self-regard. Self-respect imposes a discipline and obligations; self-esteem is a kind of flabby, bullying solipsism." He continues, "Whenever a patient claims to suffer from insufficient self-esteem, I say to him that at least he has understood his own worthlessness. Far from evoking anger, my remark evokes laughter and a sigh of relief."[41]

My earlier remarks about *noblesse oblige* are not really about the obligations of the wealthy or the privileged. Rather, they are about the need to justify self-liking. Self-liking in the absence of duty and obligation is indeed malign; self-liking justified by obligation and duty is, at the least, tolerable, if not always charming. If one mentally shuffles through the catalog of one's acquaintances who demand station without its toil and costs, the roster is mostly male. Men are more spoiled than women, and though this can return some benefits in the short term, over the long term it is difficult to sustain and usually leads to the erosion of social networks—stated differently, male loneliness.

Many men, having been relatively deprived of hard knocks, develop the expectation that they don't have to worry about the business of friendship, much as they don't need to worry about the atmosphere containing enough oxygen. They are right about oxygen, but not about friendship; what they expect to be provided is not—in fact it starts to fall away—and to compound an already serious problem, they have trouble noticing this, with untoward consequences for them as well as for those who care about them.

In a sense, marriage may collude in this process. I know several couples in which one person is essentially responsible for both people's social lives—the one handles invitations, dinners, parties, and the other just shows up as told. The vast majority of such instances involve women handling the social calendars for themselves and for their husbands. One scholar wrote of an important difference between men and women that "Once married, men . . . put their emotional needs on the backburner, or, for the most part, expect them to be met by the women in their lives." Thus, for a man, not being married "in his later years . . . may be overwhelmingly solitary."[42] Indeed, the Australian Unity Well-being Index revealed that men who live alone are much more likely than women who live alone to feel lonely.

Several friends and I recently had the pleasure of seeing blues giant B. B. King in concert. King is eighty-five years old, and still handles his guitar, "Lucille," with incredible skill. The concert included at least as much storytelling and banter as blues playing, and virtually all of King's stories were paeans to women with undercurrents of expressions of his own loneliness. The musician is world-famous and surrounded by a touring group of musicians and others who revere him; that he is also single and eighty-five is probably related to loneliness finding him even in the midst of plenty.

Marriage can be a protective shield for men, but even maintaining a very close relationship with his wife may not be enough to protect a man's health. A report on the life and death of a man who died by suicide read, "He isolated himself and did not like his wife leaving the house to go to town without him." The man kept his wife very close as all of his other relationships faded, and this was not enough to save him.

There are studies showing that friendship has as powerful or even more powerful positive effects on health than does attachment to just one person, like a spouse. For example, in a study of middle-aged men in Sweden, having a close attachment to one person did not confer much protection against heart attack and death due to heart disease. But having multiple friendships did. In this study, the protective effect of friends was as powerful as not smoking. A recent article noted, "Your BFF nowadays—at least until the divorce—is supposed to be your spouse, a plausible idea in this age of assortative mating, except that spouses and friends fill different needs, and cultivating some close extramarital friendships might even take some of the pressure off at home. Yet the married men I know seem overwhelmingly dependent on their wives for emotional connection, even as their wives take pleasure in friends to whom they don't happen to be wed."[43]

Why would grown men be "overwhelmingly dependent on their wives for connection," when the same is not usually so regarding their female counterparts? The answer posed by this chapter has to do with the atrophying effects of a spoiled interpersonal stance. Relationships require work. Forgo this work—whether because of being spoiled or, as argued in the next chapter, because of an excessive need for autonomy—and suffer the consequences.

3

CAUSES

DON'T TREAD ON ME—
THE PERILS OF INDEPENDENCE

The Gadsden flag is yellow and has an image of a rattlesnake, coiled and ready to strike. Underneath the snake are printed the words DONT TREAD ON ME (the flag lacks the apostrophe in "DON'T). The flag has, of course, been an icon of American independence and of American culture from the 1750s until the twenty-first century—it had a resurgence in the wake of the September 11 attacks and in the context of recent political discourse.

Consider the rattlesnake. It's a reptile, of course, a category of animal not known for closeness and intimacy. The rattle is meant to ward off predators and others, including people. Interestingly enough, incidentally, only older rattlesnakes have rattles; they take time to develop. The processes involved in warding-off mechanisms accelerate with age, in rattlesnakes as in men. Should the rattle's warning fail, there is the venomous bite. The bite is delivered at speeds faster than the human eye can track, and the delivered venom is hemotoxic, destructive to tissue and organs, with the potential to cause death.

Who hit upon this symbol for our country? Well, men did, and it is illustrative of both the allure of fierce independence, and its dark side, escalating loneliness. The allure is made clear by the Gadsden flag's imagery: we are self-sufficient creatures, ready to live and let live, but we're warning you, if you impinge on us, we're ready to strike and we're capable of doing so viciously—in other words, don't tread on me.

This interweaving of self-sufficiency and violent defense is instantiated in American culture, including its fringes, in many ways. For example, there are a surprising number of very extreme political groups who share, as essentially their only coherent principle, the notion of liberty in the context of an extremely minimal federal government. Here, I have in mind groups that are to the right of the Tea Party (yes, that is possible). Virtually 100 percent of the groups, almost needless to say, are male. Of course, coherence alone does not a virtuous principle make, nor does it ensure that adherents will behave in particularly coherent ways, and certainly not in virtuous ways. A man in Michigan wrote letters to his state's Department of Natural Resources, informing them that he ceased to be a "citizen of the corrupt political corporate State of Michigan and the United States of America." His reason for writing to that division of the state government is that he had affixed his signature several times to hunting and fishing licenses, and he wanted the government to understand that he was revoking all such signatures; otherwise, he feared, he would be bound by contract to the "illegitimate" government of the State of Michigan. This same individual took care to write "TDC" on all of his outgoing mail, indicating that he was using the government's zip codes under "threat, duress, and coercion." This individual's ideas, odd to the point of being laughable, led to consequences that were far from humorous. A few years after he wrote to the Michigan Department of Natural Resources, Terry Nichols responded to his perception of the government's "threat, duress, and coercion" with appalling violence. Together with his similarly inclined friend Timothy McVeigh, Nichols conspired in the bombing of the Alfred P. Murrah Federal Building in Oklahoma City on April 19, 1995, and took the lives of 168 of his fellow Americans. Nichols was sentenced to life in prison without the possibility of parole; McVeigh was executed.

This preoccupation with fierce autonomy is not just a feature of moribund if dangerous felons like McVeigh and Nichols. On the contrary, it is a clear strand of the American character, detectable even in our founding documents. The Constitution's Second Amendment, at least as interpreted by the Supreme Court in 2008, affirms the right of the *individual* to bear arms (as opposed to the right of a "well regulated Militia" to do so); a subsequent ruling extended this decision to inhibit states from passing laws infringing on the right to bear arms. The 2008 decision also emphasized the importance of self-defense, a central aspect of the right. Whatever its merits, this decision is momentous because it interprets an essential aspect of American thought in terms of "me" rather than "us." Construing the Second Amendment as being more about a standing militia than about self-defense contains the implicit message that we need guns to protect our polity and society from tyranny and other external forms of threat. In fact, in 1792, Congress approved and George Washington signed the Militia Act. The act read that virtually every white man between the ages of eighteen and forty-five was required to "provide himself with a good musket or firelock, a sufficient bayonet and belt, two spare flints, and a knapsack, a pouch with a box therein to contain not less than twenty-four cartridges, suited to the bore of his musket or firelock, each cartridge to contain a proper quantity of powder and ball; or with a good rifle, knapsack, shot-pouch and powder horn, twenty balls suited to the bore of his rifle, and a quarter of a pound of powder." This is, incidentally, of current interest in more than one way because it was an example of the federal government requiring citizens to buy something: back then, guns; in the current times, health insurance.

It is of further interest to the present argument, because the act was about—indeed, was named for—the militia; it was about the defense of the common good, not only of oneself. I am no legal scholar, but it strikes me as significant that the Militia Act was signed into law in 1792, a mere year after the passage of the Second Amendment itself. Wasn't it likely, then, that the Congress and President Washington who passed and signed the Militia Act were viewing the Second Amendment through the lens of the militia rather than of individual self-defense? More than two hundred years later, the Supreme Court thought not; or rather, five of its nine members thought not. Four justices dissented from the majority's view of the individual's right to bear arms distinct from the context of the militia. There is, of course, a natural tension between contributing to the common good and looking out for one's own, a tension that affects, if not pervades, most disagreements between conservatives and liberals in the United States. Thus, that the 2008 Court decision was very close comes as no surprise; neither does the fact that both the majority and the dissenting arguments in that case were each very compelling. I certainly would be among the last to advocate for an abandonment of self-interest; as limited as it may be, my own reading of twentieth-century history suggests that therein lie the seeds of disaster. Rather, I am arguing for a balance between the obvious and essential needs for autonomy and self-interest on the one hand, and the equally obvious and essential needs of connectedness and togetherness on the other. Martin Luther King Jr. advocated for this balance when he said, "The good and just society is . . . a social democracy which reconciles the truths of individualism *and* collectivism."[1]

This balance, as I am arguing, is more a male problem than a female one, because, in part, the allure of fierce independence woos men more successfully than it does women. The balance is made all the more precarious by a companion process, represented well by the clichéd but nevertheless fairly accurate image of men's reluctance—or is it failure?—to ask for directions. To "keep your head when all about you are losing theirs" is the way Rudyard Kipling puts it in his poem "If." Author Michael Chabon describes it rather differently in his *Manhood for Amateurs:* "This is an essential element of the business of being a man: To flood everyone around you in a great radiant arc of bullshit, one whose source and object of greatest intensity is yourself. To behave as if you have everything under control even when you have just sailed your boat over the falls."[2]

"I have it all under control" is of the same cloth as "don't tread on me." You might assume, then, that I am urging men not to act thus. But consider a scenario in which a man faces a dangerous situation, exuding confidence to his wife and children while hiding his worries and fears from them. Is this a failure of honesty or a show of bravery? When a family's beloved pet dies, and one of the parents (because, of course, it can be either one) takes care of everything—all of the arrangements, all of everyone's feelings—and does not care for him- or herself or even think to, is that a failure of "self-compassion"—a phrase I confess to finding confusing and irritatingly cloying—or is that stepping up in a time of need? I think it's largely the latter.

As with "don't tread on me," there is a sweet spot to "it's all under control." Anyone who has been on a team that is put to the test knows that belief is essential. Someone needs to say and believe that "we can do this, we have this under control."

One problem is that this takes vigor and energy, which, alas, are not enduring or boundless. The shift in identity from having everything under control to not having it under control, is, like all major shifts in identity, inherently difficult for men and women alike. Stability of self-concept serves important psychological functions like creating a predictable and smooth-running interpersonal life. It stands to reason, then, that people will resist changes to their self-concept. In fact, an entire literature on this reluctance exists—a literature that goes by the name of self-verification theory. As we will see shortly, self-verification needs present a dilemma for the person—often a male person—whose identity as fiercely independent is challenged by change in job status, financial difficulties, deteriorating health, and the like.

The claim of this line of research is that people will go to some lengths to resist disturbances to their self-views, a claim that seems lacking in profundity when considering the usual case—especially in America—of the person with high self-esteem. Obviously, someone with positive self-esteem does not appreciate blows to their sense of self and will undertake efforts to fend them off. But a very intriguing aspect of self-verification theory is that it makes the same claim of everyone, whether they are high in self-regard or low. The theory predicts, then, that low-self-esteem people will work to keep their self-esteem low. "Better old demons than new gods," as a proverb suggests.

This is a surprising suggestion. But consider the following experiment. Many hundreds of male and female undergraduate students are given self-esteem questionnaires; based on the questionnaires' scores, a few dozen with high self-esteem and a similar number with low self-esteem are invited to continue the experiment. One by one, the participants come into a psychological laboratory and are led to believe that they are participating in an experiment on interviewing for jobs. As part of this, they are given a "let's make a deal" kind of choice (*Let's Make a Deal* was a 1960s game show): three closed doors, and the task is to choose one. Behind the first door, participants are told, is an interviewer who is upbeat and positive, and who tends to issue compliments; behind the second door is an interviewer who is evenhanded and fair, who tends to call things like he sees them; and behind the third door is a more negative interviewer, one who is free with criticism. There are, in actuality, no interviewers behind the doors; studies like this are interested in which door participants choose, and how self-esteem affects such choices.

The overwhelming majority of the undergraduates with high self-esteem choose the positive interviewer behind door number one, and they do so with alacrity and with an attitude of "why in the world would I choose otherwise?" Indeed, in some studies of this sort, the percentage of high-self-esteem participants who choose the positive interviewer easily exceeds 90 percent. Notice, by the way, that this result is not only expectable and intuitive—this is apparent in the reactions of the participants themselves of "how could it be otherwise?"—but the finding is also consistent with self-verification theory: the high-self-esteem participants choose an experience that is likely to corroborate their positive self-regard.

The low-self-esteem group shows how, in fact, it can be otherwise. When presented with the same three choices, a surprisingly high proportion of low-self-esteem participants choose the door behind which they believe awaits a negative, critical interviewer. It is important to note that, were the low-self-esteem undergraduates interested in, say, the challenge of swaying a neutral interviewer or in neutrality itself, the best choice would be the door leading to the evenhanded interviewer. However, these participants seem to be primarily interested not in having their egos stroked (in which case they should have chosen the positive interviewer door), and not in a fair and balanced take (for which the evenhanded interviewer door would be the logical choice), but instead in having their negative self-views affirmed. Furthermore, the low-self-esteem participants are far from unfeeling; that is, they have low self-esteem and many of the emotions that come with it, like dejection, sadness, and dispiritedness. There is a part of them, therefore, that would like the boost that the positive interviewer might provide them. Nevertheless, they choose the negative interviewer's door, which suggests that the drive for self-verification can prevail over that of feeling good. We will return in a moment to the relevance of this set of astonishing facts for the lonely sex.

As surprising as this is to most people, a wealth of research corroborates the result, as do the anecdotal remarks of participants themselves. When asked why they made their particular choices, low-self-esteem participants who chose the critical interviewer door often offered explanations like "I just feel that he will understand me better" or "I just have the sense that we'll get along better."

These are poignant explanations, similar to ones that I have repeatedly heard myself during the early stages of psychotherapy with depressed patients. As an example, consider the following exchange that occurred between a depressed patient and me:

Patient: I did bad things as a kid; never been a nice person; there's nothing nice about me.

Therapist: Hmm . . . (doubtful look)

Patient: It's true; it *is* true.

Therapist: I'm not sure I see it.

Patient: People don't think I'm good; only those who can tolerate a lot like me. This is *true*.

Therapist: Still not sure I see it.

Patient: Well, perhaps you will . . . you know, there is no need to make me feel better; I just want you to be honest.

There are a few remarkable things about this conversation. One is how characteristic it is of the effect of depression on the mind; those who have experienced the syndrome themselves, or have seen it in depth in others, will recognize this exchange without much effort. Another interesting feature, and one that is very consistent with the claims of self-verification theory, is how insistent the patient is that I see things as he does; there is an urgency to this need. A third interesting thing about the conversation is my relative reticence—though I have had many occasions as a therapist when I did not know what to say, here the laconicism is planned. Its intent is neutrality; I did not want to agree that the patient was and is a bad person, but neither, at this early stage in the therapeutic process, did I want to disagree, at least not very strenuously, for fear of thwarting self-verification needs. The frustration of self-verification needs has the potential to reify negative self-views by provoking the patient to defend them.

A final interesting aspect to this exchange is the last phrase "Well, perhaps you will," which some may view as containing an aggressive subtext. Those of a psychoanalytic bent may concur, as at least a strand of such thought views depression as fundamentally about anger at others; here is Freud writing in 1917, claiming exactly this of depressed people: "Everything derogatory that they say of themselves at bottom relates to someone else . . . they give a great deal of trouble."[3]

I disagree. Aside from the obvious lack of sympathy in these words (and they are far from unique in the psychoanalytic canon, or in Freud's writings, in which he also expresses distaste for people with schizophrenia), there is an alternative explanation for why depressed people are obstinate and even angrily confrontational in their insistence on their own flaws: the fulfillment of self-verification needs. That the latter explanation enjoys more scientific support than the psychoanalytic one is putting it mildly. Furthermore, the depressed patient in the exchange quoted above was not prone to anger, either at me or at others, either in the throes of the illness or recovered (which he eventually was). The threat he issued toward me was never acted upon, chiefly because it was not a threat in the first place.

Self-verification findings have emerged in especially surprising contexts. Take the dilemma, for example, of those suffering from bulimia nervosa. Bulimia nervosa is an eating disorder characterized by episodes of binge eating and purging (for example, self-induced vomiting); the syndrome also includes substantial dissatisfaction with body shape, weight, and appearance. It is, it should be noted, far more common in women than men, but it nevertheless provides a glimpse into the potential power of self-verification needs. A self-verification perspective would suggest the intriguing possibility that bulimic people, in an effort to meet self-verification needs, structure interpersonal discourse in such a way that negative views about the physical self—which by all accounts are quite painful to them—are stabilized and perpetuated.

In fact, there is evidence to support this possibility. Bulimic undergraduates reported, unsurprisingly, that they found negative feedback about body appearance quite distressing. Nevertheless, given the opportunity to indicate preferences for feedback, negative evaluations of their body shape, weight, and appearance were very high on their list. The more they expressed preference for such negative feedback at one point in time, the worse were their bulimic symptoms a few weeks later.[4] This indicates a rather intractable situation for bulimic people: in an effort to meet basic needs for self-confirmation, they invite the very responses they fear, and thus propagate their symptoms. A cycle is thus established wherein a person's bulimia leads to requests for negative feedback about the physical self, which in turn leads to exacerbated bulimia, triggering still more interest in negative feedback and so on. This represents a rather confusing situation, absent an understanding of self-verification principles, for patients and clinicians alike. How else, other than by self-verification theory, to come to terms with a documented aversion to negative feedback about the physical self, side by side with a preference for that very same feedback? Vague allusions to inner conflict or ambivalence are not as penetrating as self-verification concepts.

As with bulimic people, so with child psychiatric inpatients. A 1997 study in the *Journal of Abnormal Psychology* of seventy-two child psychiatric inpatients found that the more the youth expressed interest in negative feedback about themselves, the more depressed they were and the more likely they were to be disliked by peers who knew them well.[5] A 1995 paper in the same journal, this time on undergraduates, produced very similar findings.[6]

As with bulimic people, as with child psychiatric inpatients, as with undergraduates, so with . . . chickens. Yes, chickens. In his book *Manhood for Amateurs,* Michael Chabon relates an anecdote about the behavior of "free range" chickens. They are raised in their coops for weeks, after which it would be more accurate to say that they are "free to range" rather than that they range freely. Because they do not. They are set free; many go to the edge of the structure in which they were raised and inspect the open air and grass for a while, but virtually all of them return to the cramped coops.

Presumably the chickens do this because they prefer the safety, security, and familiarity of the only setting they have known for their entire lives. Fresh air, green grass, and freedom are alluring to chickens, one supposes, but so are the continuity and comfort of the coops. According to self-verification theory, the same motives underlie self-confirmation strivings in people. People prefer stable self-concepts (even if negative) because stability provides a sense of control, cohesiveness, and predictability vis-à-vis the world at large. Our nervous systems appear to be designed in such a way that these things are desirable in and of themselves. For some people, alas, a continuing sense of low self-esteem is their chicken coop: familiar and even comfortable, to be preferred to an alluring alternative precisely because the alternative asks for the sacrifice of continuity and stability as its price.

Self-verification theorists have named this sense of stable continuity "epistemic security," which might be rephrased as "safety in the knowledge of familiarity." This is one reason that chickens do not fly their coops and that bulimic people are interested in information that they do not find alluring. There is another reason as well: interpersonal harmony.

Instability in self-concept translates into instability in relationships. To see this, imagine a very hierarchical group in which individuals' roles and statuses within the hierarchy are well defined and understood by all. Then, without warning, an individual who was near the bottom of the hierarchy starts acting as if he or she were at the top of the hierarchy. Disorientation and conflict may result; efforts may be undertaken by those atop the original structure to restore order, and resentments may arise in the hearts of those whom the individual "skipped over" in traversing the hierarchy. A change in one individual's self-concept can cause ripple effects in the surrounding social network.

Self-verification processes are akin to true north on a compass; they give us our bearings in a complicated social world. These processes occur in those with positive self-concepts and negative self-concepts alike, and in an array of surprising settings and populations. Underlying these processes are motives for keeping the world navigable by making it more harmonious, familiar, and predictable.

Self-verification ideas are of direct relevance to the plight of a person—as I am arguing, often a male person—whose identity as a "don't tread on me" and "go-to, in-control" individual is challenged by processes like decelerating energy, change in job status, financial difficulties, and declining health. If male identity overemphasizes the role of independent-minded provider at the expense of cultivating mutual relationships with friends and family, then loss of the ability to provide for others means a double blow: the loss of the role itself, combined with the emptiness that comes with atrophied relationships.

This is the basis, in part, for a generalization that I have come to see as valid: in retirement, women talk about who they are; men talk about who they *were*. The cultivation and maintenance of friendships are literally investments in the safety net of the future. As with saving money for retirement, those who regularly do it may feel some pain at the time, but notably, this pain is not just short-lived but is no longer even felt once the habit of investment has taken root. And, of course, the long-term payoff is considerable. An article on the recent recession and its disproportionate effects on men quoted a director of a career center, who said, "So many of these men were coasting to retirement, working at good jobs and earning good pay. Then, suddenly, it was gone."[7] This coasting applies as much interpersonally as it does financially.

Those who do not invest may leave themselves in the lurch. Investment in the forming and keeping of friendships and family relationships works similarly: it requires effort, the expenditure of which is compensated in the future, and the absence of which sets the stage for a bleak and unpeopled future. In living that future, people understandably look back and think about who they were then. Nostalgia can serve a positive function, but alone, it is overpowered by the untoward effects of loneliness.

Taken to excess, the "I've got it under control" attitude can prove disastrous—a sailing over the falls—just as "don't tread on me" can be isolating to the point of suffocation. Finding these sweet spots is a human problem, but one that I believe is more vexed for men than for women. The problem may also be a uniquely American one. There are cultures in which it is normative to see oneself as part of a larger whole and to de-emphasize one's own personal autonomy and independence. People in individualistic cultures take the opposite stance, prioritizing self-control and independence at the expense of being part of a larger whole.

In a set of recent studies, researchers focused on reactions on the part of Americans and Asians to the offer of a small gift from a casual acquaintance.[8] To quote the researchers, "Asians, who are inclined to think of themselves in relation to others, are more likely than North Americans to invoke a reciprocity norm in exchanging gifts with casual acquaintances, and they refuse a gift in order to avoid the feeling of indebtedness they would experience if they cannot reciprocate." By contrast, the researchers continue, "North Americans are inclined to think of themselves independently of others, [and] are more likely to base their acceptance of the gift on its attractiveness without considering their obligation to reciprocate." The independent-interdependent axis pervades social interactions in the respective cultures, including nooks and crannies of social life such as responses to a small gift.

It will not be surprising that people in the United States are rated as among the most autonomous-minded people in the world. In recent work on this topic, a team of psychologists wrote that Americans are "quite unique—even in comparison to Western Europeans, let alone Asians—in the predominance of independence and individualism, as opposed to interdependence and collectivism, in their cultural ethos."[9] In this regard, other researchers have characterized Americans as "highly unrepresentative of [the human] species."[10] A similar conclusion emerges in a piece on (American) men and friendships in which the author states, "Forgive me, guys, but we are lousy at this, and while it may seem to us that our casual approach is perfectly normal, in fact it's odd. Among people whose lives are more like those of our ancestors, for example, friendship is taken far more seriously. . . . The Bangwa people in Cameroon traditionally considered friendship so important that many families assigned a best friend to a newborn right along with a spouse."[11]

How did the American people, at first constituted in part by Western Europeans, become so different from them? The team of psychologists mentioned above answer, "The Western frontier of the 18th- and 19th-century United States was sparsely populated and entirely novel, to say nothing of its harsh ecology."[12] They go on to argue that this harsh natural environment, combined with low population and high mobility, prioritized values such as self-reliance and self-direction.

But then, how and why would values of the Western frontier permeate back eastward to the rest of the United States? The values spread back eastward in part because Easterners were impressed with images of the frontier, both in terms of the wealth accrued there and of the successes of the federal government in extending the country's reach (at the expense of Native people).

An independent strain in the American character is thus hardly a recent development. But a self-regard that is not just independent, but entitled, may be. Regarding this American phenomenon, *Daily Show* host Jon Stewart remarked on how, in contrast to his kids, he himself grew up in the "ehhh . . . you're not so special" era.[13] Stewart's views are consistent with research showing that, compared to undergraduates in the 1980s, current undergraduates score higher on measures of narcissism.[14]

A recent article offered one potential explanation of this worrisome trend. The author wrote, "Over the last half century, it can be demonstrated empirically that the new generation of elites have increasingly spent their entire lives in the upper-middle-class bubble, never even having seen a factory floor, let alone worked on one, never having gone to a grocery store and bought the cheap ketchup instead of the expensive ketchup to meet a budget, never having had a boring job where their feet hurt at the end of the day, and never having had a close friend who hadn't gotten at least 600 on her SAT verbal."[15] This description is uncomfortably true of my own sons and, to a lesser degree, of me; it is not at all true of my wife, who grew up in Mexico and thus is the only member of our family who is not the product of comfortable American suburbia. One of Elvis Costello's songs characterizes America as a good idea originally, but now a mistake. I'm with him on "good idea," am not with him on "mistake," but, increasingly, it is not hard to discern the reason for the assertion of "mistake."

There is empirical evidence that the "upper-middle-class bubble" is associated with less empathy for others. In a recent paper describing a series of studies, researchers wrote, "In three studies, lower-class individuals (compared with upper-class individuals) received higher scores on a test of empathic accuracy (Study 1), judged the emotions of an interaction partner more accurately (Study 2), and made more accurate inferences about emotion from static images of muscle movements in the eyes (Study 3)."[16] These results add scientific backing to the worry about a change in American attitudes—less empathy (at least in certain societal segments) and more narcissism does seem a recipe for cultural misadventure.

The distinct character of American self-regard may emerge relatively early in life. In the United States, if you surreptitiously place a piece of tape or something similar on the face of a toddler, in such a way that the tyke does not feel it, the toddler will, if presented with a mirror, notice the tape and reach toward it, often removing it. This happens far less frequently in non-Western youngsters, who tend not to notice the surreptitiously affixed thing in the mirror.[17] The American toddler is more self-regarding than a non-Western counterpart. When driving, I am probably above average in cautiousness, and I crane my neck around frequently to monitor what is around and behind the car; for years, one of my sons sitting in the backseat believed I was checking on him (which he complained about with definite pique only as he entered adolescence and felt I was overdoing it). A non-Western child would be much less likely to reach the same conclusion. There are a few possible interpretations of these kinds of phenomena, but one is that self-directed (as opposed to other-directed) attention is a prominent aspect of the American mindset.

One can discern the same general attitude in international rankings of things like math and science ability—and also of confidence in one's abilities, often a quite different thing than possession of actual abilities. To wit, American youngsters rate no better than twentieth in the world in actual math and science abilities, but in self-confidence, we're number one.[18]

Extreme self-regard occurs more often in American than in other cultures, but, of course, it does occur elsewhere, as does worry about cultural decline. To take but one example of extreme individualism, as described by Colin Turnbull in his book *The Mountain People,* the Ik of the uplands of northern Uganda "place the individual good above all else and almost demand that each get away with as much as he can without his fellows knowing."[19] Perhaps analogously to the American situation, there is good evidence that it was not always thus among the Ik; things became savage after the Ik were kept from their traditional hunting grounds, setting off a chain reaction of the breakdown of sustenance, tradition, and community.

As for an example of "decline worry," T. S. Eliot wrote of England in 1948 "with some confidence that our own period is one of decline; that the standards of culture are lower than they were fifty years ago; and that the evidences of this decline are visible in every department of human activity."[20] Eliot was writing of the very same time in England about which Tony Judt, sounding a different note, wrote in his book *Postwar,* "Like other amusements of its era, cinema-going was a collective pleasure. . . . In England, at Saturday morning shows for children, songs were flashed on the screen, with the audience encouraged to sing along in harmony with a little white ball that bounced from word to word."[21] Because both authors were writing about England in the late 1940s, perhaps they are referring to the same thing—decline could be exemplified by singing in the cinema.

But for at least two reasons, I do not think so; I think decline from then until now is real, apparent in the English situation and extremely so in the American. First, the singing-in-the-cinema scene is not one of degeneration; it strikes me rather as one not only of togetherness but also of uplift. Second, consider the following remarks, which ponder the modern English situation, and suggest recent decline of a more genuine character. The author asks, "When did the English become savages?" and provides a partial answer to his own question: "It isn't a question of education, for even the uneducated of a few decades ago behaved with more natural dignity and grace than the comparatively well-educated of today."[22]

Of course, misanthropic and pessimistic outlooks about decline abound over the centuries. If they had all been right, we would be a degenerate lot by now, to be sure. One should not, then, exaggerate concerns about decline in the American character or in that of other countries on this point. On the other hand, I think most who, in twenty-first-century America, reread the famed observer of early America Alexis de Tocqueville will share my own reaction, which was to be startled at the drastic change in American attitudes, from the *esprit de corps* of the 1830s to the rampant solipsism of today.

When I first pondered the scene of the English singing along with one another in cinemas, my initial reaction was that the phenomenon was a disappeared relic of a bygone time, much like the typewriter. But of course sing-alongs do still occur. I have attended more than one, in fact, each time rather by accident; in one case, a May Day party featuring songs on the solidarity of workers; the other, an Air Force chaplaincy event focused mostly on Christian rock songs. In both settings, I was seemingly the only one who did not know the words.

Both experiences produced conflicting feelings in me. The prevailing feeling was one of social awkwardness—my choices, I felt, were to fall silent (which would have been rude), to sing along lustily (which I really could not do because I did not know the songs but even if I had, it would have felt mendacious), or to awkwardly half-participate (which is what I did). In the midst of navigating these options, I also felt a mixture of admiration and envy. I admire rallying around an animating idea. And, like someone in the cold who sees a firelit room from outside, I envied their togetherness.

Segments of our culture still sing along—a hopeful thing. We probably do so, however, less than we used to. This observation applies beyond US borders, but the increasing American trend toward overly fierce autonomy—extreme forms of "don't tread on me"—renders any decrease in belongingness potentially perilous. And, as we have seen, the peril of social isolation is not equally distributed in the population. Rather, it accumulates in one segment of the population, namely, among men, and with regard to losing social bonds, among aging men especially.

TO RETURN TO THE TOPIC of the Second Amendment, mentioned earlier in this chapter, it is of course just one part of the Bill of Rights, which, in turn, is just one part of our country's founding documents along with the Constitution and the Declaration of Independence. They are not only "founding," they are binding, both in the sense that they are law and in the sense more important to this book, that they bring us together. The Founding Fathers seem to have had a very deep understanding of the balance between connection and autonomy. Many of the same guys who were fond of the phrase "Don't tread on me" produced these lines, too: "We the People of the United States, in Order to form a more perfect Union, establish Justice, insure domestic Tranquility, provide for the common defense, promote the general Welfare, and secure the Blessings of Liberty to ourselves and our Posterity, do ordain and establish this Constitution for the United States of America." These lines drip with togetherness, from the very first word, which is "we."

Togetherness, that is, not just in the moment or for themselves, but for posterity and to honor the past, too. As the journalist Tom Wolfe has noted, over the course of history, the sentiment "I have only one life to live" is of recent origin;[23] before that, most lived lives viewed as a stitch in the fabric made up of ancestors' and offspring's lives. In his 1979 book *The Culture of Narcissism,* Christopher Lasch worries that "we are fast losing the sense of historical continuity, the sense of belonging to a succession of generations originating in the past and stretching into the future."[24] For this author, the last decades of the twentieth century witnessed an "erosion of any strong concern for posterity." Should this

seem dubious, recall what Tocqueville thought of us in the first half
of the nineteenth century, when he wrote, "If an American were con-
demned to confine his activities to his own affairs, he would be robbed
of one half of his existence; he would feel an immense void in the life
which he is accustomed to lead, and his wretchedness would be unbear-
able."[25] The words are a painful reminder—and in my view leave little
doubt—that something has changed.

There are, of course, other examples than the American one in
which a people are attached to founding documents, and are sustained
by ongoing connection to them—examples that, if judged by longevity
and in context of possible American detachment from founding documents, are more successful. A *New Yorker* article from October 4, 2010,
on the Dalai Lama described a conversation between His Holiness and
Nobel laureate Elie Wiesel. The Dalai Lama noted that his own people
had lost their homeland, and asked Wiesel how his people had survived
that same experience for thousands of years. Wiesel's answer is consistent with this book's opening scene in the hills above Oakland when, in
a firestorm, people grabbed photographs of loved ones instead of material things as they scrambled out of their houses. Wiesel said, "When
we left Jerusalem, we didn't take all our jewels with us. All we took was
a little book. It was the book that kept us alive. Second, because of our
exile we developed a sense of solidarity. . . . And, third, good memory."
Wiesel's recipe is togetherness around a founding document and around
the memory of the past.

This same lesson comes from another clear example of a man thriving across the decades of his life: Mahatma Gandhi. A recent article says
of Gandhi, "Though philosophically he disavowed material possessions,
Gandhi became a savvy and serial collector of books and people."[26] Gandhi himself stated, "With each day I realize more and more that my ma-
hatmaship, which is a mere adornment, depends on others. I have shone
with the glory borrowed from my innumerable co-workers." Notice the
balance in these words between striving for success and connecting to
others. The claim of this book is essentially to advocate for this balance;
to argue only for a sacrifice of striving for status among men misun-
derstands human nature and thus would be hopeless. Moreover, in the

examples of the Dalai Lama, Wiesel, and Gandhi—whose connections to books are deep and daily—I am not suggesting that the successful male has to read like they did (or like professors are supposed to but, with distressing frequency, don't). Rather, I am pointing to the sustaining character of connection to a society's or culture's animating ideas. Books—some books—can do this, but so can immersion in the public square. And books and the public square can be one and the same: Tony Judt wrote recently, "Words [are] a public space in their own right—and properly preserved public spaces are what we so lack today."[27]

As in virtually everything, connection to books and their ideas can be intemperate. Literal readings of the Bible, for example, have been used over the centuries to justify many evil things, including some, tellingly, that contradict one another. Just as continuity around a country's history can thwart individual loneliness, so can memory of one's own individual history—put differently, nostalgia. In a 2008 study, researchers administered questionnaires to children, undergraduate students, and factory workers.[28] The questionnaires evaluated levels of loneliness, social support, and nostalgia. In each of the three groups, an unsurprising result emerged: those who perceived low social support expressed the most loneliness. Interestingly, however, nostalgia seemed to tamp down this relationship. Nostalgia took the sting out of low social support; nostalgic participants did not report feeling very lonely, even if they perceived themselves as lacking in social support. Fond memories were, in a sense, these participants' friends.

Like the good experimental psychologists they were, these researchers were not content to show only that a pattern of correlations conformed to their expectations; they wanted to go farther and show that experimental manipulation of nostalgia would produce the predicted effects. To do this, they randomly assigned some participants to engage in a nostalgia exercise, and other participants to engage in an exercise that did not involve nostalgia. Here, too, results showed that nostalgia provided a form of companionship. Even participants who are instructed to be nostalgic by experimenters experience a drop in loneliness.

Why does nostalgia confer these benefits? A researcher interviewed about the study suggested that nostalgia instills continuity of identity[29]—

a view that harkens back to the earlier discussion of self-verification needs. "Nostalgia is like looking in a rearview mirror," she said. "Do I still have the values and priorities I had before? It gives us stability when we live in a time of constant change." In his memoir *The Memory Chalet,* Tony Judt writes with nostalgia about the London of his childhood, "London . . . was my city. It isn't anymore. But nostalgia makes a very satisfactory second home."[30]

Active engagement—either with one's fond memories or with the public square—and the togetherness it inspires, should decrease loneliness and thereby measurably decrease loneliness' effects, such as suicide. When are we most involved with one another in the public square? One answer is at times of war, and indeed, wars suppress suicide rates. Another is during presidential elections—even if they are fractious, they bring us together, much as does another time of togetherness and dispute, the winter holidays (another time of low suicide rates, contrary to popular belief)—and sure enough, suicide rates drop at times of presidential elections. The country deeply mourned JFK's assassination, but together. And suicide rates fell, just as they did after 9/11. On September 9, 2001, we lost approximately eighty-five of our fellow Americans to death by suicide; on September 10, 2001, the number was the same; but on September 11, 2001, even as nearly three thousand people perished in New York, Washington, and Pennsylvania, there were far fewer deaths by suicide in the United States.

Suicide rates go down when we pull together in times of tragedy . . . and in times of celebration, too. February 22, 1980, is unique in two ways. First, it was the date of the Miracle on Ice—of all the miracles I've ever heard of, the one that seems the truest and not only because I watched it happen on TV—a victory in the Winter Olympics of the US hockey team over the Soviet hockey machine, an outcome that was unlikely, to put it mildly. And an outcome that resonated far beyond sports, as our hostages were still in Tehran at the time and the Soviets were in Afghanistan. It affected people in the United States; I have a "flashbulb" memory of it in the same way that people do of where they were when they learned of President Kennedy's death or of 9/11. The other way in which February 22, 1980, was unique is that it is the only

February 22 on record in the United States with fewer than sixty deaths by suicide. Both rejoicing and commiserating pull people together and as a function thereof sustain them, reduce their misery, and prevent the grievous tragedy of death by suicide.

"We the people" strikes a different note than "don't tread on me," and is a useful sentiment to combat loneliness, one that men in particular could benefit from reflecting on. One worries that we as a society are losing touch with the sentiment, and this is not merely because of political divides. Can kids these days even identify the Constitution, much less quote it? This worries me, which worry was encouraged by the reactions of an Air Force general, as described by a reporter.[31] The reporter had written on the influence of Christianity on the US military, and had found that, in some circles, those who were not Christian or not Christian enough were being discriminated against. The reporter wondered aloud to the general whether this wasn't against the establishment and free exercise clauses of the First Amendment (which, of course, prohibits governmental "establishment of religion, or prohibiting the free exercise thereof"). The general seemed confused by the question, unaware of the establishment and free exercise clauses, and then after consulting briefly with aides, responded that he and his aides do not focus overly on those "Constitutional things." When pressed further on the question, the general and his aides decided to pass on the question.

I heard this on the radio, driving home to dinner from work. It brought to mind the following passage from Lasch's *Culture of Narcissism*: "People increasingly find themselves unable to use language with ease and precision, to recall the basic facts of their country's history, to make logical deductions, to understand any but the most rudimentary written texts, or even to grasp their constitutional rights."[32] And Lasch wrote this approximately thirty years ago, since which time things have not improved. With a duly demoralized attitude, I queried both my sons over dinner on questions of founding documents and their content—something that we had not discussed in years if ever. Both boys get reasonably good grades and do well on standardized testing, but given the general's reply, I was expecting more fodder for my worry.

I was mistaken. They easily rattled off the three main founding documents—the Declaration of Independence, the Constitution, and the Bill
of Rights—and moreover, quoted chunks verbatim from each. In their
parlance, they "destroyed" me, meaning that they defeated me in my
quiz game. I agreed, but of course felt far from destroyed.

This anecdote is optimistic, but the general's remarks temper my
sanguinity somewhat . . . as does the possibility that my sons, who "destroyed" the quiz on "we the people" in their youth, will forget about
"we the people" as they age. They may turn instead to an overemphasis
on "don't tread on me" and other forms of excessive self-sufficiency.
They may be able to balance these two processes, as did the Founding
Fathers; a point of this book is to suggest ways to achieve this balance.
But if this balance eludes them, they, in their middle-age and beyond,
may face some of the difficulties inherent in being "lonely at the top."

"One of the fundamental axioms of masculine self-regard is that
the tools and appurtenances of a man's life must be containable within
the pockets of his jacket and pants."[33] No doubt there is an alluring
aspect to self-contained, rugged individualism. Even relatively pale experiences, such as minor exertions of self-control, are rewarding. In his
2006 book *Stumbling on Happiness,* psychologist Dan Gilbert wrote
that "People find it gratifying to exercise control. . . . Being effective—
changing things, influencing things, making things happen—is one of
the fundamental needs with which our human brains seem naturally
endowed, and much of our behavior from infancy onward is simply an
expression of this penchant for control."[34]

A well-known study illustrates this principle.[35] In the study,
nursing-home residents were given a houseplant; half were told that
the care of the plant was their responsibility, and half were told that the
plant would be cared for by staff. The only difference between the two
groups, then, was that one group exerted control over the daily care of a
plant. This difference, as seemingly minor as it was, was associated with
something not minor at all: mortality. Six months after the plants were
placed in rooms, 15 percent of those caring for their own plants had
died, as compared to 30 percent of those whose plants were cared for
by staff. This kind of finding was satirized under the headline "Man's

Loneliness Ends with Purchase of Potted Houseplant."[36] Jokes aside, though, the study summarized above showed that the simple exercise of control, in this case regarding, yes, a potted houseplant, appeared to make a genuine life-or-death difference.

A recent article about a local nursing home corroborates this perspective.[37] The home hired contractors and landscapers to build patios that oriented toward the sun during the fall and winter months, and cleared land nearby where the residents grow flowers and vegetables. The article quoted two residents; one said, "I like to sit out here and crochet and enjoy the sun and breezes"; the other stated, "I enjoy the fresh air and beautiful flowers, but, my favorite was eating the fresh vegetables." The younger of the two was, according to the article, "a youthful-looking 90."

The dark side of at least some forms of self-sufficiency, however, is also beyond dispute, and can be seen in these words on the American economy, "The cheap-oil economy has made us the first people on earth who have no need of one another. Everything we buy comes from an anonymous distance. We eat far fewer meals with family and neighbors than we did fifty years ago; we have on average far fewer close friends. The basic premise of the American economy—that the goal was a bigger house farther apart from other people—turns out to be mistaken, both ecologically and psychologically."[38] In a speech at the University of Chicago in 1966, Vice President Hubert Humphrey sounded a different note. The vice president said, "There is in every American, I think, something of the old Daniel Boone—who, when he could see the smoke from another chimney, felt himself too crowded and moved further out into the wilderness." The autonomous—and confident—strain in the American character is hard to dispute, but the point is not to dispute this; it is, rather, to point out that it may be backfiring.

There is indeed reason to worry that our relationships to one another are changing in essential—and largely distancing—ways. For example, people tend to delay marriage now more than ever before, and partly relatedly, people live in single-residence households more than at any other time in human history. Intergenerational living—a child having the experience of living with parents and grandparents under one roof—is vanishing; indeed, I myself can think of no examples of this in my neighborhood or among my sons' friends or among my own friends and colleagues. Goethe said that the failure to draw on and learn from history "is living hand to mouth," and intergenerational living was a main source of such daily history, because it linked people directly with multiple family members across generations, and thereby linked them both to the past and to posterity.[39] A fifty-year-old man who lives with his grandchild (or is otherwise connected to them) can be pulled out of isolation by virtue of that fact alone; a dilemma is that that fact alone virtually never occurs anymore.

A recent article demonstrated that late-term baby boomers (defined in this particular piece as those born between 1957 and 1964), far from having the staid and stable job careers their children imagine, have had an average of eleven jobs.[40] There is every indication that this average will not decrease and may well increase for future cohorts. Depending on one's attitude, new jobs, it should be acknowledged, can lead to friend *gain* instead of friend loss. Gain would in fact occur if one made a point of keeping friends at old jobs and making new friends at new jobs. My impression of the modern workplace, however, is that this attitude is rare, and that where it exists, it is more likely to reside in the mind of a woman than that of a man. The usual attitude, especially among men, of forgetting about many aspects of the old job (including its social milieu) means a series of work sites in which relationships are superficial and temporary.

Consistent with these speculations, over the last twenty or so years, the number of people who report having no confidant has tripled, and the average size of one's network of confidants decreased from around three to around two.[41] This same research showed that a large chunk of the decrease was specific to men, especially regarding men's shrinking relationships to non-family members; put differently, friend loss. It is worth noting that this same time period has witnessed an explosion in social media technology, suggesting that the latter is by no means a full solution to the problem of loneliness (a point to which I will return in a later chapter).

I can already see "don't tread on me" developing in my elder son in early adolescence. On his Facebook page, in the slot where one can list parents, siblings, etc., he lists instead the names of his friends—one of many statements, both implicit and explicit, that he is leaving us, not in any sort of permanent or disastrous way, but in the way of a normal quest for independence, a quest that I am arguing takes on different qualities in boys and men than it does in girls and women. When I first noticed this aspect of his Facebook page, my predominant reaction was a knowing chuckle; I have little doubt that, had Facebook existed when I was his age, I would have done something similar. Also, I am glad he has friends, and ones to whom he feels that close (though I definitely do my parental detective work on all this, behavior that my sons have termed "creeping" or "stalking"). My second reaction was to close the page before my wife saw it, because her reaction would be different; she would take his leaving us off the page as an affront, and then there would follow much gnashing of teeth. It *is* an affront actually, but it is one that is within the normal limits of the process of a boy becoming a man, a process that necessarily entails a leaving behind. Any quest requires a leaving behind, by definition. Girls also need space and privacy, but to achieve them employ "leaving" strategies less than do boys.

My elder son's need for space and privacy has skyrocketed; his wish to be fully in charge of his affairs (e.g., grades and homework) has intensified. He's doing fine (to my and my wife's great pleasure and relief), but he is a little more distant from us (to our chagrin). Is he lonely? Not in the least, if the number of friends he has on Facebook is any indication (as I have just alluded to, one of those Facebook friends is me, whom he agreed to "friend" only after *much* pleading and encouragement). He has lots of friends from school and from soccer, but then again, of course he does, they are ready-made. He is in the phase of development where blinders develop: Friends? Taken care of, permanently, or so he thinks.

This is all in contrast to his little brother, who is three years younger. Just the other night as I was working on this book, he sat down next to me—close, with physical contact—and asked me what I was doing. I told him I was working on a book and he wanted to know what it was about (with genuine, and touching, interest).

Three years ago, I had frequent interactions like this with both boys. Now, I mostly only have them with one of them, because the older one doesn't want to be trod upon. And three years from now, both boys will identify with the rattlesnake—just as their ancestors did in the 1700s—and my wife and I will grieve. Grieve mildly, that is, because this is a natural and inevitable phase of development, and what's more, we hear from parents of older sons that they "come back," to a degree, around age twenty.

That this is a normal phase of adolescent development is an important point. I am not arguing that girls do not experience turbulent teens—my friends with daughters assure me that they do. Rather, my claim is that adolescence sets boys, more than girls, on a trajectory toward and concretizes them within both the "spoiled" and "don't tread" processes.

"Don't tread on me" is an attitude of independence and self-sufficiency, and it is a mindset that is hard to maintain if the school of hard knocks has taught you how crucial interdependence is, how you will need friends to cushion inevitable falls. The "becoming spoiled" process exempts people from the school of hard knocks, places them out of it, and thus lays the groundwork for the "don't tread on me" trajectory that young boys start along.

Dogged self-sufficiency in the absence of healthy interdependence can work for a while; the energy and vigor of youth can sustain it and even amplify it into a rugged, determined, effective state of mind. Hard knocks come sooner or later, however, if not in the form of early failure and disappointments, then in the form of inevitable later struggles with fading strength and failing health (not to mention things like hair loss). The trend is evident in people's comfort in their own skin. As my colleagues and I recently showed, and as alluded to in the first chapter, just as women's intense focus on and dissatisfaction with their bodies start to fade in their forties (as compared to their twenties and thirties)—a process driven by increasing *interpersonal* connection to children and careers—men's focus shows the exact opposite trend—high satisfaction in their twenties and thirties, and increasing discomfort and dissatisfaction in their forties and beyond.[42] Ester Schaler Buchholz wrote in her book *The Call of Solitude* that "The male who hardens himself as he pushes everyone from his life allows emotional overload to force him into a retreat so complete it renders him impotent in the face of human misery."[43] This is an apt description of men I know—or on whose cases I have served as expert witness—who have taken their own lives.

The choice of the phrase "hardens himself" is an interesting one to me, in part because I have a friend whose favorite saying is "harden up," by which he means "man up" or "stop being such a wimp." He rarely if ever misuses the phrase; that is, when he says it, it is almost always the case that someone really does need to "harden up." But, as I argue in "considering the rattlesnake," the process of hardening up can be taken too far. Things that become too hard can become brittle.

North Korea is a macrocosm of this process of early and excessive focus on self-sufficiency working for a while and then failing horribly— an early hardening up overdone, leading to catastrophic brittleness. The national mantra of *Juche* (self-reliance) worked, more or less, in the country's energetic and optimistic youth, but later produced the grotesque spectacle that North Korea is today. The continued "self-reliance" policy is not only a farce (the country is far from self-reliant, of course), but it is also an atrocity, costing hundreds of thousands of North Koreans their lives. Excessive and inappropriate self-reliance can kill.

Implicit in "don't tread on me," at least potentially, is "don't touch me." In his classic 1966 book *The Hidden Dimension*, Edward Hall argues that people from "contact cultures" (Latin, Asian, Arab) prefer more physical closeness than do people from "non-contact cultures" (Northern European, North American), an assertion that has been empirically corroborated. For instance, one study has shown that Mexican-American second graders sat more closely together and touched more than their fellow Anglo-American students. I could not be more confident that this finding would replicate within my own family, in which the 100 percent American (me) has far and away the lowest need for touch and the highest need for distance, the 50 percent American–50 percent Mexicans (my sons) are intermediate (though not at the same location; indeed, the one we see as the "most Mexican" has the higher need for touch), and the 100 percent Mexican (my wife) has far and away the highest need for touch and the lowest need for distance. Here again, to quote the researchers on independent versus interdependent mindsets, Americans are "highly unrepresentative of [the human] species."[44]

I hugged a guy at my twenty-fifth high school reunion, a guy I was friends with but hadn't seen for years. His visceral flinch (which I'm assuming was not personal) was unmistakable, and I don't blame him a bit because I've done the very same thing many times. There is a section in Norah Vincent's book *Self-Made Man* in which she discusses the social environment of the monks in a particular monastery. A theme of the discussion is that these men experience a kind of closeness to one another, but one that is limited and at times hollow. In this context, she quotes one monk who affectionately put his hand on the shoulder of another: "You've never seen anyone pull away so fast and furiously."[45]

Aversion to touch can be quickly abandoned, however, if a man feels that he or his loved ones are physically threatened, in which case touch may well occur—violent touch, that is. The writer Scott Spencer recently remarked, "The simple truth is that men are somewhat violent, even those of us who abhor violence. We believe that we would, or should, be willing to die or kill for those we love. Even if we are cerebral, out of shape, or blind in one eye, many of us expect of ourselves levels of daring and aggression that would quite frankly horrify most women."[46] I think this is true, and this underlying tendency affixes an addendum to "don't tread on me"—namely, "because if you do tread on me, I will retaliate in kind, or if I fail to, hate myself for the failure." In a radio interview, Scott Spencer mentioned that his dad had always told him that women sleep more deeply than men do because the men have to be vigilant and ready to respond with force to assault and intrusion, on behalf not only of themselves but their loved ones, too (more on sleep in later sections of the book). This state of mind is preoccupying and serves to consolidate "don't tread on me" outlooks and to block efforts to connect in sustained ways to others.

The reference here is mostly to protecting others, but it might have included protecting one's very status as a man as well. Manhood, much more so than womanhood, is something that people view as earned rather than as conferred through maturity—there is empirical backing to this claim, a point I will return to. As too many people have learned over the last few years of looking at their retirement accounts and the like, that which has been earned can also be lost, and "manhood status" is no exception. To this point, psychologist Roy Baumeister recently wrote, "The fact that manhood can be lost even after it has been successfully claimed means that the man has to watch out for threats, pretty much forever. . . .You can never be sure when a challenge to your manhood might arise. You have to be on guard."[47]

Puzzling things become less so once the male tendency to prize and protect status is factored in. Consider dueling in this light. It seems an absurd thing, not just that it occurred, but that it persisted for centuries, and that dueling scars were a source of great pride. This seemingly bizarre thing becomes less so once it is realized that all of this is about the prized resource of status as a "real man"—a resource that is precarious and must be vigilantly protected. The story of Évariste Galois is of interest in this context. Not only did he die in a duel, and not only did he pioneer an entire branch of mathematics, he did both of these things before age twenty-one. Why might one spend years—adolescent years at that—immersed in mathematics with the aim of creating something revolutionary, only to die young, in a duel? Though many answers are possible, one that answers both questions with concision is "reputation." In both of these activities of course—revolutionary mathematics and dueling—men predominate, probably along the lines of a 10 to 1 ratio.

Galois was unlucky (in dueling, not in mathematics). Dueling men really did not expect to be killed or even hurt (though of course some were); rather, they intended to publicly display their *willingness* to be killed or hurt as a way to show how serious they were about their status as men of good standing. Scars did not therefore signal loss; on the contrary, they gained status for their bearers because they represented this willingness.

Dueling in males occurs across nature. Bull elk are massive creatures, with lethal hooves and antlers. An all-out fight between two such animals would end in a very grisly scene of, in the best-case scenario, one elk dead and the other wounded to the point of being near death. Like duelers, they choose a less lethal alternative: they wrestle instead, locking horns with one another and pushing each other to and fro. This pushing contest decides a winner with no need for death or injury, and no need even for the expenditure of much energy. Hervey Cleckley, in his book *The Mask of Sanity,* provides an entertaining example of these kinds of displays in discussing a psychopathic patient he had encountered: "He was found in the custody of the police, against whom he had made some resistance but much more vocal uproar. The resistance actually was only a show of resistance consisting for the most part of dramatically aggressive gestures made while he was too securely held to fight and extravagant boasts of his physical prowess and savage temper. His general demeanor in this episode suggested the familiar picture of small boys, held fast by peacemakers, who wax ever more eloquently militant as the possibilities of actual conflict diminish."[48]

I have never seen a duel in its classic sense—I suppose few have these days—but I have seen versions of them hundreds of times. A memorable example occurred in Paris, where I was staying with a friend who was living there with a French family. Times were a little tough for this family, which is why, I imagine, they were hosting my friend, as well as a German student, as exchange students—the family needed the payments they got for serving as hosts. They were therefore not necessarily delighted by my presence—not only another mouth to feed but a twenty-year-old voracious American at that—but soon enough they accepted me, in part because I shared a fondness for pear liqueur with the family's mother, whose fondness for the drink knew no bounds, and which caused the quasi-duel I observed.

My friend did not drink alcohol, a fact that plainly irked the family's mother. One night after dinner, she started in on him yet again about his attitude toward alcohol, and within an hour or so and after several ounces of pear liqueur, she decided that would be the night— "C'est la nuit," she said (the best I can do after not having spoken much French since then)—and resolved to physically force my friend to drink a shot of her favorite liqueur. This she did, in a feat of strength and alacrity that amazes me to this day.

This was not the quasi-duel. But it sowed the seeds for it by making very salient the question of one's manhood. For, needless to say, my friend's honor was continually questioned by all who witnessed the incident; indeed, even before the incident, the mother had directly questioned my friend's manhood in wondering rhetorically and loudly if lack of manhood was the reason he refused to sample her liqueur.

If my experience is any guide at all, it is the case that when one man's honor is questioned, and other men see this, it can set off a contagious wave of insecurity about one's own manhood. Understandable insecurity, really, because this resource can be fleeting, as my formerly abstinent friend learned from a smallish middle-aged French woman. This tide of insecurity, I believe, affected, more or less simultaneously, the German exchange student and the family's father, who, along with the rest of the family and me, witnessed my friend's humiliation.

It started off innocently enough with talk of shared interests in martial arts between the German student and the French father. This was an interest I did not share, which, along with the mother's favorable attitude toward my liqueur drinking, may have exempted me from this particular duel. Soon, the talk became competitive, consisting mostly of attempts by one to claim accomplishments or experiences that surely the other had not had. Then, one of them wondered aloud whether they should not have a martial arts demonstration there and then in the cramped living room, and settle this thing once and for all, "like men."

Like what I imagine a real duel would involve, the preparations for this demonstration could not have been more ornate or extensive. They went on for at least two hours—endless discussions of ground rules and how the furniture should be moved and so forth and so on. I do not mean to imply that these preparations were boring; au contraire, they were engrossingly entertaining, so much so that I forsook my nightly trip to a local grocer to compensate for the daily calorie deficit regime I was living under.

And, as I suppose probably happened frequently in real duels, the thing itself was profoundly anti-climactic, though not without its hilarity. After all the preparation and all the boasts about special skills and moves each had, when "start" was finally yelled, the German kid kicked the French dad in the shin, and he duly hopped around on one leg howling in pain. One of the main points of Roy Baumeister's book *Is There Anything Good about Men?* is that striving for status has produced a lot of important things (e.g., scientific knowledge, universities, companies). That night in Paris was about status, too, though culture was not enriched much by it.

IMPORTANTLY, IMPLICIT IN THE SENTIMENT "don't tread on me" can be the sentiment "don't connect with me." I believe it is crucial to the trouble with men that, even when one feels the desire for connection, one can give off signals that push it away. Two of the saddest such instances involve men who jumped off the Golden Gate Bridge. One, who died, left a note that read, in part, "I'm going to walk to the bridge. If one person smiles at me on the way, I will not jump." This man craved connection, but one wonders if he actually invited it. If, as he walked to the bridge, he was like the many seriously suicidal people whom I have seen in clinical settings, his expression and body language were not such that they provoked interaction of any sort, certainly not smiling. You can see as much for yourself in the 2006 documentary film *The Bridge,* which captured several deaths from the Golden Gate Bridge on film. The body language of those about to die is not inviting of care and interaction.

Another man who jumped and survived (as approximately 3 percent do) was walking on the bridge, crying. A police officer on a bicycle passed but did not stop to check on him. He recalls the thought that if only someone would show any gesture of caring, he would not jump. At that moment, a woman approached him, and he felt momentary relief and a resolve to live. When the woman ignored his tears, held out her camera, asked him to take her picture, and then coldly walked away, he ran toward the rail and leaped to what he believed would be his death.

Both these men were simultaneously desperate for connection and caring, and doing things to ward it off. To everything its season: "Don't tread on me" has legitimate allure, but can, if mis-timed or exaggerated, prove lethal.

4

CAUSES

PURSUING MONEY AND STATUS, REAPING ISOLATION

The same guys who came up with the "don't tread on me" flag were fond of another motto: "no taxation without representation." How does one most ensure not being trod upon, especially if one has been spoiled and exempted from hard knocks? See to money and status—no taxation without representation.

In their late twenties and thirties, men seem to focus on money and status, and they do so through the lens of jobs and careers. To be sure, women do this, too, but on average, men do it more. For instance, a recent study found that of all those who work more than forty-eight hours per week, 80 percent are men. A different study estimated the annual difference between men and women in time at the workplace at four hundred hours.[1] The idea here is not that men are harder workers or even that they work more overall (they may not once all kinds of work are added together). Rather, the issue is men's relentless focus on status and money. In this fanaticism, they bring to mind George Santayana's maxim that fanatics have lost sight of their goal but redoubled their efforts.

In my own early thirties, within the same year, I trained for and ran two full marathons, and I placed a scholarly article in every single issue of my field's most prominent journal (this latter feat is one that to my knowledge has not been equaled by anyone before or since). During that same timeframe, my wife was pregnant with and then gave birth to our first-born. What was going on with me?

I can imagine a psychoanalytically inclined explanation that would go something like this: "Marathons involve running; this together with the mental frenzy—a kind of running—involved in that much scholarly work means that the person in question was afraid, and was running away from the prospects of further commitment to marriage and to fatherhood." As we have seen and will see again, psychoanalytic explanations can be facile indeed. In my view, I have never run from anything and I in no way ran from marriage or fatherhood. A much more plausible explanation is that the imminent birth of my son threw my ambition into overdrive. I focused even more than before on accomplishment, probably as a way to see to my growing family's security and safety, then and into the future—in a phrase, zestful male nest-building.

This time frame, tellingly, was among the most friendless of my life. I was so focused on accomplishment—including of course in the domains of money and status—that I neglected my friendships. This anecdotal story, I am arguing here, is generalizable to many men in their thirties, and if the isolating processes continue into the forties and beyond, the consequences may include loneliness (and, if the man is successful, the experience of feeling "lonely at the top") and all of its attendant woe.

The tendency to focus on factors like status is very likely rooted in our evolutionary past. There was a profound asymmetry in the odds of reproductive success between men and women in the past. Most women reproduced, whereas only a fraction of the men did. This is not mere speculation: DNA studies have shown that, of the ancestors of all the people inhabiting the earth today, at least two-thirds were female—a fact that may seem puzzling until one considers that one man can father many children with many different women. This was very likely the norm in ancestral times, and there is no doubt that this same pattern is nature's norm today—in some species, the ratio is even more skewed, on the order of nine-tenths. This occurs because of the conjunction of a few simple facts: (1) the number of offspring possible for a female is limited by the biology of pregnancy, birth, and the immediate post-partum phase; (2) the same biological limits do not apply to males; (3) that female reproductive frequency is inherently limited renders it, like any relatively scarce thing, especially valuable; (4) valuable and scarce resources spur competition; (5) wide competition for a scarce resource produces some winners and many losers—the "musical chairs" scenario alluded to in chapter 1. In our evolutionary past, some men did all the fathering; most men did not reproduce; and most women did reproduce. All of this combines to mean that, for anyone reading these words, far more than half of one's ancestors were women. To this point, psychologist Roy Baumeister remarked, "Nature made life to seek to create more life. On this basic task, women faced good odds of success, whereas men were born to face looming failure."[2] In this light, male striving for things like status and money seems only natural—how else to have any chance in a reproductive version of musical chairs?

Moreover, as a rule, only men seem to focus on money and status *to the exclusion* of maintaining friendships and seeking new ones (and indeed there is a literature on how a focus on material goods can erode people's social relationships).[3] These trends are evident in both popular surveys and the scholarly literature: a popular magazine's survey found that five times fewer fifty-year-old men than twenty-year-old men endorsed the following definition of success: "A job that makes my family proud."[4] A mere 6 percent of fifty-year-old men chose this definition involving other people; they were much more likely to choose definitions that were self-referential and unpeopled.

It has been documented that a focus on materialism produces untoward effects. Psychologists Tim Kasser and Richard Ryan have conducted a series of studies showing that materialistic goals, far from providing the expected comforts and status, deliver instead a host of negativity: depression, anxiety, low self-esteem, feelings of low energy and vitality, and substance abuse.[5] These studies have been conducted primarily in the United States, but have also been replicated elsewhere, including Denmark, Germany, Russia, China, and India.

Consumerism can focus excessive attention on status-related objects—an unpeopling process—leaving limited energy for the cultivation of connection. Rivalries can occur between friends and neighbors over who has what, rivalries that can atomize communities. The essential problem is an either/or attitude toward wealth and status on the one hand and social connection on the other hand. This problem, I am arguing, plagues men more than it does women.

Consistent with the previous chapters on "becoming spoiled" and attitudes like "don't tread on me"—processes that begin to unfold in boys' lives and then live on to haunt their adulthoods—an exaggerated focus on materialism may start early in life. Research has demonstrated that materialism in children and teenagers has much the same effects as it does in adults: materialistic kids are more likely than other kids to have severe conduct problems, to perform poorly in school, and to engage in various risky behaviors.

Materialism, it should be stressed, can be defined as more than just a focus on money. In fact, psychologists have extended materialism's definition to include an excessive focus on status and physical attractiveness. In defining materialism in this broad manner, the key underlying dimension becomes extrinsic versus intrinsic motivation—whether one strives for things to satisfy external standards or to satisfy internally derived goals for their own sake, regardless of external standards. Extrinsic motivation, whether the focus is on status, money, or physical appearance, is associated with negative outcomes over the long term, whereas intrinsic motivation—a focus on fellow feeling, community, and accepting oneself, imperfections and all—tends to produce more satisfied people. Importantly, this work does not lead to the conclusion that any focus whatsoever on money, status, and attractiveness is doomed; rather, it indicates that a focus on extrinsic goals *to the neglect of* intrinsic ones is the process that produces negative outcomes—a process more common in men than women.

The Dalai Lama understands this concept on extrinsic versus intrinsic motivation (indeed, it is possible that he has read about it, given his well-known interest in psychological science). For all his status, the Dalai Lama is disdainful of many materialistic and status-related things, which he calls "old courtesies." A 2010 article in the *New Yorker* related that an early policy change decided by the Dalai Lama vexed many of his aides and followers; he ordered that visitors should be given a chair of equal height to his. This is consistent with His Holiness's outlook that "physically, mentally, emotionally, we are the same." Of course, this sentiment is hardly unique to the Dalai Lama; to choose one example, the psychiatrist Harry Stack Sullivan said, "All of us are much more human than otherwise."[6]

The change in chair height policy probably does make a difference to the Dalai Lama's visitors, as those, including myself, who have sat on a talk show stage on which the host's chair was almost a foot above mine, can affirm.

AN INTERESTING PERSPECTIVE on male versus female attitudes toward matters of status, reputation, and materialism comes from the unexpected direction of shoplifting. Crime in general seems to be largely a male specialty, but shoplifting occurs at roughly similar rates in males and females. Among shoplifters, however, there are intriguing gender differences, and they have to do with the phenomenon of the "proud shoplifter"—the individual who seems to care at least as much, if not more, about the reputational effects as about the acquisitive effects of shoplifting. This kind of shoplifter will tell many tales involving stealing and will often give stolen things away to friends, adding still more to the reputation. Reputation is important to the "proud shoplifters"—most of whom are male—as it is to men generally.

There is another category of shoplifter who might be characterized as the "secret shoplifter." The last thing this type wants is for people to know about the illegal activity; the motivations here are acquisitive—the coveting of particular objects and also the thrill connected with doing something risky.

I have known several shoplifters, mostly through clinical work, but also because I was a teenager with friends, and many teenagers with friends will know at least one occasional shoplifter. In the clinic, I have never seen a male shoplifter, or more accurately, have never worked with a male who disclosed his shoplifting. All of the examples in my experience are women who accessed mental health care not because of shoplifting but because of depression. Each of the women reported that they felt addicted to shoplifting, that they would prefer to stop doing it because they found it embarrassing and scary, but also that shoplifting provided some relief to their depression. This last claim may sound bizarre, but there is probably something to it; for example, the same kinds of medicines that are effective in the treatment of depression can also help people give up shoplifting. None of these women bragged about shoplifting; in fact, they would find the idea of publicizing their behavior unimaginable.

The "proud shoplifters" of my acquaintance were 100 percent male. Their exploits were done so that friends would know about them—either through their own bragging or through friends being in the vicinity when the stealing occurred. There was very little functional point to the shoplifting, if the point is viewed only in acquisitive terms. The stolen objects were an arbitrary collection that the thief himself would rarely use beyond showing them off. The point was not acquisitive but reputational, which often led to the shoplifting of physically challenging things—a memory springs to mind of a person who did not play golf but who shoplifted a golf club. To do so, the person limped stiff-legged into the store, and then a while later, limped out, now with a golf club down his pants. Men do all sorts of things—some normal, some less so—in the service of reputation.

Of course, the gender breakdown is not as total as my own experience would suggest—there are, for instance, men who steal for acquisitive motives. And there are women who are "proud shoplifters," but they are rather rare. My clinical experience reflects a valid gender difference: "proud shoplifters" are predominantly male.

What does this say about men and their attitudes toward status? I believe it indicates the value that men invest in reputation, the fact that they view it as an attainable commodity (and thus a losable one, too), and the lengths they will go to in order to claim it. Bragging about shoplifting is a pretty dumb way to attain status, to be sure, but then again, so are many things done by men in the name of reputation.

Attributions of status motives to certain behaviors like shoplifting are not always certain. The same behavior of shoplifting can be motivated by an acquisitive or a reputational motive, or by some combination of the two. Various motives for a given behavior can be multi-determined, a fact that is not always obvious. Caution is indicated, therefore, in assuming that certain behaviors are motivated by striving for status.

But some examples leave little doubt. I have already recounted the story of the kicked shin in Paris. Consider, as another example, the story told in the 2008 documentary *Man on Wire*. This astounding tale involves a group of men who, in 1974, decided to string a trapeze wire between the Twin Towers of the World Trade Center and then for one of them, Philippe Petit, to walk the wire, with no safety equipment at all. They achieved all of this, another example of men going to great lengths in the service of status and reputation. The great accomplishment of the film, however, is to make this seem a relatively small achievement compared to the caper necessary to pull the whole thing off.

Think of it. How do you string a trapeze rope of considerable weight across the substantial distance between the Twin Towers (their answer, by the way, involved a bow and arrow)? And how do you gain access to the towers and evade security all the while (they had to hide under construction tarps in immobile positions for hours)? This is the kind of overambitious fantasy that takes place every day in suburban backyards—just the other day, for example, my son and his friends "locked down" the "entire sector" of our neighborhood in a "military operation." The difference between my son and his friends, on the one hand, and the guys in *Man on Wire,* on the other hand, is the need for quotation marks: the latter did not "walk on a wire over a hundred floors up," as might happen in my backyard for instance (not to take away from the innocent charms of children's backyard capers). The guys in the film did it for real, no quotation marks needed.

As it happens, these epic feats did start as backyard fantasy, literally. The one who walked the wire strewn between the Twin Towers as a man in his thirties walked a wire as a boy of three years old, in his back yard, a wire that was a couple of feet off the ground.

As if the film needed another impressive element, the emotion shown by the men as they were interviewed over thirty years after the fact was very touching. This event was, by their very convincing telling, one of the most important things they ever experienced.

A group of people decided that one of them would put his life in mortal danger for no material gain whatsoever (in fact the whole thing cost them quite a bit of money), and not really for public fame either (but rather for private ambition and reputation, the same reason, I believe, that I went through a marathon and publishing frenzy in the year of my firstborn's birth); in order to risk one of their lives for no gain, they first needed to break several laws (trespassing and breaking and entering), putting them all at risk for further cost and for jail time; but before they could take even those risks, they had to spend months of their time scheming, learning, training, and mastering archery, physics, wind speeds at altitude, and the schedules and work habits of office workers, janitors, security guards, and others at the World Trade Center. They did all this, and the telling of it brings tears to their eyes more than thirty years later.

This is the kind of behavior that I believe Michael Chabon had in mind when he wrote in his book *Manhood for Amateurs* about "classic male modes of gratification: the mastering of an arcane lore bound up in accumulable tomes; mindless repetition (the thing that leads boys to take up card tricks, free-throw shooting, video games); and the staking of everything on a last throw of the dice."[7]

Who does things like this, risking everything to walk a wire between the Twin Towers? Although you might be tempted to respond along the lines of "mental patients," that is simply not so—for one thing, mental disorders are too disorienting and incapacitating to allow anyone to accomplish a feat like this. Even those with the intense energy of mania are too disorganized to successfully deploy that energy in the service of a momentous plan like walking a wire between the Twin Towers. For another thing, the men were each interviewed in depth by the filmmak-ers, and these interviews reveal no evidence of mental disorders, past or present (I teach a graduate seminar on detecting nuanced forms of psy-chopathology in nonfiction documentaries, memoirs, and the like, so I believe that, if mental disorders were present in *Man on Wire,* I would have noticed them). The answer to "who acts like this?" has nothing to do with mental disorders; it has to do with men on a quest. The quest in this case was not for blood or treasure, but rather for reputation and camaraderie. Put differently, they were on a quest for gangship—an important concept to which I will return shortly.

Sadly and tellingly, the two best friends among the group who pulled off the trapeze stunt drifted away from one another over the years. The two men forged a deep bond that was very meaningful to both of them, and yet even this faded. This is one anecdotal instance of a more general male tendency to neglect relationships. I am not alone in noticing this tendency. A recent article noted, "The fact is that all the women I know are better at friendships—spend more time on them, take more pleasure in them, and value them more highly—than any of the straight men. Forgive me, guys, but we are lousy at this."[8] This lousiness points up the need for workable solutions to counter this problematic and powerful tendency, a challenge taken up in the book's last section.

IN HIS PROVOCATIVE BOOK *Is There Anything Good about Men?* (his answer is "yes," in case you were wondering), Roy Baumeister relates a conver-sation that he had with a colleague who was studying career trajectories in male and female employees of a large corporation. One of the find-ings was that men identified much more closely with the company than did women. Although this is probably a positive as far as the interests of the corporation are concerned, it is not hard to imagine how it may not be in the best interests of maintaining interpersonal relationships. It should be acknowledged, of course, that people can make and maintain friends at work. "Can" and "do" are different things. Some profes-sional settings are very conducive to making friends; I would include my own job, university professor, in that category. When I hosted at an FSU football game some of my old friends from high school who are now lawyers at different firms, they were stunned that I wanted to tail-gate with a group of fellow professors. "We would never do that," one said. The other agreed, "Yeah, I flee my colleagues after work." "But why?" I asked. "Well, a lot of it is competition with each other; it can be pretty cutthroat. I guess the rest is that we just don't like each other that much." Perhaps the problem is with these particular firms (or with my particular friends), but I suspect not. I believe this is fairly typical of many professional settings, more so for men than for women, and more so in the United States than elsewhere.

I was chatting recently at a cocktail party with a couple of guys, both in their sixties. The topic was retirement, and more specifically, how to do it right. They were reflecting on the experiences of their own parents, and one of them said of his mother's retirement home that "for the women it's almost a sorority house environment—a lot of social-izing, fun, support of and care for one another. The men mostly talk about who they used to be, what their job used to be. They just don't seem to do nearly as well as the women."

I do not wish to collude in the stigmatization of aging and associ-ated things like retirement. It is quite possible to retire well. Many of my academic clinical psychologist colleagues, both those older and younger than me, look up to a man named Paul Meehl. The reverence is well earned because he made some of the most insightful and influential con-tributions to our field, in domains ranging from understanding schizo-phrenia, to the philosophy of science, to diagnostic classification and the associated mathematics. Given the prodigious nature of his work, and its scope, I was surprised to learn that the great scholar wished he had retired much earlier than he did (a main rationale for him was that if he had retired earlier, he would have had more time to read—a senti-ment with which I can easily identify as I eye the stack of books I own but have not yet found the time to read).[9] This eminent scholar retired well, but, at least in his view, late. His story is instructive, I think, be-cause in some ways he was the prototype of the person who would be bored and thus undone by retirement. In fact, he probably thought so himself and thus delayed retirement for ten years or so in the process. But he retired successfully nevertheless.

Empirical evidence backs up this example; one example is a recent study of the effect of retirement on feelings of fatigue and depression.[10] The report evaluated over fourteen thousand people, with regular assessments during the seven years preceding retirement and the seven years following it. According to the researchers, "retirement was associated with a substantial decrease in both mental and physical fatigue and with a smaller but clearly significant decrease in the prevalence of depressive symptoms." Had Paul Meehl retired ten years earlier, the odds are that he was right that he would have read a lot more, and that this would have been fueled in part by relief from things like physical fatigue.

The men in the anecdote alluded to earlier, who were looking back at who they used to be—and basing their current identity thereon—are talking about what are called "the power years" in Bob Greene's book *And You Know You Should Be Glad*. "In the power years, there's an aura around a man—he's in charge, not just of other people but of himself . . . you report to no one but you."[11] Through conversations with a friend, however, the author came to see the two-edged nature of these years and the associated attitude. When asked about the power years, the friend replied, "I don't think the forties are the power years. I think they're the fool-you years."[12] Pressed to explain, the friend continued, "You become one of those guys, thinking it's smooth sailing from then on out, and those are the guys for whom things go wrong. The power turns out to be an illusion. They get fooled by it."[13] The insidious thing about this insight is that the guys in power cannot see what is happening to them, whereas the guys referred to above in the retirement setting would recognize it instantly.

One thing that focuses men's attention on status is that achievement of even the palest versions of it is anything but guaranteed. Take, for example, the achievement of the status of manhood itself, as compared to the achievement of womanhood. Simone de Beauvoir asserted in her 1949 book *The Second Sex* that "one is not born a woman; one becomes one."[14] She had a point, she just got the gender wrong. Researchers asked college students to evaluate statements like "All boys do not grow up to become real men" and "A boy must earn his right to be called a man." The students tended to agree with the statements; note that these were university students, women and men alike, in the twenty-first century. But when researchers substituted the word "girl" for "boy" and "woman" for "man," the students tended to disagree; for instance, they tended to disagree with the statement "A girl must earn her right to be called a woman."[15] Women, according to the view implicit in the students' answers, will achieve womanhood essentially automatically; for men, the corresponding status must be earned. By "status" I am not referring to being wealthy, revered, or powerful, merely to being considered a man. If the realization of even this extremely broad definition of status remains tenuous, no wonder men's attention is fixated, often overly so and to their detriment, on status.

Memoirist Eric Wilson pondered the effects of depression on his relationships and emphasized one coping strategy, an ultimately failed one, an obsession with achievement and status through his work as a professor. He wrote, "the most pressing result of this ferocious commitment to work had nothing to do with accolades. Every minute I poured all my best energy into research and writing, I lost another opportunity to connect with my wife and found another way to calcify our alienation."[16] Calcification is an apt metaphor; so would be muscular atrophy—relationship maintenance has a "use it or lose it" character. A very well-respected professor of my acquaintance, in reply to my telling him the idea of this book, reacted in terms that affirm those of the memoirist. The prominent professor said, "I just didn't get it until I was well into my forties and my first marriage imploded. I was working all the time, mostly successfully, but I was always irritable, and my now ex-wife was miserable. After our divorce, I took a long look in the mirror, and decided if I ever got married again, I'd do things differently. A hard lesson to be sure, but it's why I'm happy now and why my second marriage has been so good." This second marriage is in its twentieth year, and at least as far as I can judge, is every bit as strong as the professor claimed.

A bedeviling fact is that money can *almost* literally become your friend. To show this, a team of research psychologists used the same social exclusion design described chapter 1.[17] The researchers randomly assigned participants to one of three conditions: "future alone"—this was the socially excluded group; "future belonging"; and "misfortune control." Those in the social exclusion condition are told, in part, "You're the type who will end up alone later in life . . . when you're past the age where people are constantly forming new relationships, the odds are you'll end up being alone more and more."

Participants in the "future belonging" condition and "misfortune control" group had it easier. The former were told, in part, that "odds are that you'll always have friends and people who care about you," and the latter were told, in part, that "odds are you will have a lot of accidents." This latter control group is often included in such study designs so that any effects of social exclusion can be specifically attributed to it and not to the receipt of bad news in general.

Unsurprisingly, the "future alone" condition was harder on participants than the other two conditions. The same held true when those in the "future alone" handled blank pieces of paper after hearing about their purported lonely futures. But if participants handled cash instead of blank paper, their negative reactions were mitigated. The researchers were telling them that they would be alone, but they did not feel so alone; money was, in a sense, their friend. A news article summarizing this work was titled "Rich People Don't Need Friends"—this is a false assertion, as this book shows, but given the experimental result, it is not hard to see why the headline occurred to editors.[18]

Social exclusion hurts, in part because it activates the same area of the brain that is affected by physical pain. According to this logic then, handling money might also alleviate physical pain. In fact, the same team of researchers found this to be the case as well. In this study, they looked at physical pain ratings of those whose arms were immersed in uncomfortably (not physically dangerously) hot water, and compared those to the ratings of a control group.[19] The groups' ratings, not surprisingly, were quite different, with the put-upon participants reporting more pain. Unless, that is, the hot-water participants were handling money, in which case their ratings began to resemble those of the control group.

Taken to one of its logical conclusions, this line of work suggests that something like Tylenol should make people less lonely, because, by affecting that pain center—a center that seems to control social pain as well as physical pain—social pain should be reduced. And psychologist Nathan DeWall and colleagues have shown that this is, in fact, the case.[20]

But of course, distributing money or Tylenol as a solution to loneliness is unworkable, to put it mildly. In the case of money, let's return to another finding in the "future alone" and "hot water" studies, which is that being reminded of having spent money did not have the same analgesic effects as handling money. On the contrary, reminders of past spending made negative reactions worse. Participants in the experiment realized, I imagine not for the first time in their lives, that the expression "easy come, easy go" is lacking in profundity and at best half true.

This is part of the reason that "money as friend" is bedeviling. It can be fleeting, and even when it's not fleeting, is not sustaining. If it was sustaining, there would be far fewer suicides among wealthy individuals, mostly men, during difficult recessions like the current one. If it were, my own dad might still be alive; he killed himself within weeks of making a very large amount of money in a stock deal. But money can *almost* be your friend, as the experiments described above illustrate, as does the example of my dad. It can be your friend long enough and even deeply enough to delude you that it is sufficient by itself for life satisfaction. As this illusion holds, time is wasting, social ability is atrophying, and friends made early in life—if they even existed to begin with—drift away.

A lucky few can coast on the friendships they made back in the day. But most can't, and over time, they drift away from friendships and simultaneously earn money and status. Recall the words of the memoirist Eric Wilson—his commitment to work was "ferocious," and yet it backfired on him. This example can be generalized to describe many men. They find themselves, after years of focus on money and status, in a puzzling and paradoxical position—they are in fact privileged and should therefore feel privileged, but instead they feel empty and lonely . . . in a phrase, lonely at the top.

5

LONELY AT THE TOP

In the last weeks of my dad's life, he was "alone in a crowd." The last time I saw him, a few weeks before his death by suicide, was on a family vacation, which included my mom, both my sisters, a friend of mine, and me. He was not alone, but it was not hard to see that he felt alone (this is not to say that I in any way expected his death by suicide; far from it, it was the most brutal shock of my life). That he felt alone, even in the midst of loved ones, was evident in his demeanor and reticence, but also in what I have come to see in clinical situations as a potentially ominous suicide warning sign, the "thousand-yard stare." Common in people who have been through a traumatic experience like combat, the thousand-yard stare involves a vacant expression in the eyes. With regard to those who have decided to end their lives, it involves an inward gaze of bemused resignation and resolution. Others often describe the person going through this as "not there" or "already gone." It is an intense form of "immutuality"—of loneliness itself.

My dad was fifty-six at the time of his death, and the kind of loneliness he experienced in the weeks before his death—"alone in a crowd"—becomes more common in men as the decades of their lives pass. I have no way of saying for sure, but I think it is a safe assumption that, in the hours, minutes, and moments before my dad's death, he not only felt alone, he was literally alone. This form of loneliness, too, becomes more common in men as they age.

Younger men, by contrast, are more prone to a third category of loneliness, which I termed earlier "alone but oblivious." My dad displayed this form as well, but in his thirties. By then, his friendships had begun to fade, so much so that even I noticed it as a young child. I even asked him about it, and he did seem oblivious (though it is possible he felt something but did not want to trouble his young son).

In the previous three chapters, I delineated distinguishable but nevertheless related sources of loneliness in men: becoming spoiled (and to some degree starting out spoiled); excessive valuing of autonomy, as typified by "don't tread on me" attitudes; and an excessive fixation on status and money. For each of the three, "alone but oblivious" forms of loneliness prevail; a person overly focused on entitlement, fierce independence, status, or money is often unable to observe that interpersonal resources are all the while draining away.

By contrast, the fourth and final source of loneliness—"lonely at the top"—usually occurs later in life, at a time when the allure of independence has worn off, and when status or money may have been acquired. But the presence of status and money, far from satisfying needs for connection, exacerbates the needs by contrast. The contrast is between a full bank account or high status on the one hand, and the emptiness of loneliness on the other.

This last source of loneliness, "lonely at the top," is distinguishable from the other three forms in another way. The first three forms— "spoiled," "don't tread on me," and "money/status fixation"—are causes, not consequences, of loneliness. "Lonely at the top," however, also has clear elements of consequence. It is an endpoint, rather than an original source.

In this chapter, the phenomenon of "lonely at the top" is described and explored. In his book *The Lonely Crowd,* David Riesman, in a section entitled "Lonely Successes," writes of the man who, at the pinnacle of professional success, is, largely owing to the consequences of that success, "miserable and frightened, waiting to be cut down from the heights." In that same passage, the author adds, "Success is fatal."[1] Words like "heights" and especially "pinnacle" imply a place of prominence and influence, to be sure, but also of isolation. There is not much room at a pinnacle's apex.

We have already seen that money can be a false friend. It can also be isolating. In her book *Bright-Sided,* which argues that an emphasis on optimism at all costs is dangerous, Barbara Ehrenreich writes of the incredible—one might even say obscene—wealth of the super-rich and the excesses it spurs. Jack Welch, upon his retirement from the position of CEO of General Electric—a pinnacle to be sure—was provided a $25 million annual salary, use of a Boeing 737 jet, an $80,000-per-month Manhattan apartment, and free security guards posted to his various homes. They are posted to his person, too; in fact, I was in the Atlanta airport when a hubbub occurred, caused by several suited men who looked like Secret Service agents. My fellow travelers and I were certain the president was coming through, or maybe a member of his cabinet, but it was just Jack Welch.

"An obvious price of this lifestyle," writes Ehrenreich in *Bright-Sided,* "is extreme isolation."[2] This isolation is attributable to the fact that subordinates of CEOs and similarly placed people are motivated to curry favor by being the bearer of only good news. One CEO is quoted as saying he is "the most lied-to man in the world." But this would explain being deceived, which is not the same thing as being lonely (though there can be overlap, as "alone but oblivious" types of loneliness show). A deeper reason for the isolation of wealthy CEOs and their ilk involves their own attitudes and behavior. They tend to be fixated on money and status, a state that was preceded in many of them by the processes described earlier of "becoming spoiled" and sensitive to being trod upon. These attitudes are inherent in the words of the lied-to CEO described above. He is wealthy and thus wields a certain power, no doubt, but his own words "most lied-to *in the world*" place him in a position of importance exceeding that of all other CEOs, not to mention the leaders of all the world's countries. The comment harkens back to that quoted in chapter 1 of a college student who opined that her dreams were the most important thing *in the world*. These statements are a reflection of our age of narcissism.

Success has been fatal for many of the men who have held the position of Dalai Lama. A 2010 article in the *New Yorker* pointed out that, unlike the current Dalai Lama, only about half of those who held the post have made it into their thirties, and several have been killed in palace assassination plots.[3] In one instance in the 1600s, a government minister hid the then–Dalai Lama's death for fifteen years, something that can only be done with a leader who is not just lonely at the top, but isolated and hidden away at the top. Indeed, the current Dalai Lama described the years of his childhood, during which he lived apart from his family in a thousand-room palace, as being "hidden away like an owl."

Of course, success need not be fatal, and people of lofty station need not be lonely. This was an obvious truth in early America. Alexis de Tocqueville wrote, "In the United States the more opulent citizens take great care not to stand aloof from the people; on the contrary, they constantly keep on easy terms with the lower classes; they listen to them, they speak to them every day."[4] This is no longer accurate, to put it mildly.

A recent article noted this same drastic change in American cultural life. The article asserted, "The fact is that American elites have increasingly been withdrawing from American life. It's not a partisan phenomenon. The elites of all political stripes have increasingly withdrawn to gated communities—'gated' literally or figuratively—where they never interact at an intimate level with people not of their own socioeconomic class."[5]

The Gallup Organization administers a group of questions on employee engagement called the Q12. The questions have been administered to millions of American workers, 1 in 260 of whom were executives at the level of vice president or higher. One of the questions is whether or not the respondent has a best friend at work. Tellingly, this question has proved to be one of the best indicators of healthy employee engagement, and interestingly, top-level executives score relatively low on this question. The title of a newspaper article summarizing this work is "It's Not Just Lonely at the Top; It Can Be 'Disengaging,' Too."[6]

Shakespeare understood this, and wrote about it in *Henry IV, Part 2*. Many will recall (not quite accurately it turns out) the King saying, "Heavy hangs the head that wears the crown," suggesting that power is a burden.

Be this as it may, the burden of power is not what Shakespeare meant; it is not even what he wrote. The actual quote reads, "Uneasy lies the head that wears a crown." The passage is not about the burden of power, but rather, the burden of sleeplessness. Henry IV is resentful that, while his subjects sleep peacefully, he cannot. At the beginning of the scene, the king laments, "How many thousand of my poorest subjects / are at this hour asleep! O sleep, O gentle sleep, / Nature's soft nurse . . ." As will become evident in the last section of the book, sleep is indeed an effective "nurse," and can serve as a conduit to decreased loneliness in surprising ways.

This is not to say that power and leadership cannot be a burden. Of course, they can, as evidenced, for example, by the accelerated graying of presidents' hair (which occurred pretty clearly in the cases of Presidents Bill Clinton and George W. Bush). In a paper published in 2011, psychologist Nathan DeWall and colleagues wrote, "Although power and leadership are by definition interpersonal roles, the people who occupy them are often faced with solitary tasks. Many such tasks are not intrinsically enjoyable, and so successful performance may require that the person override impulses to quit or slack off, so that high effort can be sustained as long as necessary."[7] These researchers demonstrated that the burden of exerting power can be observed in the laboratory; they found that research participants assigned to a high-power role tried harder at experimental tasks (like solving math problems and even playing the game "Operation," tweezers attached to a wire and all) and thereby depleted their energies. Despite this fatigue, those assigned to high-power status excelled on a second experimental task, further sapping their strength. But on a third task—one that the participants were not expecting—those in power broke down, their capacities overtaxed by exertion on the first two tasks.

This is a somewhat ominous set of findings for those who pour themselves into career development at the expense of relationship maintenance. The neglect of relationships engenders isolation and increasing loneliness and atrophies relationship-building skills; the burdens of any power derived through career success can prove depleting. The person in this scenario—more often than not, male—finds himself lonely, without the skills to do much about it, and even with the skills, lacking in the energy it would take to use them. A business consultant wrote, "I hear one comment from organizational leaders on an all-to-frequent basis: 'I wish I had somebody to talk to or work with.'"[8]

In Michael Maccoby's book *The Gamesman: The New Corporate Leaders,* the successful business manager is evidently male in the author's view—the title of the book, which came out in the mid-1970s, is not "The Gamesperson." Within this dated context, the successful manager is described as wanting "to be known as a winner, and his deepest fear is to be labeled a loser . . . to maintain an illusion of limitless options" with little capacity or time for "personal intimacy and social commitments."[9] Regarding intimacy, *The Gamesman*'s successful manager views it as a trap and gravitates instead to the office's "exciting, sexy atmosphere . . . where adoring, mini-skirted secretaries constantly flirt with him. . . . Once his youth, vigor, and even the thrill in winning are lost, he becomes depressed and goal-less, questioning the purpose of his life. No longer energized by the team struggle and unable to dedicate himself to something he believes in beyond himself . . . he finds himself starkly alone."[10]

Written decades ago, as shown by descriptions like "mini-skirted secretaries," the passage describes a man who is nevertheless still very recognizable today. The tragedy conveyed by this description is of an individual who pours himself into what he fervently believes is significant and indeed, the point of life, only to discover, too late, that he was mistaken; that he has neglected all along the only thing that is truly sustaining for a lifetime—meaningful and lasting relationships with family and friends. Once this realization sinks in, its demoralizing effects are compounded by the awareness that it is not only late in the day to fix it, but even if it weren't, he does not know how to fix it. He is in the same position as King Lear, trying in vain through force of will—a heretofore effective strategy—to beat back encroaching loneliness (and, in Lear's case, madness). King Lear cries out, "down thou climbing sorrow, / Thy element's below." As was his wont, Shakespeare has captured a book-length idea in a phrase, "climbing sorrow."

The phenomenon of self-verification, which involves seeking interpersonal feedback that confirms even negative self-concept, was described in chapter 3. One underlying motive for self-verification strivings is stability in social relations; if an individual's self-view is in harmony with others' views of him or her, renegotiations and their disruptions are not needed. Such disruptions are evident when, for example, a previously diffident individual makes an aggressive power grab. A similar process in reverse may occur when a leader begins to act submissively. The previously negotiated relationships between leader and led are thrown into question; it is not necessarily clear to everyone how to act, and efforts must be made to renegotiate a new relationship structure. Here, too, change in self-concept spurs change in social structure.

Depression is a crucible in which to examine these processes. Before delving into this, however, it is worth pausing to ponder a seeming paradox: if, as I am claiming, men are lonelier than women, shouldn't they also be more depressed than women? Loneliness is a risk factor for depression after all (though it is far from a complete explanation for depression). It is essential to recall, however, that the toll of male loneliness is delayed by the processes described in the previous chapters; that is, men are oblivious and instrumental and thus protected from depression. These protections eventually erode, however. If this is so, the sex difference in depression should conform to a particular pattern: there should be a big difference in the first half of life—when men are protected—and this difference should narrow in the second half of life—when those same protections fade. Indeed, this is the pattern.[11]

The processes of the newly submissive former leader and the formerly submissive now confident person are readily apparent in clinical settings in people who are experiencing onset—and remission—of depression. The onset of depression causes drops in self-concept, and, analogous to the situation of the newly submissive leader, relationships adjust accordingly. Perhaps even more interestingly, when people recover from a depressive episode—especially a long one—their positive change in self-concept, analogous to the example of the sudden flight up the hierarchy, can be a jolt to friends and family. Make no mistake, recovery from depression is a very good thing, but change is change. In the clinic I direct, we regularly inform newly recovered patients of this phenomenon, and it is our distinct impression that doing so heads off many misunderstandings and conflicts.

What occurs in the clinic also occurs in colonies of non-human primates. Like us, our primate cousins tend to form clear and fairly stable social hierarchies, and movements within the hierarchy are occasions of stress and disruption for the group. Incredibly, one way researchers have studied the effects of this social fluidity is to induce it, by giving an individual primate an antidepressant medicine that enhances a key aspect of brain functioning (namely, the activity of the neurotransmitter serotonin)—drugs like Prozac, Zoloft, and Lexapro, for instance. Those who get the medicine tend to rise in the hierarchy. By the same token, those who undergo experiences or procedures that undermine serotonin activity tend to fall in the hierarchy. As individuals rise and fall, whether due to Prozac-like compounds or not, waves ripple and occasionally roar through the animals' social fabric.

Focusing on one's status within a hierarchy is probably less advisable than focusing on one's connections within a hierarchy. I met a man recently at an FSU football tailgate party, a successful lawyer who was around seventy years old. Reflecting on his experience and that of his similarly aged friends and colleagues, he said, "It all goes away; you can't count on any of it. The only thing you can count on is friends." *The Gamesman* makes this same point, writing of "the gamesman" that he reaches a plateau and finds career rewards less and less satisfying. "In the achievement-oriented realm of work," writes Christopher Lasch in *The Culture of Narcissism*, too many men's attention focuses "on the struggle for interpersonal advantage, the deadly game of intimidating friends and seducing people."[12] What Lasch claimed in 1979 remains true decades later.

The struggle for interpersonal advantage need not always be a struggle for the ability to exploit others; it can also be a quest for the ability to take care of others. But this too can backfire. In her book *Self-Made Man*, Norah Vincent reports on guys who were at a men's retreat.

Often, a goal of such retreats is emotional expression, and to facilitate this, one of the activities was drawing—the kind of solution to male loneliness that I think is doomed, a point to which I will return. Two men independently chose to draw the figure of Atlas; of one of them, the author remarked, "He was really feeling the burden of being the safety net, the bread-winner and the Mr. Fix-It of his household." The other of them said, "I guess I think that if I hold it all together, if I take care of everything and everyone, that eventually I'll be loved. But the price is my life. I'm trying to do the impossible. So I guess I'm really Sisyphus, too."[13] Men and women alike can feel this way, but men in particular struggle with the "eventually I'll be loved part." Like everyone, men want to be foundational for their families; but more so than women, men struggle with opening themselves up to reciprocated love, care, or help—a phenomenon we saw earlier in anecdotal (Golden Gate bridge suicide stories) and empirical forms (the studies documenting that men in particular have trouble reaching out for care).

Our family's dog died recently, after eighteen years with us. It was not clear exactly how he died, but discovering his body was difficult, and I was deeply grateful that it was I, and not my wife or sons, who found him. I spent the rest of that day taking care of everybody and of everything, including carrying the dog's body to the car and then driving to the vet to arrange cremation. I was in control and looking out for everyone, and proud to do so though saddened at the occasion. A question didn't occur to me until days later: who was looking out for me?

WHEN YOU ARE LONELY at the top, your attention tends to get narrowed to the fact of your social isolation and its attendant negative emotions. You are beyond the "alone but oblivious" stage—people at this stage, more often than not men, have narrowed attention, too, usually focused on money and status. But for the typical man feeling lonely at the top, the questions of money and status have been answered; indeed, the presence of money and status make the absence of connection and satisfaction all the more stark.

Whatever its reason, the narrowing of attention can be productive because it can focus solutions on present problems. But it can be problematic, too, because of all the things missed that are outside of one's awareness. Is it too much to ask that people could be focused and effective problem solvers *and* have broad attention, including to the pleasures in life like sustained friendships?

The broaden-and-build theory answers "no, it is not too much to ask."[14] This theory holds that as individuals discover new ideas and actions, they *build* physical, intellectual, social, and psychological resources. Importantly, positive emotions—like those that emerge within ongoing friendships—*broaden* people's thought-action repertoires, encouraging them to discover novel lines of thinking and behavior. There is thus a reciprocity to the relationship between positive emotions and resources like interpersonal connections. Put differently, the one leads to the other, which in turn, leads to more of the first, and so on, in upward spiraling fashion. This process has been empirically modeled in a study of undergraduates.[15] Self-reported emotions and resources were assessed at two assessment periods five weeks apart. Indeed, consistent with the theory, positive emotions predicted improved broad-minded coping, and broad-minded coping predicted increased positive emotions. Moreover, positive emotions and broad-minded coping serially enhanced one another: the broadened attention and cognition triggered by earlier experiences of positive emotion facilitated coping, which in turn predicted future experiences of positive emotion. Intriguingly, there is preliminary evidence that the effect of positive emotions on broadening attention and coping is linked to increases in the neurotransmitter dopamine.[16]

The implications of this work are intriguing to ponder for the lonely man. They suggest, for example, that in order to solve "lonely at the top" phenomena, small nudges toward positive emotions might set off a chain reaction of positivity, eventually culminating in a relatively large dividend both socially and otherwise. In fact, this "nudge" perspective on behavior change is a focus in this book's later chapters on solutions to the problem of male loneliness. But, before turning to the crucial question of solutions, the next chapter highlights the reasons solutions are so critical: absent feasible and effective solutions, various forms of human misery are likely in store for the lonely man.

6

CONSEQUENCES

PATHS TO SELF-DESTRUCTIVE BEHAVIOR
(GUNS, GOLF, NASCAR, ALCOHOL,
SEX, AND DIVORCE)

When does an ongoing cause of a problem cease to be a cause and become instead a consequence? Being no philosopher, I have no ready answer to the question, but it is one I bump up against regularly in my research on the causes and consequences of various forms of mental disorders. For example, we have seen that loneliness is a cause of many problems, including suicidal behavior. Imagine a scenario in which a lonely person makes a suicide attempt, survives, and then as a consequence of the attempt, becomes even more socially isolated. Here, loneliness is implicated as both cause and consequence.

It can therefore be somewhat arbitrary to designate one set of processes as causal and another as consequential. But it can also be a useful way to keep things straight. To help keep things straight, I have described as mostly causal the four processes covered in the preceding chapters: becoming spoiled, "don't tread on me," money/status fixation, and "lonely at the top." Each of these is gender linked, with males displaying these features, on average, more than females, and each plays its part in the story of unfolding male loneliness over time. The processes have a sequential character in that spoiled and "don't tread on me" attitudes develop relatively early on, and lay the groundwork, first, for fixation on status and money, and still later, for feeling "lonely at the top," which usually occur, respectively, in the thirties and around age fifty. This seems a defensible approach, as each of the four is involved in causing accelerating male loneliness across the lifespan.

But it is difficult to consider these four processes, and indeed to consider the larger question of male loneliness, without alluding to the pernicious consequences of loneliness along the way. As we have already seen in the domain of health, these consequences are numerous and diverse. In people in general, the greater the loneliness, the worse the health. Whether the health domain is mental health, immune functioning, cancer, stroke, heart disease, or death itself, loneliness looms as a powerful risk factor.

One could say the same about some other risk factors, too, like smoking or obesity. But for two reasons, the argument can be made that loneliness is even more powerful in its negative health consequences than clear scourges like smoking and obesity. First, in studies on major health conditions like stroke, cancer, and heart disease, when loneliness is pitted against factors like smoking or obesity in explaining outcomes, loneliness has been found to be the strongest predictor.[1] This affirms loneliness's power. But the second factor has to do with its scope. Loneliness is better than smoking or obesity at explaining certain causes of death like suicide (there is some evidence, incidentally, that smoking is a risk factor for suicide, but it is clear that it is a far weaker one than is loneliness; regarding obesity, some research indicates that, far from being a risk factor for suicide, it can serve as a protective factor, for reasons that have not yet been delineated). Moreover, loneliness is also better than smoking or obesity at explaining gender patterns in morbidity and mortality.

Loneliness is thus a force of nature, as the findings on health outcomes amply demonstrate. But there are even more consequences to be reckoned with.

My overall argument implies that, although men are lonelier than women and do some stupid things that contribute to their loneliness, stupidity is not their fundamental problem. Indeed, as we have already seen, boys and girls and men and women have roughly similar intelligence levels. Even men, often in their twenties and thirties, who are in the grip of "alone but oblivious" forms of loneliness are not completely lacking in awareness. They are oblivious, yes, but relatively so, not totally so. Recall the earlier discussion of the loneliness sensor; the idea was that the feeling of emotional loneliness signals that there is a deeper problem with social loneliness. If the sensor and that which it senses are in harmony, problems can be identified and responded to. However, if there is disharmony, problems can exist, but, because they are not being optimally sensed, responses are suboptimal, too.

Men, more so than women, have suboptimally functioning loneliness sensors. Crucially, the sensor is still functioning, just not to its full capacity. It's as if a car's gas gauge accurately identified whether the tank was more than half full or less than half full, but provided no further information. The gauge is working, but not very well.

The loneliness gauge in men works in a similar fashion, but it doesn't work very well, and this has important consequences. Men are aware, dimly, that there is a problem, and dim awareness leads to dim solutions—what I in this chapter will term "failed compensations." In addition to health problems, failed compensations represent a set of negative outcomes produced, mostly in men, by loneliness. Failed compensations are attempts to address feelings of loneliness, but attempts that are misdirected, and that thus tend to exacerbate rather than solve the underlying problem. Some of these compensations are not misdirected, but half-hearted, too diluted to have much effect. These are interesting to ponder in their own right, but also because, if full-throated, they might constitute viable solutions—the focus of the two subsequent chapters.

GANGSHIP IS ESSENTIAL to men's well-being. Men evolved in gangs and still need to be in a gang. The eminent biologist E. O. Wilson said, "People must belong to a tribe."[2] The trouble with men is that they tend to lose touch with their gang. Though this will sound strange initially, this is why they watch TV, especially sports, and more particularly, golf and NASCAR. Novelist David Foster Wallace, no stranger to loneliness during his life and a suicide decedent, wrote his essay, "E Unibus Pluram: Television and U.S. Fiction," "Lonely people, at home, alone, crave sights and scenes, company. Hence television."[3] I would add that lonely men, at home, alone, crave a reconstituted gang. Hence NASCAR and golf, the attraction to and fascination with which, for men, represents an attempt to vicariously experience gangship (an attempt that, by itself, fails and really is doomed to fail).

Think of it. Men watch sports—football, basketball, baseball, and on and on. But golf and NASCAR? Why? These are not traditional team sports, where, for example, a university or a city or state is being represented, and they are not exactly action packed. The appeal of NASCAR to men, I believe, is that it is made up entirely of *great* gangs, the very thing many men lost and crave. The driver is the most visible part of the gang, but the other members of the gang are everywhere to be seen, too—the sponsors' insignias are plastered all over the car and the driver; the pit crew is at the ready, waiting to leap into action for those crucial few seconds. There are other great gangs around to compete against, and, oh yeah, there are *tools* everywhere, awesome tools in the case of NASCAR (just watch the pit crew in action).

There you have the three elements of a great gang of men—other men who like and respect each other; other gangs against which to define yourself and compete; and tools. Golf embodies this, too. You have the golfer, never alone, but always with his version of the pit crew, his caddy. The other golfers and their crew are there as well, competing away. His sponsors are not as blatantly plastered on him as they are in NASCAR, but they are there, on his hat, shirt, and golf bag . . . which, crucially, contains a great array of high-tech tools (clubs at that).

Of course, actually playing golf, as opposed to watching it on TV, has the potential to bond guys with their friends. Tellingly, I think, rates of golf participation are going down, even as TV audiences for golf are going up.[4]

Other sports like NFL football have competition, camaraderie, sponsors, and tools, but the sports themselves overshadow all this. Golf and NASCAR are understated, they boil things down to a man, his team, and his tools, and vicariously soothe a lonely male soul. They are substitutes for a man's own gang, which he has lost over the years and does not know how to reconstitute. In the next two chapters, ways for men to "get in touch with their inner gang" are the focus. The argument in this chapter is not that there is anything inherently wrong with golf or NASCAR; rather, if used *in place of* actual connections to a gang, rather than *as a supplement to* actual connections to a gang, loneliness-related problems ensue. In this way, golf and NASCAR are like vitamins, good as a supplement, not so good as main fare. A fairly typical—perhaps even stereotypical—tension plays itself out regularly in my own household, and it has to do with the bewilderment my wife feels about my sports watching, which puzzlement I reciprocate fully with regard to her soap-opera habit. Both activities, it must be admitted, have their pointless and mindless character. Should this mindlessness be doubted, I note that my wife cannot remember even the titles, not to mention the plotlines, of soaps she watched just five years ago, whereas I would have trouble naming more than two or three of the players on my favorite football team's only Super Bowl appearance. When it comes to this pointlessness, why the gender difference in soap-opera watching and sport fandom? Though I have heard NASCAR referred to as "male soap opera"—and it is true that part of the pleasure of NASCAR fandom is following the stories of the crews' activities and strategies in the days leading up to races—I do not see "male soap opera" as a very accurate description. I think male versus female attraction to sports versus soap operas has to do with the peopled nature of most women's lives, and the lonely gang-craving character of many men. Soap operas are fully peopled and are about the interiors of interpersonal lives; most sports, certainly including NASCAR and golf, are about something different, namely gangship and competition.

There are sure to be those who would counsel against competitive things as a way to allay men's loneliness. A 2007 article in the *Wash-*

ington Post conveyed the advice of psychologist Michael Addis, saying, "Join a group. . . . Instead of (or in addition to) softball leagues and poker nights, [Dr. Addis] suggests, for example, book clubs or groups focused on the outdoors.[5] They may give you opportunities for important one-on-one discussions about personal matters." This is generally sound advice—in a later section of this book I dwell on the particular power of the outdoors as an ingredient of the solution for male loneliness. But why the equivocation about softball and poker; why not say "play softball instead of (or in addition to) joining a book club?" One might reply, plausibly enough, that most men will play softball anyway, without much encouragement; what they need more of, and might not get without explicit urging, is things like book clubs.

I am concerned, however, about the underselling of things like team sports as a true tonic for many men. Christopher Lasch would be with me on this one. In *The Culture of Narcissism,* he writes of sports and games that they, "like sex, drugs, and drink, obliterate awareness of everyday reality, but they do this not by dimming awareness but by raising it to a new intensity of concentration." "Moreover," the author continues, "they have no side effects, hangovers, or emotional complications."[6] Further still, I would add, not only do sports represent a clear path of least resistance and not only are they mostly engaging and fun, but they have two distinct advantages, beyond those already articulated, over many other approaches.

First, it is not accurate to imply that one-on-one discussions about personal matters do not arise in team sports settings. Consider a conversation I have had more than once over the years with guys I play soccer with. In a usual example, we were sitting on the bench as our teammates played; we got to talking about family and such, and I mentioned that soon, my "baby" sister (fourteen years my junior) would be married, and that I was looking forward to giving her away at her wedding. One of them asked why my dad wouldn't be giving her away, and I answered that he'd passed away. Another asked, "Heart attack?" and I said, "No, he died by suicide."

To some these conversations may seem superficial or too brief to make a difference. That is false. These interactions have been a definite aid in my coming to terms with my dad's death—they are not the only things to have helped, far from it, but they are among the things that have helped. Moreover, especially as my grief has steadily loosened its grip on me over the years, and I have accordingly become more open and relaxed about what happened to my dad, these conversations often elicit in my friends a commiseration not only about my dad but also about painful losses in their own lives. All of this can occur in the few minutes before we go back in to the game. Were we to go for drinks or play poker after the game, more of it still. That is to say, authentic one-on-one interactions can occur even during the game itself, and certainly afterwards. This effect is compounded many times over, I can attest, when my friends and I are watching sports rather than playing them; this is especially so if we are at the game itself, but also true to some degree if we are watching on TV. I am not sure these same men and I would have talked similarly at a book club, putting aside the considerable barrier of ever getting them to attend one (even I, with a more than a-book-a-week habit, would be a bit of a tough sell). Ironically enough, it is not rare for my friends and me to be at an FSU football or baseball game and spend some of our time there talking about books.

Consider a related point as well. From *The Culture of Narcissism:* "Take the common complaint that modern sports are 'spectator-oriented rather than participant-oriented.' Spectators, in this view, are irrelevant to the success of the game. What a naïve theory of human motivation this implies! The attainment of certain skills unavoidably gives rise to an urge to show them off." Later in the same passage, the author emphasizes the pleasure inherent in a spectators' and performers' "shared appreciation of a ritual executed flawlessly, with deep feeling and a sense of style and proportion."[7] Spectatorship requires participation, imagination, and empathy and is therefore far from a passive activity.

Those who doubt the tonic nature of sport fandom would do well to remember the result my colleagues and I produced regarding the Miracle on Ice, the US hockey victory over the Soviets in the 1980 Winter Olympics, as I mentioned in chapter 3. It occurred on February 22, 1980. Not coincidentally, no February 22 before or since has seen a lower tally of deaths by suicide in the United States.[8] In the same work, we showed that deaths by suicide on Super Bowl Sunday were significantly fewer than deaths occurring the Sunday before or after Super Bowl Sunday, and that the suicide rates in the home counties of Ohio State University and the University of Florida correlate significantly with the football team's success; the more success, the fewer the number of suicides. I occasionally ask professors who turn up their noses at sports how their preferred activities stack up to reducing the national suicide rate; I can attest that they draw a collective blank, tongues tied (an altogether too rare occurrence).

I promise two advantages of team sports, one being that they can and do pave the way to meaningful one-on-one interactions. The other is related to the first and has to do with the kind of socializing at which men seem most adept. The sphere of one-on-one personal and intimate relationships, it is true, is not men's strong suit. This is not merely my opinion, and not only what I think those have in mind who advocate the need for men to have more such experiences, but much research corroborates this view as well. This kind of intimate socializing is absolutely essential, beyond any doubt. But it is not the only kind, and to see this, consider three sets of research results. First, an experiment is conducted in which participants, as they are ostensibly on their way down the hallway from one experimental room to another, come across a person who seems to be in pained distress. This person, unbeknownst to the participants, is actually not in distress, but is a confederate of the experimenter and is only acting. What do the participants do?

That depends, in part, on the participants' gender. Perhaps surprisingly, the males are more helpful to the supposedly distressed person, on average, than the females. This effect is not limited to the laboratory. For my research and lecturing on suicidal behavior, I have amassed a collection of video clips in which people clearly intend their own deaths and set in motion their plans to bring about their deaths only to be saved at the last moment. A harrowing example is of a woman in Israel whose actions were caught on security cameras. She approaches train tracks and kneels before an oncoming train, her gaze averted. At the last moment, she looks up, sees tons of steel barreling toward her; at that instant, mortal fear grips her, and she flings herself backward. Several seconds elapse on the video as the train rushes by; it is hard to endure these seconds because the viewer assumes that once the train passes, there will be a gruesome scene. What actually happens, however, is that once the train passes, the woman stands up ånd walks away, apparently unharmed. Subsequent investigation reveals that she is not only unharmed, but does not have so much as a scratch on her.

The video reveals something else. As she approaches the tracks, several people signal to her and call out to her, trying to help her. All of these strangers are men. In other videos in which people intend to jump to their deaths from a bridge but are prevented from doing so by Good Samaritans, all of the latter are men. In January 2011, a woman driving in Georgia hit an ice patch and ended up in her car in a pond at night. Her car was sinking fast, and she was panicking for many reasons, including the fact that she could not swim. Moments before her car went under, a stranger appeared and pulled her to safety. The stranger was not a police officer; simply another driver who saw the woman's car skid into the pond. The stranger was male (and likely Southern, a point to which I will return). Apparently, he was also not interested in fame or money—no one knows who he was; police reports have his name listed only as "Joe."

When it comes to helping a stranger in the public sphere, odds are that the helper will be male (and this is so whether the person in need of help is male or female). As you ponder why this may be, I'll describe two other research findings, which, even though they are on different topics, lead to a similar bottom line. In a study on the New York City subway line, psychologist Stanley Milgram and his team approached strangers and, without any preliminaries or explanation, asked, "Excuse me, may I have your seat?"[9] As we will see later, a surprising number of people complied with this request, but for now, I note that far more men than women complied. In response to a request from a stranger (usually the stranger was young and male), there was more male responsiveness. Taking a different tack, researcher Mark van Vugt and colleagues have conducted studies on factors that influence whether and how men and women participate in "public good" games.[10] In one experiment, undergraduates were each allotted a small sum of money, which they could either keep or pool with others in a simulated investment venture. If at least two-thirds of the group contributed to the pool, then everyone would receive double their allotment, even if they did not pony up. Half of the participants were led to believe that their group was competing against groups from rival universities.

Without competition, men and women contributed to the pool more or less evenly. But rivalry affected men's participation in the "public good" far more than it did women's. Under conditions of competition, 92 percent of male participants anted up, as compared to 53 percent of the women.

Charles Darwin might have predicted this finding. He wrote, "A tribe including many members who, from possessing in a high degree the spirit of patriotism, fidelity, obedience, courage, and sympathy, were always ready to aid one another, and to sacrifice themselves for the common good, would be victorious over most other tribes; and this would be natural selection."[11] Competition has a bad reputation in many circles, sometimes with reason. But we should not fail to appreciate that it can foster virtues, such as loyalty and bravery.

In one set of findings, men help a distressed individual more often than women do and are more cooperative with a request from a stranger; in another, men join together for the public good more than women do. These results make men sound great, but an additional set of findings makes them sound less so. Men fight in public far more than do women—think "bar brawl" and if you have even the briefest acquaintance with bars or just with people you will picture men—not women—fighting. These examples of helping a stranger, pooling one's money together with strangers, and fighting strangers, share the common thread of relating to strangers. There is relating—so it's not that men are asocial—but it's a different kind of relating than the one-on-one intimate type with which many men struggle mightily. This "public square" form of relating is probably not intense enough or close enough to be sufficient in itself to solve male loneliness. But it can serve as a way station, a means to the end of closer friendships.

A man featured on NPR's *Morning Edition* would likely agree. Around twenty-five years ago, he found himself at Thanksgiving with a dilemma involving the recent bitter divorce of his parents: go to his father's house, and thereby alienate his mother; or go to his mother's and alienate his father.[12] There are, of course, solutions to this dilemma: flip a coin, tell the parents that you will alternate Thanksgivings with them, go to some other relative's or friend's Thanksgiving dinner, or stay at home alone. The overall argument of this book might imply that many men would choose the latter option, and that is so—many men would. But, consistent with the "public square" relating that men tend to do with strangers, the man in the NPR piece chose another option: he put an ad in the local paper offering to host Thanksgiving dinner for twelve people. He got a good response, and the dinner has caught on as an annual tradition; in 2009, he cooked for eighty-four people, and expects a similar number at subsequent dinners. Again, "public square" forms of relating are probably too diluted to cure male loneliness by themselves. But my guess is that the man featured in the NPR piece has formed year-round friendships with some of the dozens he serves on Thanksgiving, and in fact there are many people who have attended the dinners across multiple years. "Public square" relating, then, has a role as a means to the end of closer friendships.

It can also be an end in itself, which brings me back around to team sports. Male sociality, as the various "stranger" studies show, is diffuse and varied; there is a grazing aspect to it. Team sports set up an arena for this kind of sociality, one that includes competition—as the study on pooling money showed, competition, far from driving a wedge between men and fostering things like resentment and anger, can bring men together (it brought women together less so).

Consider another male-dominated arena, one that is also relevant to team sports: the use and provision of nicknames. In one of his weekly pieces on *60 Minutes*, Andy Rooney lamented the fact that people call him Andy—he would prefer Andrew.[13] Having had much personal experience with this very issue, my ears pricked up. He went on to mention how frequently nicknaming occurs in men, and how rarely in women. There is an episode on *Seinfeld* in which Jerry's friend Elaine is posing as someone else, who happens to be named Suzie. Someone calls her "Suze" instead, and Elaine's displeasure cannot be overstated. I had always thought the scene was funny because of the intensity of Elaine's reaction, combined with what she was reacting to: a very minor change in a name that wasn't even hers. But maybe it's funny for the additional reason that it violates gender norms in nicknaming.

To further understand this marked gender difference, consider the example of perhaps the most well-known figure of my hometown, Tallahassee, Florida: Coach Bobby Bowden. Coach Bowden retired after the 2009 football season, and will be remembered by FSU fans and in college-football circles more generally for two national championships (1993 and 1999) and for an even more impressive and unrivalled accomplishment: fourteen consecutive appearances in college football's top five.

Coach Bowden will also be remembered for his near-constant use of the name "buddy" to address fans, reporters, really anyone he came across (as long as they were male). The practice seems harmless enough and hardly surprising from a Southern football coach who strives to appear affable and who meets thousands of new people a year. Nicknaming is often meant to convey and—depending on the context and tone—can convey, friendliness and good will. But, again depending on the undercurrent of the conversation, it can also be hollow and superficial and off-putting and distancing to boot. Coach Bowden's nicknaming sometimes did have this character. And, though he clearly has a family around him that loves and cares about him, it was not rare for people in Tallahassee to see or hear about episodes when the coach seemed very isolated, even in the midst of hundreds of people, alone in a crowd.

Why did Coach Bowden reserve his nicknaming mostly for men? For one thing, he might have had some awareness that it would not go over well with women, that he could elicit the same kind of reaction displayed by Elaine in the "Suzie-Suze" incident. For another thing, when challenged or angered by a female reporter, he would occasionally fall into the "joshing-around-so-as-to-distance-or-retaliate" mode, such as when a female reporter asked him about the sensitive subject of whether or not he planned to retire, and the coach replied, in a tone that he apparently intended to be humorous but that was tinged with obvious irritation, "ain't that just like a woman"—a comment so blatantly sexist that one marvels that more fallout did not ensue (that there was not more fallout was not for lack of Tallahassee media coverage). And, on rare occasions, the coach would break out female nicknames like "missy" or "darlin'."

These latter nicknames are diminutive, and it is easy to think of several in this category that seem apt for women, and far harder to think of them for men. Bowden's "buddy" is as close to diminutive as it gets for male nicknames—along with other names of that genre like "pal," "sport," or "champ"—and as we have seen, he often did not really use it to show affection but rather to keep people at arm's length. In fact, the easiest male diminutive to think of is the insertion of "-y" or "-ie" at the ends of certain names, like Jimmy or Jamie for James, Tommy for Thomas, and Andy for Andrew. Tellingly, many men resist these names, especially as they age, as the examples of Andy Rooney and yours truly show.

My name, Thomas, has been made more diminutive by my Mexican wife and her family, who call me Thomasito. The Spanish language has many such forms, and in this context, two things about the language have always intrigued me, and my intuition is that they are not coincidental. The first is the distinction between familiar and formal pronouns; for instance, for the pronoun "you," *tú* is used for familiar people such as family and friends and *usted* is used to show respect. Other languages such as French (*tu* and *vous*) make this distinction, but English—the mother tongue of the men I have in mind in writing this book—does not. In the book's last chapter, I will return to this point, and reflect on whether there is something distinctly American or Anglo-American about the problem of the lonely sex. It is built into the very structure of the Spanish language to be able show familiarity and closeness by the use of the familiar pronoun (though it should be acknowledged that, in theory, the same statement could be said about formality and distance through the use of *usted* being built into the language's structure; my experience of Mexican culture at any rate suggests that this is true in principle but not in practice, as my next point illustrates). Another aspect of the language relevant to closeness is the intensity of feeling behind the imagery of diminutives. In English, nicknames like "honey" and "sugar" have a certain sweetness both literally and figuratively, but they lack the vastness of common Spanish-language expressions like *mi cielo* (my sky) or *mi vida* (my life). My wife and I call each other "my love" (though once in a bout of distraction she called me "my lunch"; distressingly, this occurred at lunchtime), and this amuses our Tallahassee friends in part because of the image's vastness as compared to expressions like "sweety" and "darling" and "dear."

Nicknaming is rampant among men, and it is clearly more of the "buddy" type than of the *mi vida* type. Nicknames among men can denote genuine affection, it should be noted; but quite often, they represent a compensation for the problem of the lonely sex. Many instances of nicknaming among men, like Coach Bowden's "buddy," represent the superficial appearance of familiarity and intimacy, with none of the substance.

Things like nicknaming and watching golf and NASCAR on TV are pale substitutes for genuine interpersonal connection, and are thus ultimately failed compensations. They fail for two principal reasons. First, watching something on television is often too vicarious, too removed from actual interaction with others. In this context, a recent study of forty-five thousand Americans conducted over thirty-five years by University of Chicago researchers found that, of ten or so daily activities, happy people tended to do them more than unhappy people, with one exception: watching television.[14] One of the researchers stated, "We looked at 8 to 10 activities that happy people engage in, and for each one, the people who did the activities more—visiting others, going to church, all those things—were more happy. TV was the one activity that showed a negative relationship. Unhappy people did it more, and happy people did it less."[15]

A second reason that watching NASCAR and golf on television fails as a compensation involves the allure that NASCAR and golf hold. Yes, part of that allure is ganghood, as I've already noted. But another reason men are attracted to these sports is their rugged individualism. The sports are "mano a mano," and indeed this particular phrase is virtually guaranteed to be used at least once per event by NASCAR and golf TV commentators. Men are attracted to these sports in part because they leave individualism intact and glorify it, but they also place individualism within the milieu of gangship.

Men need gangs and are particularly prone to lose them as they age. Some compensate through NASCAR or golf. They drink, too— and this works somewhat because some of the elements are there; for example, there is a tool-like air to the care and knowledge with which some men discuss, peruse, and buy scotch (if you doubt this, take a look at the magazine *Malt Advocate*). And, as with golf, there is a difference between doing an activity alone or watching it on TV and doing the activity with others. Playing golf with friends can solve or at least allay the problem, whereas watching it alone on TV will not; drinking scotch or beer with friends could help, whereas drinking alone may not. Alcohol, of course, has been vilified in many sectors of society and over history—to some degree, with reason. Alcohol can kill and maim, to be sure. Banning it, however, was an obvious disaster. Evidence suggests that Prohibition might have led to *increased* levels of alcohol consumption, in part because stronger liquor was more profitable to smuggle and thus more available and popular. Moreover, of course, a very violent black market for alcohol thrived, with none of the proceeds going into tax coffers.

Except in excess, alcohol probably does more good than harm, as experimental and anecdotal evidence alike shows. From the experimental perspective, consensus is growing around the view that moderate levels of alcohol intake are better for health than are excessive intake *and* no intake. As Daniel Okrent documents in his book *Last Call,* the Founding Fathers were regular and, in some cases, fairly prodigious drinkers. Even as he was crafting "We the people . . ." and the rest of the US Constitution, James Madison drank a pint of whiskey every single day. Thomas Jefferson, even as he came up with "We hold these truths to be self-evident" was similarly fond of alcohol.

I am aware of several examples of people who have banned alcohol from their lives, with very untoward effects. The poet John Berryman and the novelist Jack London each stopped drinking in the weeks and months before their deaths by suicide; sobriety, far from contributing to their well-being, seemed to accelerate their social isolation and thus fuel their deterioration. In his very insightful memoir about depression called *Darkness Visible,* William Styron points to a similar process in his own life: alcohol suddenly and inexplicably began to make Styron physically ill, and so he decided, reasonably enough, to quit drinking. He believes, however, that this decision set in motion processes that culminated in a near-fatal depressive episode. In clinical settings, I have seen several psychotherapy patients whose experiences were similar to that of Styron.

What is at play in these examples? I believe the mechanism involves alcohol's effects on socializing. Alcohol intake facilitates socializing, which, in turn, tamps down loneliness. Remove the alcohol and, for some people, the desire to socialize plummets, and soon thereafter, loneliness and the toll it takes set in.

A parallel exists to men who rely fully on their wives for social opportunities, and indeed for social skills. When such men lose their wives, their loss is compounded by the loss of socializing. Similarly, when (some) men lose alcohol, they also lose the desire to socialize, which, as the cases of Styron, Berryman, London, and others show, can end very badly.

The issue here is not really about *reliance* on alcohol (or wives), but rather, about *over-reliance*. If alcohol is a mere setting condition, grease for the wheels of socializing, problems tend to be minimal, and the benefits of enhanced social connection can be considerable. If all social connections, however, depend on drinking, and if, in the absence of alcohol, all socializing withers away, the dangers are by now, I hope, clear.

Alcohol has some of the same alluring properties as guns: like guns, alcohol has a "take things into your own hands" quality, has a dangerous side, and has a cachet associated with its long history, its various types, its production, and its use (e.g., "shaken or stirred"). Alcohol use, like watching golf and NASCAR on TV, seems to many men like a potential solution because it allays somewhat the vague feelings of loneliness that penetrate through men's mists, but still leaves self-reliance unfazed. There is an empirical association between loneliness and problematic drinking, and this association is the basis for a negative snowball effect in which loneliness can lead to more drinking, which leads to more loneliness, and so on.

IN A POPULAR MAGAZINE'S survey of male attitudes, one thing that was *not* very different between twenty- and fifty-year-old men was their attitudes toward guns (assessed with a very brief and broad question on "gun control" in general). In both groups, less than half felt at all positive about gun control.[16]

Men are, as a rule, enamored of guns, just like thousands of earlier generations have been of weaponry more generally. As with alcohol, this can work somewhat, because some of the elements are there: tools to be sure, but potentially camaraderie and competition, too. But in the worst-case scenario, they shoot guns . . . at themselves, resulting in very high suicide rates for men, mostly older men.

Though not an older man at the time of his death, Nirvana musician Kurt Cobain's life and death illustrate all of these elements of men's relationships to guns. Cobain developed a taste for gun ownership and enjoyed hanging out with friends at shooting ranges. "Developed a taste," is, I think the right phrasing, because as a kid of about thirteen or so, he believed guns were barbaric and wanted nothing to do with them. But through repeated exposure, he lost his distaste, which was replaced by an active appetite. This process is similar to that in which people start out as very averse to things like coffee, nicotine, or extremely spicy food, but not only lose their aversion to the substance but develop cravings for it. For Cobain, as for a lot of people, guns represented an enjoyable pastime—an activity that absorbed him and that also connected him to others who felt similarly. Unfortunately, in a time of deep disconnection and alienation, he turned one of his guns on himself. He died in 1994 at the age of twenty-seven.

Cobain and others view guns in the same way that some see tools or cars. They are alluring for many reasons: they express instrumentality and thus are means through which to express autonomy; in some circles, they are also a way to express status; and, perhaps relatedly, they have an edgy and dangerous side. But along with all this, they also provide opportunities for connection via immersion with fellow enthusiasts in the attendant subculture. These connections can be sustaining, but if they fall away, it is not uncommon for men to turn the tools on themselves, just as they do with guns. Deaths by self-inflicted knife or puncture wounds, from hanging in garages, from carbon monoxide poisoning in cars or garages, and from purposeful motor vehicle accidents (or from gunshot wounds self-inflicted in a moving vehicle—oddly, not vanishingly rare) are all examples of guns, tools, or cars changing from the instruments of immersion and connection to the handmaidens of death.

Men's interest in things like tools may seem stereotypical, but there is truth to it nevertheless. In Clint Eastwood's movie *Gran Torino,* the main character has a garage full of tools, which he plainly enjoys in and of themselves, but he also takes pleasure in passing on his knowledge about the tools (and some of the tools themselves) to a neighborhood boy. This is not just fiction, as I can easily bring to mind many real-life examples of my personal acquaintance who fit this image.

Consider, in this context, an article entitled "10 Offbeat Places to Meet Guys," directed at women and revealing about men.[17] The piece opens with a good and funny point, "Heard about the woman who met an amazing guy browsing placemats at Williams-Sonoma? Me neither." It then transitions to the first offbeat place, "your local hardware store." The article continues, "Your neighborhood hardware joint is a hangout for not just handy condo-owning types, but all guys. . . . Being surrounded by tools brings out any man's masculine side. . . . Ask for his advice on a DIY project ('Do I need special hooks to hang a giant mirror?')." Oh, and offbeat place number two, after the hardware store? The driving range.

ONE ROOT CAUSE OF male loneliness is that men are not fully aware of the looming problem as it begins to overtake them. But they're not completely unaware either, and as they start to sense the inklings of a problem, they resort to solutions that feel right to them, but that ultimately are not. These solutions—things like fascination with guns, and watching golf and NASCAR on TV (which men do in droves)—feel promising because they leave intact prized independence but have aspects that smack of connection as well.

The fiery and fierce independence of NASCAR drivers and many golfers, too, is well known. But they are also embedded within a team of many people—dozens of people for NASCAR drivers, once all support and sponsor staff are accounted for. How appealing for someone who is beginning to sense his loneliness, but values his independence. Men identify with these athletes, and it soothes them. But soothing is not solving. However, soothing can point the way to solving. As expanded upon in the section on solutions, lasting behavioral change is easiest and most successful when it builds on already ingrained habits. The habit of watching NASCAR or golf on TV alone can be shaped into watching NASCAR or golf with friends, traveling to races or tournaments with friends, playing golf with friends, and so on.

As another doomed compensation, men have affairs, a temporary and destructive solution that contributes to their elevated divorce rates. *Esquire* magazine's "Survey of American Men" (October 2010) reported that more fifty-year-old than twenty-year-old men endorsed the following statement about divorce, "It's an option, and I don't think there's anything wrong with it."

Like alcohol, sex can be a powerful diversion, and sex per se (as opposed to intimacy and closeness) allows, to be sure, for a connection . . . of sorts. Without emotional intimacy, however, sex represents a fleeting if intense connection. Its intensity belies its temporary nature; it allows the illusion of connection even as it allows self-focused gratifications like sexual release and sexual conquest. Like alcohol use, the use of sex to solve accelerating loneliness is doomed unless it is accompanied by genuine and sustained interpersonal connection. Absent that, it leads to serial affairs, wrecked marriages, and fractured families.

Much more than women, men tend to struggle in late life after divorce or after being widowed. A recently widowed man said to me, "My male friends don't seem to know what to do or say. Women seem to rally around each other in the wake of such things. I wish I had that."

SECTION III

THE SOLUTIONS

7

SOLUTIONS

THE LOVE OF NATURE AND NUDGING
MEN BACK INTO HEALTH

s there any hope for the rather dire state of affairs constituted by male loneliness? William Faulkner was writer-in-residence at the University of Virginia in the late 1950s (about which position and the many attendant invitations he received to speak, he said, characteristically, that he was writer-in-residence, not speaker-in-residence, and then proceeded, again characteristically, to be gentle with audiences, sometimes touchingly so). At one question-and-answer session, a young woman asked Faulkner, "It's been said that you write about the secret of the human heart. Is there one major truth to the human heart?"

The question plainly affected Faulkner. He paused, and then said, "Well that's a question almost metaphysical." He paused again, and then, with increased seriousness and choosing his words with obvious care, stated, "I would say if there is one truth of the human heart, it would be to believe in itself, believe in its capacity to aspire to be better than it is."[1]

Faulkner's hesitation was certainly not due to his not having thought much about the question. As the young woman pointed out, the overarching focus of his fiction was to try to answer this question. Not only that, he had had this to say in Stockholm a few years earlier upon receiving the Nobel Prize:

It is easy enough to say that man is immortal simply because he will endure: that when the last dingdong of doom has clanged and faded from the
last worthless rock hanging tideless in the last red and dying evening, that
even then there will still be one more sound: that of his puny inexhaustible
voice, still talking. I refuse to accept this. I believe that man will not merely
endure: he will prevail. He is immortal, not because he alone among creatures has an inexhaustible voice, but because he has a soul, a spirit capable
of compassion and sacrifice and endurance. . . . It is [the writer's] privilege
to help man endure by lifting his heart, by reminding him of the courage
and honor and hope and pride and compassion and pity and sacrifice
which have been the glory of his past.[2]

Art like Faulkner's can elevate the human soul and heart, and thus draw out things that are active barriers to loneliness, things like compassion and sacrifice. But art like Faulkner's fiction and paintings in the Louvre is no solution to the problem of male loneliness posed in this book—art is available, in realistic terms, to too few people, and even for those to whom it is available, relatively few are inclined to engage with it. That's a pity, but nevertheless true, so solutions to the problem of the lonely sex have to attempt the cultivation of Faulkner's verities like compassion and sacrifice, but do so in ways that target men generally, not just some elite subset.

Psychologist Alan Kazdin has come to a somewhat similar conclu-
sion about a related issue. Regarding the problem of making quality mental health care widely available, the psychologist characterized a usual form of mental health treatment, individual psychotherapy, as too "elite."[3] He stated, only half-jokingly, "If the goal is to reach a small number, and to exclude those in need, particularly those in minority groups, particularly those in rural areas, especially those who are elderly, especially those who are young—if that is our goal, we are

doing great." What might work, by contrast, are approaches that one might describe as taken to the people by the people. The article states, "Internet programs and smartphone apps can reach people over a wide geographical base. Lay therapists, such as adolescent peers, can bring aid to young adults. Messages in everyday settings like offices, schools, and stores, can serve as new avenues of delivering interventions." The article posed the question, "Why treat people in everyday settings?" and provided the answer, "Because that is where psychopathology is." He might have added, "and that's where people are."

This argument is similar to the one made above about art; the problem is not really art or psychotherapy per se—although both fields have their problems, to put it mildly. Rather, the problem involves access and dissemination. Solutions that depend on men to attend individual or even group psychotherapy, or to take art classes or go on regular tours of museums, are, for most men, born into a sea of barriers they will never surmount.

Another approach to this question of whether there is any hope in taking the edge off male loneliness is to pose the question: Are male brains simply wired differently, with loneliness and the tendencies that cause it imbedded in the hardware? Again, yes, there is hope, and no, these tendencies are not hardwired. On the latter point, a series of studies by researcher Greg Hajcak and colleagues is informative.[4] These researchers are interested in immediate electrical signals given off by the brain when people are presented with various stimuli, especially visual stimuli that have emotional content. These signals are recorded fast enough that little deliberate conscious thought is captured; what is measured is more akin to immediate orienting responses. When the images contain people as opposed to inanimate objects, the electrical signal is loud and clear; the brain is interested. The brain remains more interested in images of people even when the comparison images of inanimate objects are particularly interesting, complex, or colorful. Within the category of images of people, the research team divided the pictures up into three groups based on content: erotic images; affiliative images (called by other researchers nurturing images); and exciting images. An erotic image from this series might show a woman and a man under a sheet clearly in the act of having sex; an affiliative image might show a mother caring for her baby; and, an exciting image might show a close-up of a sea-sprayed person surfing within the tube of a wave. Which kind of image does the brain orient to most strongly?

Two intriguing results emerge from this kind of research. First, the brain response is similarly high to the erotic and affiliative images, and not as high to the exciting images. This makes a certain amount of sense if one views the brain as an essential part of our survival equipment (in the evolutionary sense of survival in the service of passing on one's genes); in this context, our nervous systems should preferentially orient to scenes involving reproduction and nurturing, as those are evolutionarily more important stimuli than are exciting things like skydiving and surfing. Second, these studies reveal no gender differences. To be more precise, they produce no gender differences regarding the immediate orienting responses of the brain, but they do produce differences in participants' post hoc reactions when asked to rate the intrinsic interest of the photos to them.

Imagine, if you will, a typical nineteen-year-old male college student participating in an experiment such as the one alluded to above. He will need to be informed of the study, sign an informed consent form, and be prepped for the experience, including being fitted with an electrode cap. The electrode cap is in place, and an image of a mother gazing into her baby's eyes is shown; both mother and child are smiling. Within milliseconds, the apparatus records the young man's brain's orienting response to the image—a healthy one, as is usually the case for such affiliative images. Then, a few seconds later, the research assistant asks the young man to rate the picture's intrinsic interest to him, on a scale from 1 to 10, with the latter indicating very high interest. He responds "six" after a quick thought process that goes something like this: "I have to rate it above five else I'll seem like I'm against babies and mothers, and anyway it is a nice image, but I'm not rating it too high, else I'll seem, I don't know, like I'm too interested in things like this and not enough interested in masculine things." That is to say, "six."

An erotic image presents no such dilemmas. The brain orients with force within milliseconds, and the usual male undergraduate quickly rates the image a "ten."

Next up is an image of a young person in very attractive skiwear, including a full helmet with a mirror visor. The person is snowboarding, leaning hard into a turn, spraying snow prodigiously against the backdrop of evergreen trees. The apparatus does its work and records a response to the image that shows a healthy orienting response, but a response that is not as pronounced as that recorded in response to the image of the mother and baby and to the erotic image. This is as it should be, because this is how the hardware of human brains is engineered. Then, the young man is asked for his 1 to 10 rating; here, he does not even have to think much, and yet, in contrast to his response to the mother and baby, he states his thought process aloud: "Snowboarding's awesome; I love to snowboard; the picture's cool. I give it a nine."

What has occurred here is both vexing and promising. At some level at least, the man's brain understands the essential power of affiliation; this can be seen in his immediate orienting response to the image of the mother and baby versus the image of the snowboarder, and in this, his brain's reaction is similar to that of his female peers. Promise and potential inhere in this result because it suggests that the basic hardware for decreased loneliness is there in the male brain.

The vexing aspect, of course, is that males learn to override this hardwiring, and they do so precisely via the processes described in the preceding chapters. But if they can learn to act in loneliness-inducing ways—and I think that they do so is not in dispute—then perhaps they can unlearn these ways, or learn new things that may offset the attitudes and behaviors that produce the lonely sex. This unlearning and new learning are the focus of this section of the book.

NATURE'S POWER

Some of this has the potential to sound like the idyllic frolicking in woods and meadows that are precisely the unrealistic kind of thing I would like to avoid recommending. And it is clearly possible for solutions to be so watered down or implausible that they have no hope of working. In her book *Bright-Sided*, Barbara Ehrenreich points to one such example. The setting is sales training at an insurance company, and each day of training began with the requirement that everyone shout, "I FEEL HEALTHY, I FEEL HAPPY, I FEEL TERRIFIC," while throwing punches in the air. A punch of this sort was called by the training leaders "a winning punch."[5] The same kind of thing occurs at sales rallies for the company Amway, with one side of the crowd shouting "Ain't it great" and the other side shouting in reply "Ain't it though." Most would view these as vapid approaches to solving much of anything, superficial and ineffective on their face.

But why are they so? They are not lacking in positivity; they have emphatic features; the insurance training slogan even refers to health. The problem, however, is that they contain no authentic reference to the outside world, either to other people or to nature. It would be a challenge to create a slogan that is higher in self-regard than the insurance sales-training example, or a glibber chant than the Amway example.

It is simple to chant inanities, just as it is simple to satisfy one's innate affinity for the natural world. But there's a difference; one should not doubt the power of connecting to nature. There are other potential solutions for men's accelerating loneliness besides connecting to nature, some no doubt more likely to work than others. But a focus on the outdoors strikes me as particularly promising, especially if it involves other people, but perhaps even if it doesn't, because it can spark interest in reaching out, in getting out of one's skin and engaged in the larger surround.

Eminent evolutionary biologist E. O. Wilson called biophilia "the innately emotional affiliation of human beings to other living organisms,"[6] and I would extend the definition to include other natural phenomena, too (even some man-made phenomena can serve). Eric Weiner's book *The Geography of Bliss* underscored the power of a love for nature by noting that each year more people visit zoos than attend all sporting events combined. This author also mentioned a famous study of hospital patients, some of whose rooms overlooked trees, and some of whose rooms overlooked the brick face of an opposite building. The former patients had shorter hospital stays and fewer physical and other complaints, harking back to the study in which caring for a houseplant was associated with decreased mortality in nursing home residents.

In her book *Packing for Mars,* Mary Roach writes, "People can't anticipate how much they'll miss the natural world until they are deprived of it." She continues, "I have read about submarine crewmen who haunt the sonar room, listening to whale songs and colonies of snapping shrimp."[7] In fact, one of the things that the captains of submarines use to motivate and reward their crews is "periscope liberty"—a chance to lay eyes through the periscope on the coastline, stars, clouds, and birds. Deprived of contact with much of the biosphere, a craving for basic connection to simple parts of the natural world develops.

The same thing happens with astronauts. According to *Packing for Mars,* "Astronauts who had no prior interest in gardening spend hours tending experimental greenhouses." The book quotes a cosmonaut who was speaking of tiny flax plants he and his colleagues were growing on Salyut 1, the first Soviet space station: "They are our love."[8] This craving and love that develop in submarine and space environments alike is an indicator of the power of connecting to nature, and the fact that the craving emerges most acutely in rare contexts like space travel or submarine duty points to a dilemma.

The dilemma is that virtually everyone—even lonely men; even, for that matter, people in most prisons—have enough contact with the biosphere that they do not develop intense cravings for it and thus underestimate the salutary effects of increased contact with it. I have taken active steps to isolate myself lately, mostly in an effort to finish this book on time, and nevertheless, I regularly fail to fall off the biosphere's grid—or rather, it rarely fails to come and get me. Even when I am relatively successful in my efforts at solitude, the sun shines into my office through cracks in blinds. When I am less successful, I am summoned by a child, a dog, a cat, or a wife, to do, discuss, or clean something, and I am struck by how the immediate stab of irritation can (note I do not say "will") melt away in the glow of their expressions, their anticipation, their humor (which I would claim even for the dog and the cats)—that is to say, their "biosphericity."

The world's most isolated person is immersed in the biosphere. Somewhat like an astronaut, he is confined to his own small space, locked into it, utterly by himself. And he has survived thus for approximately fifteen years. He is not in outer space, but rather in the wilderness of Brazil, the last surviving member of a tribe that has never made sustained contact with the rest of us. He fends off intrusion, occasionally with force—he has shot at least one outsider with a bow and arrow, recalling our earlier discussion of men's reactive violence. How does he survive? How does he tolerate his solitude?

Evidence suggests that he keeps up an active interpersonal life, even though he is quite alone. He does this via regular interaction with the spiritual world, probably deceased ancestors, for whom he leaves regular ritual markings on trees. And he is deeply embedded in the biosphere, hunting game, tending to a few crops like corn, and gathering honey from wild bees.

Some of my childhood friends have long understood the power of immersion in nature, and I have doubted them until recently. When I visit them in the Smoky Mountains, they think, quite naturally, that they should take me hiking. Which they should, and which is wonderful, but which I doubted the first few times I visited them. They seemed to me charmingly woodsy, but a little out of touch. Of course, it was I who was out of touch, and not particularly charmingly so. I believe I am representative of many men in this regard, in the fact that the natural world is around me enough that I do not crave it intensely, and thus misunderstand an opportunity for even more connection to it and thus for enhanced well-being. Most men get by with a version of the submarine crewman's "periscope liberty"; they get by on an occasional glimpse of nature, when more immersion—and not all that much more—is usually readily accessible and would noticeably increase health and happiness.

I anticipate that some will reject connecting to nature not only as weak medicine, but also as hopelessly naïve. How can interacting with nature make a difference at all, and especially a difference regarding potentially dangerous and even lethal states of mind, like severe loneliness and the mental disorders often associated with it? It made a difference to a memoirist who nearly killed himself in the throes of a severe form of depression. In his memoir on the experience, Eric Wilson wrote that he began to "engage in the larger world . . . out of my solipsism and into the air. This began in small ways. In imagining, for instance, how my daughter might see leaves or pinecones or mockingbirds, I started to take a new pleasure in nature." In the same passage, the author remarks, "Nature was easy. Reaching out to people was harder."[9] This is an important insight: connecting to nature can have loneliness-reducing effects in and of itself, but its main value is as a means to the end of connecting, or reconnecting, to people.

In *Packing for Mars,* Roach relates an anecdote she learned from a man who had spent a winter at a research station at the South Pole. The man said that he and others who had been at the South Pole with him spent a couple of days, upon return, simply gazing at things like flowers and trees. When one of the group spotted a woman with a stroller, he shouted to the others in excitement, "A baby!" The group rushed toward the baby, causing the mother to turn the stroller and flee. This occurred in broad daylight in a safe and peopled area.

This anecdote is instructive for at least three reasons. First, it is an obvious illustration of the natural world's sway over us and how we can come to take it for granted; like water, it seems a little mundane until its absence reminds of its essential power. Second, the South Pole researchers were very interested in things like flowers and trees, but these things did not make the men literally shout with excitement. A baby did. All aspects of the natural world have the potential to satisfy our love of nature, but some experiences are more satisfying than others, and at the top of this particular hierarchy is interacting with other people. Third, consider what might have happened in this same anecdote if the group of South Pole researchers were all women. Would the baby's mother have been alarmed? I doubt it, because it would not have been the first such experience for her, whereas it probably was the first time a group of men acted like that.

"Acting like that" seems odd for men, at least when pondered superficially. But considered more deeply, it seems odd to me that lack of interest in response to the glory that is a baby is expected enough among half of our species that, when men seem uninterested in babies, it barely registers on awareness. The males among many of our primate cousins do not share this apathetic tendency—at least not to the same degree as humans. There are, of course, examples in nature in which males turn viciously on the newborn—this happens, for instance, when an adult male attacks the offspring of his male rival, so that he can have reproductive access to the offspring's mother. Even here, the male's attitude, though it might be called malign, cannot be called disinterested.

In day-to-day life, enough of the biosphere is present that intense cravings for it are unlikely to develop. This is too bad, in an important sense, because of the difference between the concepts "barely good enough" and "optimal." Men walk around their daily lives much as coalminers do in a mine; if the canary is still alive, "good enough." There are two profound problems with this tendency, however. First, the canary is a dull sensor; that is, the canary will die and thus signal the coalminers of a problem only in the most toxic of environments. In a similar fashion, men walking around their environments with "good enough" attitudes toward the biosphere will avoid intense cravings for it, but will also neglect the benefits of more intense engagement with it. This discussion harks back to that in chapter 1 of men's dulled loneliness sensor. Second, and relatedly, unless men are in a submarine or in space, the canary never dies, and the message they therefore absorb is "good enough." No need to go see my grandchildren or nieces or nephews, no need to go for a walk and notice the particular quality of that season's light against the trees, no need to notice what plants are growing around the area . . . "good enough."

But it's good enough only in the sense that it will avoid the deep cravings of astronauts and submarine crews. This is a quite strange criterion to use for daily life, but this is what men do. One approach, then, to male loneliness is simply to revert to a more natural state of regular interaction with nature, even if in only small doses. Staring out the window for ten seconds, for instance. Or walking outside and physically touching something in the natural world like a stick or a leaf (taking care, of course, not to touch the leaves of things like poison ivy). To be clear, this is far from a comprehensive cure for intense loneliness. A main point of this book, however, is that there really are no comprehensive cures for loneliness; the approach is not to engineer from the outside a new sociability that was not there to begin with. Rather, the idea is to spark natural internal tendencies that inhere in virtually all human cells and souls, but that have atrophied in men. Interaction with the biosphere is one such spark. Put enough sparks together, and you get a fire, assuming there's combustible material around. Here, the flammable material that is around is human nature, which is innately gregarious.

Not all sparks are created equal. Literal sparks are easy to come by in nature. Bang any two rocks together and usually, sparks will fly. But some sparks are too fleeting and cool to actually set anything on fire. By contrast, the sparks that result from banging flint against rocks containing iron or sulfur are excellent fire starters—they are hot sparks. What are the "hot sparks" that kindle the fire of social connection? What are the flint, iron, and sulfur in the production of social flame? Human gregariousness is combustible enough that even reaching out to a leaf or a star can stoke it.

The night after writing the preceding paragraphs, I awoke in the middle of the night, for reasons that I do not know. For a second or so, I was disoriented, my frequent travels having deranged my default assumption of "you're at home." A few milliseconds after I realized I was at home, I glanced at the red numbers of the clock, which said 3:49 AM; next, I noticed that I was alone, but then immediately remembered that my wife was on a trip. To this point, I believe that I had been awake for a total of approximately three, maybe four seconds. In past experience, this is the time window in which insomnia can kick in. More precisely, it is at this point that I feel a pang of irritation in my gut, then have the thought "oh no, I'm awake now and it'll be hard to get back to sleep," followed perhaps by ruminations about my next day's work or whether my wife is okay on her trip.

But this night was different. Literally as my stomach muscles began to tighten with irritation, an awareness dawned on me of how very dark and silent it was. As is not always the case, all of our house lights were off, as were those of our neighbors. The moon was not out. I relaxed a bit, and then noticed I had been mistaken about the silence. A very gentle drone of insects was whirring, so softly that it struck me as another version of silence. I sank back into the darkness and the quiet, and was asleep again within a minute.

This is obviously anecdotal and perhaps merely coincidental. But I wake up in the middle of the night at least a few times a month and find it to be frustrating and irritating. It is not at all like me to be sentimental about or to even notice things like the gentle quality of insects whirring. Yet on the very day I was writing about the effects of a love for nature, the notice of soothing things like the quiet occurred to me, and did so within a few seconds. Moreover, it made me feel better. One thing that is not merely anecdotal or coincidental is that simple things can work very well for sleep problems, and for other problems, too, a point to which I will return.

Things can, of course, be simplified to the point of inanity. Although it is surprisingly difficult to track down an original source for this quote, the statement "Things should be as simple as possible, but no simpler" is often attributed to Einstein. That is an apt description of my goal for this part of the book: simple but not simplistic.

The new British government's Big Society agenda includes a program called "Active at 60"; the program may be an example not of simplicity but of being simplistic. It may well fail if it doesn't get more specific. The minister for pensions described the program, saying, "We hope Active at 60 will make a real difference to the quality of life of those approaching retirement or who have just retired, by helping them get out and about in their communities, improving their wellbeing and preventing the risk of social isolation as they grow older." He continued, "Each local community organisation within the selected areas will recruit at least one Active at 60 Community Agent who will volunteer their time to help motivate, encourage and organise people within their own communities to become more active, physically, socially and mentally."[10] Encouraging people, urging them to get out and about, and improving their well-being are all laudable goals, but they are not achievable without specific and feasible steps toward those goals.

SIMPLE WAYS OF REACHING OUT

Small doses of social connection are strong medicine. You take your statin medicine every day, you take a third of an aspirin every day—well, take your social medicine every day, too, and *call somebody*.

A man I knew, a revered psychological scientist and professor, lived into his eighties, and at a series of lectures celebrating his career, colleagues and former students from all over the country jammed the lecture hall, so that there was standing room only. Why? Partly this was due to the excellence and influence of his work, but another factor was at play. He avoided email and insisted on talking to people on the phone instead. He rarely made social phone calls; they were almost always about work. In this, his approach was probably mistaken. However, at the end of each and every one of these professional phone calls, he religiously extended the call to chat about family, hobbies, and the like.

In her book *I Remember Nothing,* Nora Ephron wrote of her father as he aged and started to forget things that "one thing he never forgot was a phone number, and in his later years he made at least a hundred phone calls a day." If he could do one hundred, everyone can manage one.

The research of positive psychology researchers like Sonja Lyubomirsky has shown the potential power of simple things like reaching out over the phone. In one of their studies, these researchers had participants call a research hotline once a week to report on people or events that made them feel grateful.[11] The effect of these calls? Detectably lower blood pressure, less hostility, and more success at things like weight loss and quitting smoking. If a weekly call to a stranger manning a research line has these effects, I think it's safe to assume that a daily call to friends would, too. A recent article stated, "Adults who frequently feel grateful have more energy, more optimism, more social connections and more happiness than those who do not, according to studies conducted over the past decade. They're also less likely to be depressed, envious, greedy or alcoholics. They earn more money, sleep more soundly, exercise more regularly and have greater resistance to viral infections."[12] The effects even extend to kids; those who are more grateful get better grades, feel more satisfaction with their friendships, and report fewer stomachaches and headaches. Taken together, this is quite a list, and corroborative of the claim that regular reaching out to others really can have beneficial and profound effects. Cicero appears to have had a point when he said, "A thankful heart is not only the greatest virtue, but the parent of all other virtues."

Every Thanksgiving, the following quote attributed to H. U. Westermayer circulates on the Internet: "The Pilgrims made seven times more graves than huts. No Americans have been more impoverished than these who, nevertheless, set aside a day of thanksgiving." There are people, needless to say, who have been dealt very difficult blows, and for whom gratitude might therefore seem a lot to ask. Anecdotally, however, these same people have little trouble with gratitude; in fact, it often comes quite naturally from them, more so than from some of their coddled and spoiled counterparts.

A problem with the daily phone call solution is, in a phrase, call who? Almost always, it's a weak excuse to say, "I don't have anybody to call." Malcolm Gladwell, in his book *The Tipping Point,* reports on a test that roughly estimates how many friends and acquaintances one has. He lists around well over two hundred somewhat unusual last names (no Johnsons, Joneses, or Smiths), and the task is simply to go through the list and give yourself a point for each name that corresponds with someone you know. Gladwell has given the test to many groups of people. In adult samples, the *lowest* score he reports is nine names recalled from the list of over two hundred (and the average is over thirty). Of hundreds and hundreds of people, the worst-off person can call a person a day for over a week and not run out. When aunts, uncles, cousins, nephews, nieces, brothers, sisters, wife (yes, you can call her, too), and in-laws are added in—and we haven't even mentioned people from grade school, high school, college, previous jobs, or business/graduate/law/medical school—"I don't have anyone to call" is weak indeed.

A related excuse is that there may be some awkward moments on the phone—"why are you calling me?" kinds of moments. Quite true, but I have a few counterarguments. First, which is preferable: occasional awkwardness in the context of ongoing connection, or sustained loneliness? Second, just as hands become calloused in response to ongoing labor, so do souls become inured to the occasional bout of social awkwardness. And third, people can tolerate an enormous amount of social discomfort with very few lasting consequences.

I know this last fact from clinical work with patients with social anxiety disorder (also known as social phobia)—an impairing and painful condition characterized by intense fear of social situations such as going to a party, carrying on a conversation, public speaking, and the like. An essential feature of social anxiety disorder is extreme anxiety about being judged by others or behaving in a way that might cause embarrassment or ridicule. The person who suffers from social phobia believes that everybody is watching him or her. In social situations, anxiety escalates, even to the point of panic attacks, including symptoms like heart palpitations, shortness of breath, and profuse sweating. Because of these difficult experiences, people with social phobia usually go to some lengths to avoid feared social situations. Because social situations are such a key part of life, fear and avoidance of these situations causes an array of difficulties, including loneliness and reduced opportunities for love and work.

Despite what pharmaceutical companies may imply in TV advertisements, or what anyone else may claim for that matter, the clear treatment of choice for this condition, by far, is a behavioral one that involves gradually increasing exposure to the very thing patients fear—in this case, the fear is of social scrutiny and negative evaluation. Put differently, patients are put on a planned program of social awkwardness, with the goal of getting them used to it and thus unconcerned with it.

Consistent with the overarching theme of this book, social anxiety disorder is not at all rare in men, and there is evidence that, in treatment-seeking samples, socially anxious men outnumber socially anxious women. There is one form of social anxiety disorder that is undoubtedly more common in men—and this form of the condition illustrates the "planned social awkwardness" aspect of treatment—and that is difficulty urinating in public bathrooms. (The condition occurs in women, too, but is rare).

A couple of questions usually rush into people's minds: Is this really a big enough deal to count as a mental disorder? If so, why is this viewed as a form of social phobia?

With regard to the first question, yes, it is a big deal; use of public bathrooms is necessary for many social and travel activities. Men with a severe form of this fear may plan their activities based on bathroom access and may refuse to participate in activities where access is questionable. Going to a restaurant, a movie, a sporting event—these are all very vexed activities for the sufferer. This is not even to mention the difficulties this form of the disorder can cause with regard to occupational functioning. Imagine working at a place in which you feared the bathroom to such an extent that you would rather suffer the considerable discomfort of not using it rather than face it.

With regard to the second question about why this is considered a form of social anxiety disorder, the difficulty is caused by performance-based social fear (i.e., "what will everyone think if I'm standing here at the urinal but can't urinate?"—the syndrome is also called paruresis but, emphasizing the fear element of the condition, is also known as "shy bladder syndrome" or more colloquially as "stage fright").

A highly effective treatment involves bouts of planned awkwardness in a public bathroom. This is planned carefully beforehand by therapist and patients, including the therapist carefully explaining what will occur, obtaining the patient's understanding of the plan's rationale and an agreement to the plan, preferably in writing (in the clinic I direct, we obtain an additional informed consent form—beyond the usual general one—for procedures like this one, in part because of the seemingly unusual setting of the treatment, but also because the therapist cannot fully guarantee confidentiality in public settings).

Here's the plan: the therapist enters the bathroom, followed a few seconds later by the patient. For this first session, the patient's role is that of observer, and so he waits around by the sink, checking himself in the mirror, washing his hands, etc. Even at this initial stage, clinical progress has occurred: the patient has entered a public bathroom for probably the first time in months or even years, and is staying there despite the fact that the setting makes him very nervous.

The therapist's role is to approach the urinal and stand there, apparently trying to urinate. This behavior is something that the patient finds difficult even to observe, because, he believes, the therapist is subjecting himself to severe humiliation. Important to the treatment, the therapist does not seem to be humiliated or even much affected; on the contrary, he is acting like the situation is not particularly unusual. Observing this is literally amazing to the patient, and is also therapeutic to him.

The patient's sense of amazement is about to increase because the therapist waits for a stranger to approach the adjoining urinal, turns to the stranger, and exclaims, "I don't know what is going on, I just can't urinate!" This can be a mildly awkward experience for the therapist—part of the point of the treatment is to show that mildly awkward exchanges are no big deal—but the world stops for the patient because he expects the next few moments to involve humiliation of a catastrophic scale. Yet, what actually happens is that the stranger mutters something like "ok," or "sorry," or—and this is the worst case, at least in my clinical experience—"why are you telling me that?" The contrast between what the patient is sure will happen—disastrous embarrassment—and what actually happens—lack of interest, perhaps a mild awkwardness—could not be sharper.

This scenario is repeated a time or two in the next weeks, and then the roles reverse so that the patient is the exclaimer. In every case of this sort that I have treated, supervised, or heard about, the problem has been resolved within six sessions of this behavioral treatment. And, I can attest, it is a very rewarding experience to be the therapist in these kinds of cases—not only is the treatment inherently interesting and even a little adventurous, but, more importantly, it substantially relieves patients' suffering, not over the course of years but of weeks.

Different forms of social anxiety disorder call for different kinds of prescribed social awkwardness. For people who are very concerned that others are scrutinizing them while they eat, so much so that eating out at a restaurant seems impossible and even eating at home with others is a severe test, the plan would include purposeful social errors around meal time—for example, dropping one's fork or having ketchup on one's face. For those who fear public speaking, the plan would not only include giving speeches to others, but making a mistake in doing so. When patients with social anxiety disorder engage in these kinds of tasks, they are, needless to say, anxious . . . at first. But then the anxiety fades, even within a given experience and certainly across repeated experiences. This is fairly remarkable, because it means that engaging in things patients believe will be catastrophic has the opposite effect of reining in social anxiety.

This example illustrates a simple intervention—getting someone back on the path to health and thriving. Moreover, if patients with social anxiety disorder can go through these tribulations, and they can—it happens every day in clinics around the world, including mine—then it strikes me as implausible that the "phone a friend per day" exercise, described above, is not doable because of the occasional experience of awkwardness on the phone. If these patients can face fears that they initially view as disastrous in consequence, it is possible to endure the occasional "why are you calling me?" In her book *Voluntary Madness,* Norah Vincent nailed the relevant issue when she wrote, "I often don't feel like socializing, and I often find myself on the verge of cancelling engagements with friends. Sometimes I do cancel them. But almost invariably I regret it." The author continues, "I resent the effort it takes to maintain relationships . . . and yet I know that isolation is very bad for me. I know that my happiness depends, in large part, on human contact and intimacy. And so, as with everything else, I do it and reap the reward, or I don't do it and suffer the consequences."[13] This is spot-on, and I have seen some version of this same sentiment in virtually every psychotherapy patient I have ever seen. In fact, the realization that this is so is not a bad landmark for progress in psychotherapy; the failure to appreciate this or, perhaps even worse, to appreciate but not act on it, by contrast, is not a promising prognostic indicator in psychotherapy.

Still, the phone exercise won't work for everyone, mostly for the same reason that physical exercise doesn't work for everyone—lack of motivation. It is remarkable, nevertheless, what you can accomplish when you set your mind to it. One of my favorite examples in this regard is the writer Flannery O'Connor, who wrote every day for two hours, even after she was diagnosed with lupus, even after she understood she would die from it, and even after receiving the sacrament of the dying.

Not everyone can muster this motivation; let's say, then, that "phone a friend" will work for only about a fifth of US men—that's well over 30 million men so it's nothing to scoff at. But that leaves around 125 million men unattended to, and perhaps more importantly, many millions of desperate wives and others wondering what else to try. There is at least one other option that has a good chance of working.

It is to reconnect the man with his best friends from his youth. Some time between age twelve and age twenty-five, people come into their own; their identity consolidates, and they become pretty much the person they'll be for the rest of their lives. When this happens, the friends they have at the time are the ones most people look back to as their best friends from youth. These are frequently high-school or college friends, but they can be junior-high friends, friends from post-school jobs, or friends from post-college school. If the man himself can't tell you when this happened for him, you can figure it out with questions about times when he had the most fun back then. Stories that make him laugh or that light up his face—those are the ones.

He needs to have a reunion with them. It needs to be as juvenile a time as the guys can muster, and ideally it needs to occur regularly, approximately annually (just like an annual physical or a visit to the dentist every six months). The goal of the reunion is to resurrect the man's social connections when they were at their peak. To put it more succinctly and accurately, *the goal is for him to be part of a gang again.*

Apparently, former Dodgers and Yankees manager Joe Torre agrees with this philosophy. One of Torre's annual traditions was described in a newspaper account as follows: "Torre's getaway started in the mid-'90s with a few friends. It was a way for a few men to be boys again. No wives, no girlfriends and no children. The concept of male bonding appealed to him. This year the getaway features 18 men, some with ties that stretch over half a century."[14] The fact that Torre has known some of his gang for more than fifty years is not inconsequential, nor is the fact that, when Torre was still managing, he prioritized this annual tradition over baseball's winter meetings, which he skipped. "It is a trip that will keep going as long as he does."

And they have raucous fun, experiences that the men plainly view as more than just fun. The article states that "Torre said the trip's dinners were sacred, boisterous affairs that could last three hours." The other members of Torre's gang obviously prize it, too. From the article: "Frank Torre, Joe's brother, will soon be 77, but he gushes about the gathering like a 6-year-old raving about Santa Claus."

Some people, unsurprisingly including a disproportionate number of men, may be inclined to dismiss the value of friendship. They may, for instance, question whether friends are worth it beyond family relationships. Family is important, but so are the friendships, maybe even more so. A professor of sociology was quoted in an article on research on family relationships versus friendships: "There is just scads of stuff on families and marriage, but very little on friendship. It baffles me. Friendship has a bigger impact on our psychological well-being than family relationships."[15]

Or, sure, critics might say, there are intangible benefits to friendships, and maybe even some tangible ones such as a ride home from work in a pinch or help moving. But really, after all, what is a friend worth economically? In 2009, the Institute for Social and Economic Research answered that question: each additional high school friend is associated with an income gain that is equivalent to a half year of extra education.[16] Put differently, eight additional friends in one's youth are as valuable as an entire college education, and a college education, in turn, easily translates into an extra million dollars of income over the course of a lifetime. For bottom-line types then, each friend is worth about $150,000 of extra income—that is, a $5,000 bonus per friend per year for a thirty-year career.

THE OTHER DAY AS I was getting lunch to go at a self-serve cafeteria on the FSU campus, I was in my own world and didn't realize that one of the guys behind the counter was talking to me. Several words into what he was saying, I snapped out of it, and we had a brief, superficial chat about FSU football. As I walked back to my office, I noticed that my mood was noticeably brighter than it had been before I went to the cafeteria. Was I looking forward to lunch, which I was carrying with me? Maybe, though I'm not the sort of person who gets any sort of jolt from food or its prospect. As I reflected further, I attributed my mood boost to the brief talk about FSU football. Yes, it was brief and superficial, but it had an effect on me, which should come as no surprise, as our biology is geared toward making socializing reinforcing.

It may not be coincidental that this occurred as hot lunch was on my mind. Hot food and drink can take the edge off of loneliness. In social exclusion experiments—the ones we have encountered before that randomly assign some participants to receive feedback that they are likely to have a lonely future—the excluded participants are more likely than others to choose a hot rather than cold post-experiment beverage, and the hot beverage undoes some of the effects of the exclusion. In an essay titled "Improvable Feasts," Alain de Botton wrote, "The moments spent during the ingestion of food are especially propitious to moral education. It is as if the prospect of a bowl of zucchini fritters or a plate of gravlax and buttered toast can seduce us into showing some of the same generosity to others that the table has shown to us."[17]

As a general rule, in hunter-gatherer societies, mealtimes are occasions when any display of competition is actively discouraged; a sense of consideration and interpersonal delicacy is the norm. This description of the Nyae Nyae !Kung is representative: "We observed no unmannerly behavior . . . and no encroachment about food. . . . The polite way to receive food . . . is to hold out both hands and have the food placed in them. To reach out with one hand suggests grabbing to the !Kung. I found it moving to see so much restraint about taking food among people who are all thin and often hungry, for whom food is a constant source of anxiety."[18] In my view, one reason that this is moving is the !Kung's stitching of togetherness into the basic rituals of eating, by which they achieve the elevation of social harmony even above the essential matter of food.

Characteristically mistaken, Freud thought that fire was important in human evolution because it instilled restraint. More specifically, he believed that self-control emerged because people needed to learn to resist the strong urge to extinguish the life-giving fire with a stream of urine. How it actually worked is described well by Richard Wrangham in his book *Catching Fire*: "Clustering around a fire to eat and sleep would have required our ancestors to stay close to one another. To avoid lost tempers flaring into disruptive fights, the proximity would have demanded considerable tolerance."[19] Those who were too aggressive or otherwise surly to benefit from the fruits of the campfire and the cooperative attitudes they require, would have, over time, lost out and thus died out.

Sharing food is characteristically human. Writing of how men and women in hunter-gatherer societies tend to search out distinct and complementary sets of food items, Wrangham notes in *Catching Fire* that "each sex eats not only from the food items they have collected themselves, but also from their partner's finds. Not even a hint of this complementarity is found among nonhuman primates."[20]

Male-female complementarity may be uniquely human, but sharing food—and the openness inherent in it—is not. Our primate cousins, the bonobo, can be generous with each other where food is concerned. In a typical demonstration of this, pieces of fruit are placed in a test room. Adjacent to the test room is a caged-off area in which an individual bonobo sits and observes the scene. The bonobo in the caged-off portion cannot open the door to the test room, but a bonobo in the test room could, if so inclined, open the door from the inside. A second bonobo is let into the room with the food, and has a choice—to eat all the food, or to open the cage and let the other bonobo in to share. Typically, bonobos share, and fairly generously. For example, an individual bonobo could eat almost all the food and only then open the cage to let the other have the remnants. But opening the door is usually one of the bonobo's first actions.

To be receptive to food, one has to literally be open; usually of course, it is the mouth that's open, but one can be fed through other openings, too, such as a tube to the stomach or intravenously. A literal openness of one sort or another is required, and a principle of cognitive science is that literal bodily movements and processes often ripple out and lead to associated psychological reactions, a view that is compatible with my emphasis in this book on simple and concrete things that "spark" and "nudge" back toward health.

For example, a person instructed to contort the face into a smile will often feel a slight mood boost, as will the person who can no longer furrow the brow because the attendant muscles have been paralyzed by Botox. The motoric acts of smiling and of not furrowing the brow ripple out and lead to the psychological state often associated with smiling and not furrowing. FSU psychologist Mike Kaschak and colleagues have reported an example of this general phenomenon involving language comprehension, which they named "the action-sentence compatibility effect."[21] The researchers asked participants to read simple sentences and judge, as fast as they could, whether or not the sentences made sense. The sentences of interest either involved action away from the body (e.g., "close the drawer"—doing so involves moving one's hand away from the body) or action toward the body (e.g., "put your finger on your chin"—which involves moving one's hand toward the body). If the participant judged that a sentence made sense, she or he pushed a yes button; if not, a no button. Remarkably, if the yes button was farther way from the participant than the no button, participants hesitated in their judgments of "toward the body" sentences. Similarly, if the yes button was closer, participants took longer to judge the "away from the body" sentences. This effect even applied to abstract sentences like "Liz told you the story" (a "to the body" sentence). The researchers noted, "The data support an embodied theory of meaning that relates the meaning of sentences to human action."

The effect extends well beyond language comprehension. People who tell harmful lies about others want to use mouthwash more than do others; those who write the lies down wish to use hand sanitizers more than do others. Researchers at the University of Chicago have shown, in at least two ways, that movements can affect people's preferences. A study of non-Chinese speakers examining Chinese text characters expressed distinct preferences for script examined when the participants were pulling up on a table (hands under the table, pulling towards one's face) as opposed to those examined when pushing down on the table (pushing down on the top of a table, away from one's body).[22] This presumably occurs because of the motoric signals of "pulling to = attraction" and "pushing away = repulsion." In another study, participants expressed decided preferences for two-letter typing combinations that were motorically easier to type.[23] It may seem very obvious that people would prefer the easier combinations, but a key point is that it was not obvious to the participants themselves. In both the study on typing and that on Chinese text characters, participants were unable to explain their preferences, suggesting that the body is contributing to mentation, but is neglecting to tell the mind about it.

In a similar fashion, the process of opening ourselves to the literal act of ingestion may well open us up to other things, too, like kindness, generosity, and empathy—antidotes all to loneliness.

THE RITUAL OF EATING TOGETHER is supplemented by other rituals that bring us together as well. I have spent some time recently on US military bases. Late afternoon usually finds me alone in my hotel room, working on my computer or reading. As the clock strikes 5:00 PM, the national anthem starts; you can hear it anywhere you happen to be on the base. Even though I have experienced this many times, it never fails to first surprise me and then, as I look out the window and see the busy base come to a complete standstill, move me. In those few moments, I am alone but feel far from alone. Engagement in shared ritual, particularly rituals tied to an animating idea and a meaningful history, is loneliness-reducing.

My friends and I have season tickets to FSU football games, and the rituals there are no exception to the rule—that ritual can unite. Here, as on the military bases, the national anthem is one such rite, as is the boyish fascination that my friends and I (all men in our forties or older) take in the "flyover": a military plane or formation of jets that flies thrillingly low over the stadium, timed precisely to coincide with the last few words of the national anthem (by far my favorite example of this involved the stealth bomber).

Soon thereafter, yet another ritual brings the entire stadium together (except for the fans of the opposing side, of course). An undergraduate student, usually male, who has been selected and groomed for the role, rides Renegade the horse to midfield. The student is dressed in full FSU Seminole regalia and is carrying a flaming spear; the horse is decked out to match. As the players excitedly jump up and down en masse nearby, the student has Renegade rear up on his two hind legs. The student then plunges the spear into midfield, right in the middle of the Seminole logo; as he does so, the FSU fans yell "whoomph!" (The propriety of this of course worries many but the university has the full support of the leaders of the Seminole tribe in Florida.)

I was in Cleveland recently on business, and it so happened that my (original) hometown Atlanta Falcons were in town to play the Browns. I brought one of my sons on the trip with me so we could both go to the game. Browns' fans have their rituals, too, we discovered. An unfortunate one is to single out an individual wearing enemy colors, and as he (it's usually a man, I assume, and hope) is, for example, on his way to the concession stand, a considerable portion of the entire stadium crowd points to him and repeatedly chants "Asshole!" This affirmed my decision for my son and me not to wear Falcons garb, which saved us from the chanting ritual as well as from being the direct recipients of a very sincere "Go fuck yourselves!" delivered to Falcons fans seated near us. (The Falcons prevailed, perhaps the reason for the venom of the day.)

Browns fans were, no doubt, together in these sentiments, in that they were physically in the same locale and expressing a similar reaction. But I doubt they *felt* especially together in these particular rituals, in the sense of being in synchrony with one another. Belonging—loneliness's antidote—occurs not just in the presence of other people (though that can help), and indeed, it can occur in their absence. As has been mentioned, people can most definitely feel alone in a crowd. Togetherness seems to require not just other people, but a harmony with others (or with remembered others, or with the natural world).

There is a discord in anger, and a harmony in cheering in unity. Browns fans were in the same stadium during the angry chants and outbursts, but not really in harmony. That changed when a song came over the loudspeakers, during which they chanted O-H-I-O and for each letter put their arms over their heads to form the letter (Ohio State fans do a similar thing). This ritual was harmonious and cast a palpable sense of friendliness around the stadium.

Another activity that occurs at many stadiums and that illustrates both our propensity to rally together and the way in which some forms of togetherness are more meaningful and lasting than others is the bobblehead race that is depicted on the Jumbotron video screens during a commercial time-out in a football game. Three bobble-headed cartoon-like characters are shown on the screen; they are, unimaginatively enough, labeled "Number one," "Number two," and "Number three." They are shown stretching out and warming up in preparation for a race, a hundred-yard sprint from goal line to goal line. A significant portion of the crowd chooses their favorite, cheering fervently for their chosen cartoon character to win the randomly decided race; those who have chosen "Number three," for example, hold three fingers up in support. Those whose character wins seem genuinely pleased by it, high-fiving others who have chosen that same character. (I recognize that non–sports fans feel that the sports themselves have this same random quality, a sentiment I do not share.)

People enthusiastically participate in "the wave" at ballgames (and, it should be remembered, the majority of the people at ballgames are male); "the wave," a standard these days but a relatively recent innovation, occurs when one after another group of spectators stand and raise their arms. The successive nature of the process creates the impression of a wave roiling around the stadium . . . or as the British would call it, a "Mexican wave" (a reference to one of the wave's creation stories, which has it coming into being at a soccer game in Mexico in the 1950s; the earliest origin story that I am aware of is at bullfights in Spain in the 1930s). The wave is an example of a metachronal rhythm, a kind of movement that can be seen across nature, including in the movement of a millipede's legs, the motion of the hairlike structures called cilia that single-celled organisms use for locomotion, and the undulating nature of many body organs (e.g., intestines, stomach). It is mildly fascinating to view a stadium's wave as having the same underlying structure as, say, the patterns of movement in a bacterium. The same movement by which a bacterium gets around can be writ large, at, for example, the Indianapolis 500, the grandstands for which hold approximately 250,000 people, and which has a claim to be the site of the world's biggest stadium wave.

What do things like the wave and bobblehead race say about us? One thing I think they indicate is that we are wired for—prepared for—togetherness. Any opportunity, small or not, random or not, will serve. But of course, not all opportunities are equal. The "bobble-head" experience certainly does not harm anyone, but the together-ness it inspires is probably not particularly deep or lasting (though, as I am arguing, surprisingly simple things can and do serve the purpose of bringing people together in significant and enduring ways). The wave, if my repeated experience of it is any indication, seems to imbue crowds with slightly more cohesion than the bobblehead race. I be-lieve this has to do with its tie to nature. Unlike the race of the bobble-heads, the wave arises from the joint contributions of the crowd, and it is an accurate mirroring of a process—a metachronal rhythm—that pervades nature.

Our biology is evolved to make friendly encounters rewarding, as John Cacioppo and William Patrick nicely show in their 2008 book, *Loneliness*. These authors also suggest remedies for loneliness, and the gist of their recommendation is essentially captured in my anecdote about chatting about FSU football with the guy on the other side of the lunch counter: be nice to other people. I think this suggestion is both quite true and problematic. Its truth can be seen in my mood boost after a brief talk with a stranger about FSU football, to take one small example. Its problematic character is noted in a review that compares the book's recommendations to a late-night TV infomercial, and states, "You already know the advice that [the authors] are recommending, so let me save you the price of the book: do unto others as you would have them do unto you. . . . It's great advice, of course. Time-tested. Easy to remember. And I don't doubt that it works, for those able to follow through with it. But it will be useless to those too trapped by circumstances, habits, or brain chemicals to change their ways by mere will power."[24]

I see this same dynamic virtually every day in the psychotherapy clinic I direct. We often recommend very simple, obvious steps that re-ally do work, with amazing results in some instances . . . if people would only do them. In this, we sympathize with Samuel Johnson's advice as recorded by his biographer Boswell: "If you are idle, be not solitary. If you are solitary, be not idle."[25]

Consider sleep hygiene, for example. As we will see, one is neither idle nor (necessarily) solitary when asleep. And sleep problems are remarkably responsive to a few rules and habits: try to go to bed and wake up at roughly the same time every night and morning; use the bedroom only for sleeping (and sex); if you find you can't sleep, don't lie in bed but get up and do something relaxing; if you are a clock-watcher, turn your clock around so that you can't see it; and so on. These really do work, and improving sleep is very helpful in many conditions, including major depressive disorder and bipolar disorder. . . . I'm also quite confident that improving sleep would not exacerbate, and probably would help somewhat, male loneliness. The same can be said for exercise.

People have at least some dim awareness that the right amount of sleep and exercise is good for them. And if pressed, most people can be made to articulate these facts and to agree with them. But people also tend to dismiss these solutions as obvious and thin gruel, so they don't even try them. Or, more precisely, they try them half-heartedly, or for a day or night or two, with results similar to those of taking an antibiotic for only one day when you have a bacterial infection. Things like sleep hygiene and exercise are obvious, but they are also stunningly strong gruel if done persistently, and so the trick is getting people to believe this and buy in—*really* buy in, not just do the hand-waving version.

In *The Divine Comedy* Dante wrote, "A great flame follows a little spark." The maxim might be rewritten to read, "A great flame *might* follow a little spark, and some sparks more so than others." The sparking of connection is both simpler and more difficult than it sounds. It is simple, because there are literally hundreds of activities that spur connection. In the clinic I direct, we keep a list of such activities in all of the consulting rooms. A patient's complaint that there is "nothing to do in Tallahassee" is met with a list of over 250 things to do in Tallahassee (we have recently been outdone is this regard by a blog called "Tallahassee365," which lists an interesting local activity for each of the 365 days of the year). This is difficult, however, not because of what to do or even how to do it, but rather, the will to do it, the motivation to try and persevere. This is a particular difficulty for older men and is the reason that all the stops need to be pulled out to help them overcome it.

We approach this dilemma by starting easily and slowly. For sleep hygiene, maybe just start with the clock-watching rule: how hard is it to turn a clock around? For exercise, maybe just start with easy in-home exercise: at least once a day, if you are sitting in a chair watching TV or web-surfing, stand up and sit back down at least five times. Doable, and it's a start.

We also tell compelling stories, like those mentioned already of the two men who jumped from the Golden Gate Bridge, one to his death, the other to severe, but survivable, injuries. Both men claimed that a simple personal gesture like a smile or a show of concern would have been literally life-saving, and that not having received any such gesture (and, a crucial point, probably not having solicited any), both men jumped. Simple things—a smile, a brief chat—can make a big difference. Here again, not much to ask, and a start.

We back ourselves up with rigorous research. Of the three leading and most studied psychotherapies for major depressive disorder (i.e., behavioral activation; interpersonal psychotherapy; cognitive-behavioral psychotherapy), two can be legitimately summarized by the phrase "get more active and connected" (behavioral activation and interpersonal psychotherapy). The third, cognitive-behavioral psychotherapy, includes these components, but adds a focus on challenging negative thoughts. Tellingly, I believe, there is evidence that this addition does not do much, that, for instance, behavioral activation alone is as good as behavioral activation plus cognitive-behavioral therapy.[26] It stands to reason that if these are effective approaches to the treatment of a major, serious illness, they will be effective in addressing male loneliness (serious in its own right, as documented in the book's opening chapter).

We also seek the path of least resistance, in the sense that we look for current behaviors, already habitual in nature, that can be remolded into more adaptive behaviors. Smoking and drinking, for instance, for all of their potential health costs, can also pay a health dividend if the behaviors become conduits for social connection, an important perspective for a number of reasons, including the evidence that becoming less lonely can be as or more powerful for improving health even compared to quitting smoking (which should, of course, be seriously considered).

If you smoke alone during breaks at work, try seeking breaks with other smokers; if you drink alone at home, invite someone over for drinks, or go to a bar (safely, of course), hang out, and maybe even offer to buy someone a drink.

And we are patient and persistent. We are mindful of the fact that the usual number of unsuccessful quit attempts for something like smoking is six before success occurs, and that this is a general truth regarding behavior change. Habits do indeed die hard—trite perhaps, but also, like many trite things, quite true—and this is so whether the habit is smoking, sleep behaviors, exercise, or socializing.

In *Hamlet,* Shakespeare wrote, "Assume a virtue if you have it not. . . . For use can almost change the stamp of nature." In addition to getting rid of bad habits, one can cultivate good ones. Forcing oneself to do simple, positive things, day after day, thus has the potential to "almost change the stamp of nature" (characteristically, Shakespeare captured an important truth with one word—"almost"). The patient cultivation of virtue is analogous to taking sandpaper to wood: it will not change the essential structure of the wood, but it will remove edges that catch. The comedian Louis C.K. learned this lesson after his divorce when he was thrown into a new role with his children: "I'm a person who tends to fall into depressions and sleep a lot and eat a lot; I can't really do that because when my kids are with me there's no one to cover for me. At six o'clock in the morning they are there waiting to seize life and I can't just go back to sleep. I have to get up and drag them to school."[27] His forced habit grew into a virtue; he came to view himself not just as dragging himself out of bed and his kids to school, but as a better, more engaged father. He assumed a virtue and it became, almost, his nature.

The forcing of habit and routine can, according to this view, instill virtue. If this is so, then one extreme implication is that at least some people not only benefit from but actually enjoy aspects of incarceration. This may sound outlandish, but in the psychotherapy clinic I direct, I have seen this very phenomenon many times. The modal situation involves someone who has been convicted of a crime; before sentencing, the person's lawyer recommends psychotherapy as a way to signal seriousness about a new future, perhaps thereby persuading the judge to hand down a relatively lighter sentence. The focus of the psychotherapy in the weeks before sentencing, and certainly after it, is dread of imprisonment. A few weeks or months later, sentence served, we see the person again, and he often reports having learned something from prison. The staff person asks, "How so?" The usual reply: "I was surprised how I took to the routine of it. I slept more deeply and well than I can ever remember. I felt physically better, more healthy, more able to concentrate, my mind was clearer." Some of this can be accounted for by the absence of drinking and drug-taking, but not all of it. A large chunk of this effect has to do with good habits and routines—going to bed and getting up at more or less the same time daily; eating regular meals; exercising at least a little bit more days than not.

I am by no means the only person who has noticed this phenomenon. In his book *The Victims Return,* historian Stephen F. Cohen writes of those being freed in the 1950s from Stalin's Gulag, "Years of imprisonment had deprived them of their families, careers, possessions, and sense of belonging. Some even preferred the routines of the Gulag . . . to the uncertainties of freedom."[28] In another passage, the author writes, "Distraught returnees sought comfort in circles of other victims, who were 'like a family.' Some even expressed nostalgia for the survivalist comradeship of the Gulag."[29] The attractions and power of rhythmicity—and of togetherness—are such that they can be felt by some even in the midst of atrocity.

The psychiatrist A. M. Daniels—who writes under the pen name Theodore Dalrymple—has commented on this effect numerous times. He has had ample opportunity to observe it in his work as a prison psychiatrist. In his collection of essays, *Second Opinion,* he relates the following exchange between a prisoner and himself:

Dalrymple: "Is this going to be your last sentence?"
Prisoner: "I hope not."
"You mean you want to come back here?"
"I've only been outside prison one out of the last ten years, doctor."

"You prefer it here?"

"I do, really."

This is far from a unique exchange, even if the field of experience is limited to Dalrymple's, never mind my own and that of many of my colleagues who have noticed a similar thing. In another passage in *Second Opinion*, the psychiatrist described a man who had spent three months of the last sixteen years out of prison. "Do you prefer life in prison?" he asks the man, who replies, "I feel safer."[30]

One may certainly express a pang of sorrow about this state of affairs, that there would be not a few people in our society whose happiness seems assured only behind bars. One may share this sentiment, but then respond "surely this principle of extreme regimentation only applies to the criminal; for others, it would be an affront to our liberty and thus to our pursuit of happiness."

I'm not so sure. For one thing, this effect was observed among Gulag prisoners (a very small minority of them, of course), few of whom were criminals in any true sense of the word. For another thing, there are many thousands of people—the vast majority far from criminal—who look back with favor on their time in an extremely regimented environment—the military. General Stanley McChrystal, who commanded US forces in Afghanistan during Operation Enduring Freedom, advocates a regimented schedule through personal example. McChrystal goes to sleep most nights around midnight, and arises at 4:00 AM. On work days (that is, almost every day), he puts in six to seven hours of work (surrounded by many staff and aides), and then breaks for his only sit-down meal of the day (here again, with a large group of people), a large combination of breakfast and lunch. He works for another couple of hours, and then goes on his daily eight-mile run (again, not alone). He usually returns to work thereafter, and except for an occasional break or snack, works straight through until midnight, when the daily pattern repeats.[31]

The Dalai Lama's daily schedule bears some resemblance to McChrystal's. His Holiness arises at 3:30 AM and meditates. Meditation is followed by full-body prostrations, which include elements of both physical and spiritual exercise. Next, he walks for exercise, either outside or on a treadmill. He has breakfast, and then meditates some more and reads, mostly in philosophy. The Dalai Lama then puts in a full day of work, meditates for an hour or two more, and then goes to sleep, at 8:30 PM.

McChrystal and the Dalai Lama are, needless to say, extraordinary, and thus it is unrealistic to expect everyone else to regiment a schedule to this extent. My guess is that the general's reply might be along the lines of "what you ask of yourself determines the extent of your achievements," and that His Holiness would likely agree. Some associate this kind of regimentation with stoicism and remoteness. However, General McChrystal and especially the Dalai Lama are not very remote. In the latter case, an article quoted someone familiar with His Holiness: "We were in this hotel in downtown L.A., and they're trying to get him from point A to point B . . . all of a sudden, boom! He breaks off and goes into the gift shop, where they're selling chewing gum and 'I Love L.A.' teddy bears, just to say hello to the shopgirls."[32]

The extremes embodied by McChrystal and the Dalai Lama are not at all necessary for optimal social relations and health; the principles, however, are. Regularizing sleep schedules, building physical activity into daily schedules, constructing life patterns so that social interactions are inherent—these are not a lot to ask, and can be lifesaving.

Also consider the following anecdote, reported by a psychiatrist at the National Institute of Mental Health. The doctor had come into professional contact with a patient who had bipolar disorder—a condition that can include extreme and destructive "highs," or manias as well as profound depressions—and who was not particularly adherent to his medication regimen. When this particular patient experienced manias, they were especially florid, even as compared to the manic phases of other people with severe forms of the illness (which, as anyone intimately familiar with the condition will attest, is saying something).

During a time when the patient was symptom-free, the psychiatrist obtained his and his family's agreement to the following arrangement. The next time the patient became severely manic, he was to be brought to the NIMH and installed in a room that, from most outward appearances, resembled a nice hotel room. The room was monitored by clinical staff through direct observation, as well as through video and audio, and various monitors were placed on the patient himself (e.g., to keep track of blood pressure and heart rate). One of these monitors resembled a bulky wristwatch; its purpose was to provide the staff with actigraphy—an ongoing read, somewhat like a seismograph, of the man's activity level. If he was asleep, the actigraph would record a value near zero, and if he was jumping up and down, a far higher value. It is important to note that the man was medication-free during his time in the room, not a trivial fact given that he had bipolar disorder, and a quite severe form of the illness at that.

The room had some other special features as well. It was locked from the outside so that the man could not leave. It was made safe, with padding on the edges of tables to protect from injuries in a fall and to guard against suicidal behavior, should it develop. And most important of all, although temperature was maintained at a comfortable level, all of the room's electricity was otherwise cut off at 10:30 PM, and was turned back on at 6:30 AM. The nightly cut-off was dramatic: it was literally lights out, all lights out, pitch black. Lights-on was dramatic, too (and measures were available to wake the patient if lights-on did not succeed, including staff going into the room and shaking him awake; as we shall see, this was unnecessary).

On the first night, the man stayed up all night, walking around and talking in the absolute darkness. His actigraphy resembled the seismograph of a disastrous earthquake. His staying active throughout the night, incidentally, is a testimony to the gravity of severe forms of bipolar disorder, if any were needed. On the second night, a similar pattern recurred, although the patient did get into his bed for about an hour total, during which he slept approximately thirty minutes. The third night continued the trend: mostly up and about, but some time in bed asleep. By the fifth night, the ratio of time awake to time asleep had shifted to sleep's favor, and by the seventh night, the patient's sleep-wake cycle had normalized: he would fall asleep within a half hour of lights-out, and remain asleep throughout the night until the 6:30 AM lights-on. Just as important and as remarkable, as his sleep patterns returned to normal, his other manic symptoms remitted as well: he ceased the non-stop flight-of-ideas talking he had done upon admission, and his mental status cleared.

A man with a particularly severe form of a grave illness—an illness that regularly agonizes and even kills (through suicide) its sufferers—and who found himself in an acute and dangerous phase of the illness, a florid mania, was brought back to health, medication-free and within a matter of days, through nothing more than the regimentation of his daily schedule. In this anecdote, a true force of nature—bipolar illness—squared off with what I am arguing is also a force of nature—regimentation and rhythmicity of daily schedule—and the latter won.

For her dissertation, one of my PhD students hooked around fifty undergraduates up to actigraphy devices and monitored their sleep over the course of three weeks. From this, we plan a paper to be titled something like "The Natural Sleep Habits of Undergraduates in the Wild," because there clearly was some wildness. One finding that may disturb the sleep of college students' parents was that the *average* time they went to bed was well after 2:00 AM. To reiterate, this does not mean that they occasionally went to bed late; rather, after 2:00 AM was when they *usually* went to bed. Moreover, there was a 1.5 standard deviation around this average, which means that for a large chunk of these students, average time to bed was well after 3:00 AM and for virtually none of them was the average time to bed before midnight.

They did not sleep much, either. The average amount was just over six hours per night, and the standard deviation around this average was rather small, meaning that for virtually all of these college students, less than seven hours per night was a usual routine, and for many of them less than six hours was pretty common.

A main goal of the dissertation was to assess the link of sleep indices to suicidal thinking—a point that is germane here because I am arguing that improved sleep should be one goal of the lonely sex, who, as was made clear in earlier chapters, are prone to suicidal ideation and behavior. The project did in fact uncover important links: actigraphy-assessed sleep problems were associated with increased suicidal thoughts across the three-week study, and, importantly, this association was observed even when accounting for depression.

This is intriguing because it rules out the idea—one that is plausible enough—that sleep problems and suicidal ideation are associated merely because both are features of depression.

Perhaps even more intriguing, especially in light of the previous discussion of General McChrystal, the Dalai Lama, and the manic man who underwent severe sleep-wake regimentation in a hotel-like hospital room, is the fact that, of all the sleep indices examined in the dissertation, *sleep variability* was the most consistent and strongest correlate of suicidal thinking. Sleep variability was defined as the irregularity in time-to-bed and time-to-wake, an irregularity that General McChrystal and His Holiness do not allow themselves and that the man experiencing mania was discouraged from by lights-out and -on. The sleep variability actigraphy readout would read "zero" for McChrystal and the Dalai Lama; it would read "zero" as well for the manic patient after his mania remitted. As a predictor of suicidal thoughts, sleep irregularity was more important than how long or how efficiently one sleeps.

A similar finding emerged in a recent study of African Americans over age fifty.[33] Sleep variability—which the researchers defined as amount of deviation on a particular night from one's ongoing average sleep duration—predicted cognitive performance on the next day. Cognitive performance was measured with an array of memory, verbal fluency, and other tasks, including the clock drawing test, described by the researchers as measuring "a participant's ability to draw a clock to a specified time (i.e., 10 after 11, 3:25, 10 after 9, 6:55, 10 after 6, 1:45, 5 after 4, and 9:40)."[34] That sleep variability can significantly affect performance on a task like this underscores its importance.

So does a quotation from the concluding paragraphs of the dissertation alluded to earlier: "The Substance Abuse and Mental Health Services Administration (SAMHSA) lists sleep complaints among the top ten warning signs of suicide, and our results are consistent with these recommendations. In the present study, indices of disturbed sleep predicted acute increases in suicidal symptoms, conferring risk even above and beyond the influence of depression. In this way, disturbed sleep may be a warning sign for suicide. Alongside other subjective or objective sleep complaints that predict risk, such as insomnia and nightmares [more on nightmares shortly; they are quite important], our results specifically suggest that sleep variability may be an appropriate risk factor to evaluate and integrate into current suicide risk assessment models. Compared to other suicide risk factors, sleep is modifiable and amenable to treatment. It may also be less stigmatized than other symptoms of psychological distress."

The points in these last two sentences are essential and represent the future of mental health care: simple, effective, and acceptable to patients.

The point of this dissertation work was to link sleep problems to suicidal ideation; the focus was not on differences between the young women and men in their sleep. To have a glimpse at this, I asked the dissertation's author if she would reexamine her data. She graciously obliged, and some of the findings were illuminating with regard to this book's thesis on the lonely sex and the various sources of and solutions to the problem.

Keep in mind that these participants were undergraduates; the average age of the young women and men was approximately nineteen. Even at this tender age, gender differences were starting to emerge: this research shows that men slept a bit less overall, slept less efficiently, and took longer to fall asleep once in bed. These findings bring to mind the anecdote, alluded to already, of the writer who recalled that his dad always told him that men sleep lightly because of the need to be vigilant protectors.

IT HAS BECOME INCREASINGLY apparent to me through recent clinical experience and through scientific research on suicidal behavior—especially within the military but outside it, too—that nightmares represent their own special, stand-alone problem. It is not just that nightmares disrupt sleep, although that is part of it. It is also that they are upsetting and demoralizing over and beyond causing sleeplessness. Samuel Taylor Coleridge wrote that nightmares represent "the night's dismay" that "saddened and stunned the coming day." In *Hamlet,* Shakespeare wrote, "I could be bounded in a nutshell, and count myself a king of infinite space—were it not that I have bad dreams." Nightmare sufferers would agree. Many patients who suffer from frequent and disturbing nightmares will say something along the lines of, "If I can't be comfortable when I'm asleep, if terror and horror come at the time when I'm supposed to be the most comfortable and peaceful, what hope is there for any comfort or peace for me?"

As this last phrase implies, nightmares are a documented risk factor for suicidal behavior.[35] And, as with many such risk factors, their ominous possible outcome belies the simplicity with which they are clinically managed. It is not particularly difficult to substantially reduce or even eliminate nightmares. The technique, supported persuasively by an impressive clinical trial, involves rescripting nightmares and then rehearsing the newly rescripted image throughout the day.[36] Take, for example, a nightmare of being followed into a dark alley by an imposing figure whose footsteps become a run; the nightmare sufferer turns just in time to see a knife coming at his chest, at which point he awakens with a start. The task is to literally rescript, in writing, the nightmare, in such a way that control and power are in the hands of the dreamer. So a patient might write about the above example, "I was in a dark alley, I heard someone behind me, he began to walk faster toward me, then to run. I wheeled around and saw that he had a knife. I immediately yelled that I had a taser and would tase him if he came any closer. He did not heed the warning, and I stopped him in his tracks with a taser shot in his chest." This rescripted image—the issuing of the warning followed by the successful taser shot—is to be mentally rehearsed a few times throughout the day. As this example shows, and despite the voluble claims of many, simplicity and effectiveness often go hand in hand in the mental health arena.

At recent speaking engagements in which I lecture on the importance and relative simplicity of relief from nightmares, I have been approached by more than one psychiatrist, each of whom said that multiple patients with frequent nightmares have obtained considerable relief from the antihypertensive drug Prazosin. Satisfyingly, research corroborates these claims.[37] It is not at all clear, incidentally, why an antihypertensive medication should alleviate nightmares; research studies aimed at answering this question should prove revealing indeed. In the meantime, frequent nightmare sufferers have two solid therapeutic options: imagery rehearsal and Prazosin.

What do nightmares and other sleep problems have to do with the problem of male loneliness? I recall a college acquaintance of mine telling me that he and his girlfriend had such busy lives that they hardly saw one another. To try to solve this problem, they moved in together, and this helped, but not in the way they anticipated. They were so busy that even living together they hardly saw one another, but they slept together every night . . . and my friend didn't mean sex, or rather, he didn't mean only sex. He meant instead that they benefited from the closeness and togetherness of sharing a bed even while asleep. I recall thinking this was a little preposterous—how could a genuine togetherness really exist without talking and doing things? Yet again, I was wrong; there is something to my friend's experience, and to his credit he understood it despite his gender and his youth. To my knowledge there are no research studies on this particular issue, but, true to the theme of this book, I'd expect a majority of twenty-year-old males to react like I did, but only a minority of college-age females to do so. I can certainly attest to the fact that my wife has understood this principle far more deeply and for a far longer time than I have.

There is an emerging research literature corroborating the fact that belongingness while asleep not only exists but is important to health. To quote a prominent sleep researcher, "Sleep can be considered as a fundamental attachment behavior, in that it is a behavioral state that requires a relative cessation of awareness and down-regulation of vigilance—processes that are optimized when one feels a sense of physical and emotional safety and security. Throughout history, humans have derived physical and emotional safety and security, particularly during times of real or imagined threat, through their connections with close others."[38] These connections, research like this makes clear, do not cease at night.

Sleep researchers conducted a sleep diary study of twenty-nine heterosexual couples; the diary data were supplemented by actigraphy, the same technique used to assess the sleep of the man in the throes of mania who was described earlier, as well as in the dissertation study of "the sleep habits of undergraduates in the wild." In addition, the researchers tracked couples' daytime relationship behaviors using a technique called "ecological momentary assessment." This latter method involves participants carrying around BlackBerry-like devices, which signal them several times per day to respond to a few questions that pop up on the devices—questions, in this particular case, on relationship closeness, cooperation, and conflict. Couples completed sleep diaries, were monitored with actigraphy, and responded to the ecological momentary assessment signals daily for seven days.

Some intriguing results emerged. For instance, the degree to which a couple's sleep was harmonized—that is to say, the extent to which they fell asleep at approximately the same time—was related to the next day's harmony in the relationship. Sleep onset concordance appeared to lead to fewer fights and more relationship contentment the next day. There was also some similar evidence regarding overall sleep quality: for both partners, better sleep tended to predict better relationship quality the next day. This association went both ways (at least in some analyses): relationship quality during the day tended to lead to better sleep that night.

Contrary to the view articulated in a psychoanalytic treatise that "Sleep is the great protector of alonetime,"[39] these findings and many others support the view that we relate even as we sleep. What gregarious creatures we are; not even sleep can prevent our socializing.

Sleep is an essential aspect of biorhythm, and when it is harmonized, people are more in tune socially. Another key aspect of biorhythm is food intake, and, like sleep, this undeniably biological phenomenon has taken on social and cultural significance. Meals, especially the evening meal, are, in virtually all human societies, a time of both bodily and social sustenance. The evening meal is a ritual with a rich and ancient past, and, alas, at least in some parts of the world, a dubious future. This description of modern-day hunter-gatherers is one that is highly likely to be generalizable across the human history of at least the last 100,000 years: "The hunters return to camp in the semidarkness, and each family eats supper around the fire after darkness has fallen. . . . Only in the evening does the whole family gather to eat a solid meal."[40]

There is a simplicity and groundedness to a family together after sunset around a fire or a table for dinner. Solutions to the problem of accelerating male loneliness need to heed the same organizing principles inherent in simple and effective things like the power of closeness at meals and even when asleep, and things, noted earlier, like imagery rehearsal therapy, and Prazosin. Solutions have to be simple, with gradual, easy beginning steps, using paths of least resistance if possible; they have to be backed up by compelling rationales, either with scientific data, engaging anecdotes, or, preferably, both; and their application must include patience and persistence.

Plausibility is essential, too. A promising program developed by the US Marine Corps to combat a growing problem with suicidal behavior does well on the dimension of plausibility. The program charges junior officers to personally engage their troops and thus come to be alert to their problems, including mental health problems. A newspaper article described the program, quoting program leader Master Gunnery Sgt. Peter Proietto thus: "We're not going to give each other a big group hug." Proietto, a four-tour war veteran, continued, "But we're going to address it like Marines. We're going to say, 'What's going on there, Devil Dog? If you got a problem, let's get it fixed.'"[41] Incidentally, should this strike you as a glib and superficial approach, I would understand the reflex, but can assure you that the military could not be more serious about suicide prevention. They have invested considerably in suicide-prevention efforts, including, as alluded to already, the multi-million dollar Military Suicide Research Consortium, which I direct at Florida State University.

A major aim of the Consortium is to contribute to an understanding of suicidal behavior in military settings, and then to propose solutions that are feasible even in remote places, such as the mountains of Afghanistan. An initial working hypothesis of the Consortium—and one that is consistent with the theme of this book—is that a signature of many military suicides involves an individual suddenly experiencing alienation even as everyone else enjoys a prevailing sense of camaraderie (e.g., a person who has let his/her unit down).

Down-to-earth plausibility and simplicity represent vexed issues in mental health care. Many of the psychiatrists and psychologists in the field have spent much of their adult lives training in things like psycho-therapy (not to mention funding that training), and view themselves, often with reason, as sophisticated and wise people. It can therefore grate on their self-views if they are viewed as dispensers of advice like "get up at the same time every morning." I have witnessed this firsthand among senior psychotherapists who were being trained to do a form of psychotherapy that is quite regimented. The trainers could not have been more insistent that the therapists conduct the technique exactly as formulated, and could not have been more frustrated by the therapists' regular departures from script. I see it in young therapists, too, includ-ing those who are just a year or two into their clinical training. When both the beginning and senior therapists are asked about the reasons for their improvisations, virtually all express some version of the feeling that departing from regimen allows them to display things like intu-ition, insight, and wisdom.

Many therapists of this ilk are indeed quite intuitive and insight-ful; a problem, however, is that these things, in and of themselves, do not translate into lasting behavioral change in patients, even if they do impress patients and make them feel that they are doing hard psycho-logical work. I agree with Randall Jarrell, a poet quite familiar with psychological misery, who died by suicide. One of his poems asserted that it is misguided to confuse pain with wisdom, because pain can be needless, inchoate, and lacking any redeeming qualities. And I agree with Tony Judt, who, writing of the effects of amyotrophic lateral scle-rosis, stated, "Loss is loss, and nothing is gained by calling it a nicer name."[42] It is no coincidence, in my opinion, that these statements were made by people intimately familiar with actual suffering (severe depres-sion in one case; ALS in the other), as opposed to people thinking of abstract or romanticized versions of agony.

A quote from a psychological evaluation that recently came across my desk and that is far from atypical, read, "she attended unstructured individual therapy to talk about her emotions. She found this experience to be helpful at the time but feels it was ineffective in the long term." I believe it was this kind of experience Christopher Lasch had in mind when he wrote in *The Culture of Narcissism,* "People have convinced themselves that what matters is psychic self-improvement: getting in touch with their feelings . . . immersing themselves in the wisdom of the East . . . learning how to 'relate,' overcoming the 'fear of pleasure.'"[43] He noted that there was nothing much wrong with any of these things singly but that, if viewed jointly as a way of life, they undermine true connection (notice the scare quotes around "relate"), both to the public square and to the rich history thereof.

How can insightful professionals fail to notice a glaring thing like the fact that there is no improvement in the very condition for which they are treating patients, sometimes for years? I have no ready or overarching answer to this question, but a partial answer involves a lack of appreciation of the need for humility in the face of nature. Intuitive, insight-oriented psychotherapies are based on the notion (appealing to some) that human nature can, to a degree, be engineered or re-engineered, much as a heart, hip, or knee can be replaced or a cancer irradiated. The "re-engineering of souls" does not have a very impressive track record as psychotherapeutic stance (not to mention as political philosophy of twentieth-century despots).

An alternative attitude is that the human mind is a frontier that, relatively speaking, has not really even been successfully explored, much less mapped or mastered. We are not advanced enough to construct it or reconstruct it, even if we can construct or reconstruct other things (including very intricate things like hearts). A proper attitude, then, is to let nature take its course, and when this fails, to attempt interventions that simply try to nudge things back on natural course. "Nudging" people back onto natural course can be viewed as its own school of psychotherapy, a point on which I expand below. Simple things can have a force that is surprising initially, until a moment's reflection makes them very obvious—a passable definition for truth itself, incidentally. This attitude requires a humility that can be hard to embrace for the highly trained.

Consider two findings in this regard, one highly anecdotal, the other less so. As we have seen, an approach to the treatment of depression is simply to arrange for people to become somewhat more active. The treatment, called behavioral activation, involves planning simple, mildly pleasurable activities and troubleshooting obstacles that may stand in their way. Robert Burton, author of the charming, massive, and at times prescient *Anatomy of Melancholy* (any lack of prescience should probably be forgiven in light of the book's publication date, 1621), endorsed this view in personal terms. He wrote, "I write of melancholy by being busy to avoid melancholy."[44] The approach of writing a tome is not workable for everyone, but a walk around the neighborhood, a call to a friend, some work in a garden, some time with a book: one assumption of the treatment approach is that things like these, if done frequently and regularly, can significantly reduce the painful and impairing symptoms of depression.

Is this assumption tenable? We have already seen the power in simple approaches in the form of sleep regularization in a very manic individual. Behavioral activation has been subjected to rigorous empirical scrutiny. In a clinical trial, the treatment was compared to two imposing rivals, namely, cognitive therapy and antidepressant medication.[45] Patients in the trial were followed over the course of two years, so that not only the effectiveness of treatment, but also the durability of any treatment effects, could be evaluated—this is crucial because the point is not just to get people better and to do it quickly but to do so lastingly. The trial was designed in such a way that some patients in the medication arm of the study were withdrawn from medication and put on placebo, whereas others continued on the medication (under conditions of informed consent, all patients knew about this aspect of the study, but did not know whether they were placed on placebo or were continuing on the medicine). Of all patients in the trial, those who began on medication but were placed onto pill-placebo experienced the most depression relapses. Those in the other three conditions—continued medication, prior cognitive therapy, or prior behavioral activation—did equally well.

This is a remarkable pattern of findings for two main reasons. First, two treatments that were discontinued—behavioral activation and cognitive therapy—nevertheless had lasting benefits, even as compared to a strong treatment (medication) that was continued. Second, no treatment outperformed behavioral activation. A quite simple approach performed at least as well as approaches that were more complex either psychologically (cognitive therapy) or biologically (antidepressant medication), and this occurred, it should not be forgotten, regarding a disorder that can be agonizing and indeed deadly.

I believe this all adds up to mean one of two mutually exclusive things: either depression, as well as human nature itself, is a very simple thing, so much so that behavioral activation can affect it rather profoundly; or, behavioral activation can serve as a nudge, to get a very complicated and poorly understood system—our emotional and mental equipment, the consequences of eons of mammalian and primate evolution—back on track. Even the most superficial reflection on human nature, not to mention a consideration of the complexities and misery of depression, points clearly to the latter conclusion.

This finding—and the replications that affirm it—represent an empirical basis on which to believe in the "simple nudge" school of psychotherapy. This perspective assumes that re-engineering souls and psyches is beyond us; much better, then, to nudge people back into normal and natural rhythms of health, which will unfold by their own inherent momentum. How to nudge? Coaching people to sleep, eat, get active, and relate to others more healthfully—to show up, reach out, and join in—is one reasonable answer. As noted in an earlier chapter, small doses of positive emotion tend to broaden focus, opening up other avenues for positive experiences, leading to more positive emotion, and so on, in a positive chain reaction. Small nudges can lead to major change via such chain reactions.

I promised another, more anecdotal reason, to endorse "nudge" thinking. It involves my treatment of someone in the throes of depression—as it happens, someone who was male and in his fifties and very lonely. Indeed, it was his loneliness that finally brought him into treatment after years of regular episodes of depression. Our first session occurred in January of a given year, a detail that will assume some importance. He had experienced severe depressions starting in his mid-thirties and had had an episode virtually every year since then. To his recollection, all of these episodes started around November and ended, on their own, in the spring.

Allow me to pause at this stage of the story to point out a couple of remarkable facts. First, my patient's age of onset was unusual: those who experience recurrent major depressive episodes usually have their first such episode at around age twenty or so, whereas my patient had his in his mid-thirties. Second, his episodes followed a winter pattern, raising the possibility that he had seasonal affective disorder, a syndrome that is highly similar to major depressive disorder. However, true seasonal affective disorder is fairly rare at southern latitudes (where we were at the time) because it is related to winter paucity of sunlight—this is not such a problem at southern latitudes. Moreover, when true seasonal affective disorder is present, patients tend to experience sleep and appetite disturbances in the direction of oversleeping and overeating, whereas for patients with non-seasonal major depressive disorder, insomnia and lack of appetite comprise the typical presentation. My patient experienced sleeplessness and loss of appetite, which, along with our southern location, raised questions in my mind about seasonal affective disorder.

I didn't linger on these questions long, for the man was severely depressed and deeply lonely, and treatment needed to begin as soon as possible. One indication of the severity of his depression was high suicide risk, high enough that involuntary hospitalization was something I strongly considered. One factor in favor of immediate hospitalization was that his ideas about suicide were violent—they involved exsanguination—and yet, his discussions of these ideas were level and cool, as if they did not daunt him at all. A disadvantage of hospitalization—and a primary reason he was not hospitalized and instead carefully monitored through safety checks—was that he was very concerned about the impact of his hospitalization—and indeed of his potential death by suicide—on his son, who was around fourteen years old at the time. This child clearly meant everything to him, and indeed, seemed to represent nearly the sum total of my patient's interpersonal connections.

Many questions should have occurred to me at the time, but, through a combination of inexperience and urgency to initiate treatment, they did not. For instance, was it coincidental that the child was fourteen years old and that the father's episodes had started up around fourteen years ago? Why was my patient so extremely terse about the child's mother, stating only that they had separated years ago, and that he preferred to move on and not discuss her? He was taciturn and stoic by nature—at times a positive resource for him—but why did stoicism turn to stubborn refusal when it came to discussing his son's mother? And what about the relatively late age of onset and the winter pattern that did not seem to fully add up?

We started cognitive therapy—a reasonable and empirically supported approach, as the clinical trial on behavioral activation showed—but after five weeks of treatment had little to show for it other than his continued connection to his son and a growing rapport with me. Five weeks is sufficient to see at least a little symptom resolution, and when there is none, it is cause to reflect on the treatment approach and perhaps change tactics. I went back to my notes from the original assessment and finally noticed the lingering questions about, among other things, his child's mother. I resolved to have answers to these questions in our next meeting.

My resolve, and my patient's response, resulted in one of the most memorable clinical experiences I have ever had, and one that is a clear demonstration of a psychotherapeutic "nudge" helping a lonely man. The first half of the next session was a tense affair, with me insisting on more history about his child's mother, and my patient deflecting, evading, and becoming increasingly tense and angry. Then he started crying.

At first, there were rivulets of tears running down his still stoic face, but then the stoicism broke and gave way to painful sobbing. This lasted for what seemed to both of us a long time, but in reality was probably five minutes or so. During these few minutes he tried two or three times to talk, getting out one or two words before sobs overcame him again. I'd murmur things in response like "There's no rush, take your time."

The sobs relented, replaced again by steady rivulets, and he said, "I never really talk about this, but she left me, just a couple of weeks after our son was born. I think something went wrong with her in her mind after the baby; she just left. She'd send a postcard now and then that didn't make any sense, and I tried everything to call her and track her down. I got her on the phone once; her voice was full of hate and she said she didn't ever want to see or talk to me again. I think I said something like 'But why, and what about our son?' She hung up. I tried some more after that, but eventually I just gave up. I haven't talked to her or even heard anything about her in over ten years."

"When did this happen?"

"Just after my son was born, like I said."

"Yes, but when was that, what is your son's date of birth?"

"Fourteen years ago October; she left that November."

"November. Huh. You must have been a wreck."

"I didn't have time to be. I had a new baby to feed and clothe, I had to keep my job, find someone to help me with him . . . and I made looking for my wife a second job."

"You didn't have time to grieve then."

"I guess not."

I told my patient that I had formed a new idea about why he was depressed, why it started when it did, and why the episodes had their onset in November. My idea, in a phrase, was "unfinished grief."[46] An effective treatment approach for this particular condition is, consistent with the "nudge" school of psychotherapy, greasing the wheels for the natural grief process to resume and to resolve. The nudge and the greasing consist of exchanges much like the one I just described in which I insisted that my patient tell me about his loss. In "cruel to be kind" fashion, the therapist's task is to probe, remind, and even gently cajole the patient into reminiscing about the lost person, trusting that, with time and persistence, this will dislodge the stuck grief process.

It certainly did so in the case of my depressed patient, not just in that one session, but in subsequent sessions, too, each of which followed the pattern of initial reluctance, breakthrough emotional pain of high intensity, and then a lessening of that intensity with time and talk. But as sessions progressed, the reluctance waned and so did the intensity of pain. By the time we had put in eight sessions or so, he could talk about his loss in terms that retained emotion but that were tolerable and manageable. And, absolutely essentially, as this process unfolded, his depressive symptoms dissipated. Also essentially, he started making new friends.

We agreed to stop psychotherapy soon after that, around late March, but I asked if I could call him next November or December to see if the treatment took. This was important not only because I wanted to ensure that his treatment response was lasting but, relatedly, because I wanted to rule out the possibility that his improvement was merely due to his usual pattern of spontaneously getting better in the spring. He agreed, and when I phoned him in December, I was relieved to hear that he was depression free and that his personal life was continuing to gain momentum. I asked him to call me if anything changed, and suggested that if I didn't hear from him, I would call the next December just to see how things were, which I did. He remained without symptoms and increasingly well connected to friends and family.

Consider the extent of my contributions to his recovery; once, that is, I finally understood what I took to be its main obstacle. I asked him questions about a difficult time in his life; I urged that we stay on topic; I said things like "take your time" when he was sobbing. Put differently, it ain't rocket science. Recall also that I started with an approach—cognitive therapy—which, though also not rocket science, was more complex than the treatment I settled on and with which I got nowhere. My role was merely to serve as nature's nudge.

Judging from my irregular glimpses at the *New York Times,* there are regions in the United States that incline toward complicated approaches to psychotherapy (New York City, and, to a lesser degree, New England, come to mind). "Everywhere is somewhere else's nowhere."[47] But is it a coincidence that complicated understandings of mental disorders and their treatment regularly appear in the *Times,* and prevail in the northeastern United States (and much of Europe), but not in the regions like the US South? Thinking in ways that are unmoored from day-to-day life can stem from lack of genuine contact with people; recall the character in Sartre's *Nausea* whose isolation led to doubt of reality itself, or consider the participants, if they can be called that, in isolation chamber experiments. New York City is no isolation chamber, safe to say, but there is evidence that people there are somewhat lonelier than in other areas of the United States. Some people there are lonely in the midst of millions.[48]

Karl Marx commented on "the idiocy of rural life." Perhaps, but big-city folk, in addition to being a little more lonely, are also demonstrably less helpful to their fellow citizens, as compared to the "idiots" Marx perceived in the countryside. In a clever demonstration of this fact, psychologist Stanley Milgram and colleagues placed phone calls to people in New York, Philadelphia, and Chicago, as well as to people in small towns in the corresponding states. The caller pretended to have dialed the wrong long-distance number, and started the call by expressing curiosity, because of upcoming travel plans, about the weather in the call recipient's area. The caller then said, "Please hold on" and put the phone down for one minute. If the recipient was still on the line, the caller inquired about hotels in the local area. Researchers rated the helpfulness of call recipients on a scale that ranged from "hung up immediately" to "cooperated fully with all requests." Small-town call recipients scored more toward the "cooperated fully" end of the range than did big-city dwellers. Helpfulness and openness are spurs to togetherness and thus antidotes to loneliness.

My research group noticed this same phenomenon in a recent study on "lost letters"—a technique, as it happens, also borne of the fertile mind of psychologist Stanley Milgram. The technique is used to unobtrusively assess the public mood on controversial or sensitive topics, and involves intentionally "losing" letters that are pre-addressed and stamped. I'll describe what my research group did using this technique in Tallahassee shortly, but first, to get a sense of the approach, consider the following example. A third of a set of letters are addressed to, say, the Democratic Party, a third to the Republican Party, and a third to the Communist Party; all addresses have a P.O. box that is the same for all letters and returns to the researchers themselves. The researchers know how many letters they "lost," can count how many are returned, and thus can compute a percentage of returned letters based on whether the address was "Democratic," "Republican," or "Communist." The assumption is that if people go out of their way to make sure a lost letter finds its way back into the postal system, they have, on average, some care about the topic in question, and thus a higher percentage of return reflects a more positive public mood about the topic. For example, were one to run the "Democratic" versus "Republican" versus "Communist" lost-letter study, approximately equal percentages of "Democratic" and "Republican" letters would find their way back to the researchers' P.O. box, whereas a much lower proportion of "Communist" letters would, reflecting current public opinion.

Our lost letter study was on public attitudes to suicide prevention, and we found the encouraging result that as many letters addressed to a suicide prevention organization were returned as letters addressed to comparison organizations focused on things like heart disease and diabetes.[49] For the present discussion on the geographical distribution of things like helpfulness, however, that is beside the point. What is very much on point is how high the overall return rate was in the Tallahassee, Florida region. Nearly 70 percent of the six hundred letters we "lost"—and it should be noted we "lost" them in areas of Tallahassee that are representative of the local population regarding things like income, age, ethnicity and so on—found their way back to us, whereas in similar studies in the northeastern United States, for example, far lower overall return rates are observed (around 40 percent is usual). Southern hospitality, it turns out, is demonstrable in many ways. This attitude, common in small town America and not just in the South, is a conduit for connection and thus a bulwark against loneliness.

The point is relative: it is, of course, not the case that people in big cities do not help one another at all. In fact, researchers demonstrated that they do, in an interesting experiment in the New York City subway system, alluded to earlier. A member of a research team would approach people riding the subway, and flat out ask them, without further explanation, "Excuse me, may I have your seat?" The research team produced the startling result that nearly two out of three people were cooperative with the request, either giving their seat up outright, or scooting over to make more room.

LARGE CITIES DO NOT necessarily lend themselves to a simple lifestyle. It is tempting, particularly to those who are drawn to sophistication, to be dismissive of simple things and their surprising effects. This is a dangerous attitude, however, and one that can even prove fatal. The shuffling off of this attitude seemed to be a key factor in Eric Wilson's overcoming mental disorder (which very nearly occasioned his death by suicide). Referring to the temptation to dismiss simple things, he wrote, "I pushed against this temptation and learned that the most pervasive cliché of all—the simplest things are the most pleasurable—had an unexpected profundity. In relinquishing my crude distinction between high and low, elegant and ordinary, subtle and obvious, I found that common experiences, such as playing with one's child, can become, if attended to imaginatively and energetically, endlessly engaging."[50] This author makes an important distinction: simple things do not mean effortless things (nor do they mean clichés). Learning to put forth effort—in simple things and in relationship maintenance—is an essential dimension of solutions for the lonely sex.

SOME SOLUTIONS TO MALE LONELINESS are touched on above: a phone call to someone every day; reunions; sleep regularization; and connecting to nature. A spin on immersion in nature was mentioned in a recent article. The author wrote, "A couple of years ago, a pair of sociologists followed shoppers, first around a supermarket and then around a farmers' market. They found that at the latter, shoppers had *ten times* more conversations than at the Piggly-Wiggly."[51] A specific and doable mini-solution, where available, then: go to farmers' markets.

Relatedly, and also a version of the connecting to nature solution, I recently started growing cucumbers in my backyard (another activity that puts me in occasional contact with our neighbors). This can be a solitary activity at times, when the neighbors are not out, but it is important to keep in mind a key aspect of the connecting to nature solution: being alone and connecting to nature is better than just being alone. Moreover, dabbling in gardening has given me another thing to talk about with others, especially others who do not find my pet interests (sports, beer, work) as fascinating as I do. Some people are very passionate about gardening, and thus become interested in and animated toward anyone who can talk at all knowledgeably about fertilizer, pest control, and the like.

Still in the domain of a love for the natural world, and a clear example of taking a bad, unhealthy habit and shaping it to have at least some healthful aspects, it is possible to grow your own tobacco, though of course this is easier to do in some regions of the United States (e.g., Maryland, Virginia, North Carolina) than others (and of course it is not healthful to smoke tobacco, though growing it is another matter). Some are surprised by the idea of growing tobacco, but of course it is a plant, and it is perfectly legal to grow and use your own tobacco (though it is illegal to grow and sell your own tobacco, untaxed). And there are advantages to doing so, including the avoidance of additives and of paying the ever increasing cost of a pack at the store. Needless to say, my counsel about tobacco is to quit it altogether; but for committed smokers, especially ones who are lonely, my counsel would be to grow your own, and to reap the several benefits, including biophilic benefits, as well as those derived from talking shop with other smokers and other people who tend gardens. Notice, also, the appeal of something like growing one's own tobacco to someone partial to "don't tread on me" attitudes.

Staying with the theme of taking a potential vice and turning it into a hobby—a hobby that is engaging in and of itself but is also a way to relate to others who share that particular interest—beer- and wine-making are activities that also impart intrinsic pleasure, capitalize on nature in action (in this case the natural action of yeast), serve as a basis to relate to others, and appeal to "don't tread on me" types. I have dabbled in this, too, and am impressed by the vistas of conversations and social events it opens up.

If, for weeks or longer, not just for a day or two or three, an extremely lonely person takes the counsel of this chapter—heed the power of the natural world and a daily phone call, to take two feasible and demonstrably effective examples—the person will be nudged out of loneliness. This is a high virtue, given the scourge that loneliness represents. More ornate approaches have been recommended—psychoanalysis, for instance—as have simple approaches—do unto others, for example. But ornate things will not work (unless you are interested in them for their own sake, in which case, you are probably not terribly lonely, or else addressing loneliness would be your priority); neither will advice that is lacking in specifics and is thus overly simplistic. There is an "eat-your-vegetables" quality to things that actually work, at least in this domain, and there is a reason that parents exhort kids to eat their vegetables, as abundant research shows. The advice of this chapter is sufficient as a nudge, but in the next chapter, I identify still a few more "vegetables."

8

SOLUTIONS

REALISTIC WAYS TO CONNECT TO OTHERS

Silence and other forms of interpersonal disconnection can be deranging, even fatal, as the preceding chapters have shown. Not all have endorsed this view. In the book *Politics, Philosophy, and Culture,* historian and philosopher Michel Foucault stated, "I think silence is one of these things that has unfortunately been dropped from our culture. We don't have a culture of silence . . . I'm in favor of developing silence as a cultural ethos."[1] I'm not much impressed with the famous philosopher's thinking generally, and I disagree in particular with a general cultural emphasis on silence. But, it is not hard for me to imagine that, with all the talking that undoubtedly surrounded a figure like Foucault, he craved silence. In this one specific thing, he and I would see eye to eye. We might also agree on the value—really a sacred privilege—of being left in peace to read, think, and write. As one who tries to do a lot of these activities, and who has two sons and more than two pets streaming in and out of the office where I attempt to read, think, and write, I get the impulse toward the hagiography of solitude that Foucault advocated. But, for a very advantaged academic like him to elevate silence to a cultural value is akin to a billionaire bemoaning wealth and averring that everyone should have less money.

A recent article advises, "Silence is 'something that we can do!' It is something that we can seek. We decide what we listen to every day. There are hundreds of noises to catch our attention, and we selectively attend to those which we deem important. What if we came to see that silence was something important to search for? What if we came to believe that we had the right, and I would even suggest the 'responsibility' to create a balance of silence/noise in our lives?"[2] Another article sounded a similar note—one that I know plays well in academia but that I think rings very false in many other settings: "On the journey of life, no real progress can be made without making the time for reflection. Solitude is essential. It gives us the time and opportunity to explore and know ourselves."[3] The equation of progress with "exploring and knowing ourselves" is stated as if those two things are obviously the same. From many clinical and other experiences, I can assure you that they are at least as often antonyms as they are synonyms, and that a self-congratulatory navel-gazing attitude is very often an active impediment to what most would regard as progress of any kind.

Still another article claimed that, "Without loneliness, life ceases to exist."[4] These words show a lack of even faint acquaintance with genuine misery.

Philosopher Foucault and the authors of these articles are united in their regret that silence has been dropped from our culture; one should be careful of what one asks for. Silence can kill. The Korean word *muksal* means "to kill with silence," and it was the tactic used by North Korean dictator Kim Jong Il to display his displeasure when a pro-American candidate won the South Korean presidency in 2007. The North Korean regime simply kept silent about the event for many weeks—an attempt to kill with silence, figuratively (which, as with much of what the North Korean leadership does, was not particularly effective). The author Octavio Paz said, "Man is the only being who knows he is alone"—achieving two profound misunderstandings with considerable parsimony.[5] Man is *not* alone, or is at least not optimally, when thriving and healthy. And try convincing a socially isolated non-human primate that it should buck up, that it doesn't know it is alone—you will fail. It knows it in its bones and cells, and its aloneness will be reflected in its emotion, behavior, immune function, and other health indices, too, because, like us, the non-human primate is wired for gregariousness (as are many other animals).

One psychoanalytic perspective on loneliness argues that people need more time alone and claims that "we are already versed in the grim fears associated with being alone."[6] On the contrary, I don't think we're versed enough. These writers represent a subgenre of thought on the virtues of solitude and silence, but all seemed either unaware or insufficiently appreciative of the problems and even catastrophes that silence can cause, both figurative and literal. To take a literal example, a Midwestern man's wife left him, which pained him so much that he withdrew from family and friends and became depressed to the point of incapacitation. He has silence, and plenty of it.

In fact, he spent his last days in silence, and killed himself on his farm. This is a true case, far removed from cultural criticism and philosophy. One of the articles just alluded to advised, "The discipline of solitude and silence is a crucial component in a healthy life. Learn to embrace it."[7] There may indeed be people for whom this is sound advice—for whom silence and solitude are actively helpful—but it is certain that there are others for whom this advice would produce laughter, if only they had retained the capacity to laugh (which the man on the farm almost certainly did not retain and which many people with severe forms of depression do not retain). One recent article gets this issue right; the author states, "Silence is sometimes torture, as much as noise is."[8]

The body of the man on the farm was not found for days. This grim fact brings to mind an anecdote from a quite different context, described in a book on former prisoners of Stalin's Gulag, one of whom was married in her sixties, post-Gulag, and discussed the experience with an interviewer.[9] Having herself witnessed fellow prisoners left for days after they died, she said "At least when you're married, someone will bury you straight away." This is not necessarily the most ringing endorsement of marriage, but there is wisdom in the statement—the kind of care that persists even after death is sustaining indeed in life.

The philosopher Foucault's error—mistaking a thought that happened to have occurred to him for something generally true or profound, with no rigorous and systematic way to tell the difference—is a common one, particularly in some corners of the academy. A related mistake is to postulate as a universal truth something that is merely an individual's temperamental preference, such as a preference for (relative) solitude. Very intricate thoughts on the part of theorists like Foucault, especially those unmoored from the lived lives of general folk—including those on farms in the American Midwest—are thus likely to be unhelpful in addressing the trouble of male loneliness. Some such ideas, moreover, are not just inertly unhelpful but actively misleading. Consider an example from a psychoanalytic treatise on the need for solitude. The passage begins in a distinctly unpromising way: "Putting aside Darwinian perpetuation of the species . . ." I have learned that whatever follows openings that are in any way dismissive of Darwin's ideas is not going to be especially illuminating. The passage continues, "the death instinct is on a day-to-day level best understood as the need to balance the stress of perpetual connectedness to outside stimuli with a restorative aloneness."[10]

Despite weed-like proliferation of claims to the contrary, there is no death instinct, and even if there were, why would it have anything to do with the fact that people occasionally need to rest? My approach throughout this book has been to tend toward the simple, the down-to-earth. I understand that this approach does not suit everyone's temperament; I observe this fact every day in clinical settings among patients and clinicians alike. Ideas like "silence as a cultural value" and "the death instinct" may be sophisticated, but that is not worth the price of misunderstanding human nature.

IN THE SAME PIECE alluded to in the last chapter regarding farmer's markets, the author states, "We eat far fewer meals with family and neighbors than we did fifty years ago."[11] Here, then, is another mini-solution, and one that is certainly doable. Our next-door neighbors invited us over for dinner. During the evening, it emerged that I and my neighbors are both on Facebook. We promised to try to remember to "friend" each other on the site, one of us remembered, and we're now Facebook friends. Our houses were maybe thirty feet apart, but after that, I "saw" our neighbors on Facebook far more frequently than I do around the literal neighborhood, a point to which I will return. Our neighbors have since moved to another house in the same neighborhood, about a half-mile from our house—a trivial difference in some contexts, but enough of one to assure that I now never see them . . . except on Facebook.

Is it hopelessly idealistic, even naïve, to expect families to eat dinner together more, to chat more on suburban or urban sidewalks, or even on virtual ones? The charge of naïve idealism is a serious one to the project I am urging in this book, and there are certainly ways to go about connecting to others that are hokey or otherwise unworkable. But on this, I agree with a recent article's assertion that, "Age-old human wisdom has understood that a life well-lived requires engagement with those around us. That is reality, not idealism. It is appropriate to think that a political Great Awakening among the elites can arise in part from the renewed understanding that it can be pleasant to lead a glossy life, but it is ultimately more fun to lead a textured life, and to be in the midst of others who are leading textured lives . . . that requires once again seeing the American project for what it is: a different way for people to live together, unique among the nations of the earth, and immeasurably precious."[12]

I am a member of a group of seven friends, all connected to the university where I work, all men in their forties, fifties, and sixties, and every time we get together (on average once a week), Anheuser-Busch stockholders get richer. We do not engage in particularly healthful activities together—cigars can also be involved, for instance—but a very telling fact is that our wives, without exception, openly encourage our drinking sessions. Do they want to get rid of us for an evening? Perhaps that plays a role, but I think it's mostly that they see friendship's positive effects on us—our moods are better, we are less in our own little worlds after we get home and for a while afterwards, too. Our wives don't want us to drink more—some of them want the opposite—but they want us to interact regularly, because they know it's good for us, and thus for them and our families. The drinking is worth it to them. I've already implied another telling fact, incidentally: each of us is married, and has been, for a minimum of ten years.

I can tell essentially the same story about my high-school friends. We get together about annually (e.g., at the Indy 500), we do not act very healthfully, and our wives all encourage it. Every one of this group of around ten is married and has been for over ten years—a reasonably remarkable fact given usual divorce rates of approximately 50 percent.

These two groups of mine illustrate the "something bad turned good" principle, but also dispel a myth, popular among some men, along the lines of "my wife would never go for that." On the contrary. She'll not only allow it, she will encourage and like it, because your improved state of mind—and the positive ripple effects on the marriage and the family—are easily worth it to her.

In addition to being a member of these two groups of friends, there are others, too, and one of them is made up of all the guys I play soccer with these days. If friends are ready made in third grade and in Little League baseball, it stands to reason that they would be as well in the weekly, over-forty soccer game. Just show up most weeks, and a year later, you're friends with several, a version of club-joining (also a productive strategy). Showing up is a tried-and-true recipe for success, and one main reason is that it sets the stage for making friends.

Reunions with friends can be powerful. This fact is amply demonstrated by psychiatrist Larry Dewey in his excellent book on combat veterans, *War and Redemption*. Writing specifically about reunions after combat—but I think the words are applicable to reunions generally—the psychiatrist stated that reunions "give the original events a new and healthier meaning. They often bring some clarity, peace, and release."[13] A veteran said of a reunion with brothers-in-arms, "During the three days we were together, it seemed we never stopped talking. There is no question we all felt a release of old pressures."[14] Of the effects of reunions, the psychiatrist continued, "Memories are processed and better understood. Friendships are reaffirmed. Grief is displayed and processed. Hearts are eased."[15]

This psychiatrist is not referring to group therapy (though he advocates this as well for those who struggle with combat experiences).

He is not even referring necessarily to reunions during which painful experiences are constantly rehashed. He is writing, rather, about fellowship. One can feel this fellowship even when alone (albeit in attenuated form). I have already mentioned a novelist friend who claimed not to have much need or interest to be around people, which claim I disputed by reminding her she spends hours per day steeped in the lives of the people she is writing about. Philip Roth was interviewed about his new novel *Nemesis*.[16] Asked about his choice not to write from the point of view of just one character, Roth, who like my friend writes alone several hours per day, answered, "I liked the we, and the our, and the us in the telling. The whole community is being represented."

If my own experiences of "the we, and the our, and the us" are at all representative—for example, a weekend gathering at a lake house after a friend's wife had succumbed to a long illness; a road trip to a ballgame with several friends, one of whom needed time away from troubles at home—immersion in struggle and pain is not necessary. In fact, it can chase some men off. What is necessary is simply one another's presence; in most cases, not all, a sense of companionship emerges organically. An unstated understanding develops, along the lines of "we're here with one another having fun at this game/this show/this casino/this whatever" therefore "we'll be with one another in the future" and therefore "we'll be here for one another in times of need." Genuine friendship is the crucible in which this companionship emerges best, but as we will see, even surprisingly fleeting relationships may have some effect.

It is a legitimate question as to whether such experiences are enough to make a real difference in peoples' lives. I believe that this question has been definitively answered in the affirmative, and the answer comes from the "caring letters" study.[17] This study—landmark but in my view underappreciated—included several thousand people hospitalized due to suicidal thoughts or behaviors, or because of depression. About a month after patients were discharged from the hospital, they were contacted to gauge their interest in ongoing outpatient treatment as a follow-up to their inpatient hospitalization. Such follow-up, recent thinking and data indicate, is absolutely essential to good mental health care, in part because the timeframe following release from psychiatric hospitalization is a documented window of elevated suicide risk. As often happens, however, many people declined ongoing care (techniques to enhance the likelihood that people will pursue continued treatment—which can mean the difference between avoiding rehospitalization and indeed between life and death—are a frontier of current mental health research). The participants in the "caring letters" study included all those who declined ongoing care.

It is worth reiterating how high risk these patients were, on average. They had experienced a very recent psychiatric hospitalization, in itself a marker of severity of illness and thus of heightened suicide risk. Moreover, they had refused ongoing treatment, which not only indicates that they would miss the active benefits of ongoing care, but also that they would not have ongoing contact with someone who could evaluate any re-escalation of risk and intervene accordingly. Further still, by virtue of their turning down care, the patients had engaged in "help negation," a behavior shown by past research to be predictive of relatively poor clinical course.

All study participants therefore had some things working against them. One might imagine, then, that only an intensive and extensive intervention would make any difference. A plausible assumption, but wrong, as we will see.

Patients were randomly assigned to one of two groups. Nothing was done for one group, an approach that might produce some ethical concern, a concern perhaps allayed somewhat by remembering that patients in this group had already been offered—and had declined—follow-up treatment. The other group, also composed of people who had been invited to and declined subsequent treatment, received a "caring letter" in the mail, a few times per year for around five years.

The letters were brief, consisting of three to four sentences that expressed interest in patients' well-being and contained reminders that treatment was available should patients decide to pursue it. The letters, moreover, were individualized, usually personally signed by a health-care professional with whom the patient had interacted when in the hospital, and efforts were made to word each successive letter slightly differently. Some letters included responses to any questions or comments made to previous letters, and all letters included an envelope, unstamped, with the researchers' address.

The researchers believed that caring would be an active antidote to suicidal crisis, and they calculated that, if notes were not sufficiently personalized, they would not convey the proper sense of care (a reasonable assumption, but as we will see, a subsequent study shows that it may be a questionable assumption). Their definition of the crucial variable of caring was "a feeling of being joined to something meaningful outside oneself as a stabilizing force in emotional life."[18] This definition emphasizes, it should be noticed, mutuality over autonomy. On the point of caring as an effective antidote, the researchers wrote "[an earlier paper] expressed this concept clearly after recounting suicide prevention measures over 600 years and contemplating what is really new, observing that 'there is surely at least one common theme through the centuries—it is the provision of human contact, the comfort of another concerned person, often authoritative but maybe not, conveying a message of hope consonant with the assumptions and values relevant to that particular time.'"[19] As noted in chapter 1, John Sym made this same point in a book published in 1637.

Caring matters. Even a small bit can have noticeable effects: patients who received the letter had a lower suicide rate in the five-year interval after discharge as compared to patients in the control group. The only other study to date on a clinical intervention, subjected to a randomized controlled trial, that has produced an effect on deaths by suicide also involved caring follow-up contact.[20]

I raised the question of whether relatively insignificant experiences of interpersonal connection can nonetheless have detectable effects on well-being. The "caring letters" study is one of the clearest demonstrations that they can.

As small a dose of treatment as an occasional brief letter is, it is possible that still smaller doses have positive consequences. A study from Australia replicated many of the features of the "caring letters" study, but changed some aspects, too.[21] More specifically, the letters were not personalized; in fact, they were not even letters—they were automated postcards. Beyond the recipients' name and address, the postcards had no personalized features at all and contained no reference to previous comments or questions patients may have had. What they did contain was computerized statements like "we hope you are doing well, and want to remind you that we are here if you need us." In a charming wrinkle, each postcard also contained a simple computer-generated image of a happy-looking dog.

The caring automated postcards worked: vulnerable people who received them engaged in fewer suicidal behaviors than did those who got no postcards (and several participants commented favorably on the image of the happy dog). It is as if our receptiveness to caring is on a hair trigger, perhaps not fully sated by very small doses, but sufficiently satisfied to make a detectable difference. (I am aware, incidentally, of an ongoing study of this same sort, on "caring texts.")

I began the discussion of the studies on caring letters and postcards as a reply to the question "can small social connections really make a difference?" Before I return to my affirmative answer to that question, I want to first situate the discussion within the hard contours of reality. The argument here is emphatically not the Pollyanna-ish or utopian one of "let's just all get along better and/or be a little nicer and paradise will descend." Earlier, when referring to the slow and steady cultivation of virtue by, day in and day out, acting virtuously and thus developing virtuous habits, I drew an analogy to sandpaper and wood: sandpapering does not change wood's essential structure, but it nevertheless has important and easily noticeable effects. The analogy applies as well to the effects of caring on social alienation in men and indeed in everyone: something like caring letters is not proposed as a full cure for things like profound loneliness, depression, and the like. Rather, it is proposed as something that will take the edge off those things, making life more bearable in the short term, and giving the chance for natural processes of social connection to kick in and improve things further in the long term. Don't doubt that caring can do at least these things: the findings from the caring letters studies suggest that a touch of caring took some catastrophically suicidal people from the precipice of death itself to a safer place.

Very small instances of connection can make a significant difference. The caring letters/postcards studies showed this, as did a study
done at the beach. Researchers had actors place their beach towels a
few yards from beachgoers; the actors set themselves up in the usual
way, including placing an expensive-looking device to play music near
their area. In half of such scenarios, the actors were instructed to make
pleasant yet very brief small talk with nearby beachgoers, and then pre-
tend to doze off to sleep. For the other half, all was similar, except that
the actors were instructed to ignore everyone nearby.

In all cases, after the actors were seemingly asleep, the researchers
had other actors sneak up and steal the music player in a rather obvious
way. The researchers were interested in the reactions of the beachgoers
to the theft. Redeemingly, in most instances following the small talk—
which again was of the most fleeting nature—beachgoers intervened.
But beachgoers were much more likely to ignore the theft happening to
actors who had ignored them. As in the caring letters/postcards studies,
the briefest of connections made all the difference.

I AM NOT ONLY A member of various groups of friends, but also of my family
of origin, with whom I have found it somewhat difficult to stay connected, much more so actually than with friends. But Facebook helped.
The entire point of Facebook is social connection, and many people, including a growing number of people over forty, can attest that it works.
Eighteen months ago, I was not on Facebook, and thought I never
would be. Now, I check the site daily, and I have hundreds of Facebook
friends, many of whom are high-school friends whom I invited to join,
and who in turn invited others; many are my cousins and other relatives. For any of my friends or family who think it's "too young" for
them, I shame them into joining by telling a true story: my mom is now
on Facebook, and loves it—of course she does, she's "friends" there
with her children and grandchildren.

Facebook can be like a newspaper, made personal to you, and
brought to life. Updates on your friends' and relatives' lives are served
up by the minute, easy to read in detail or to skip over at your pleasure,

just like with the newspaper. And as with the newspaper, there are an-
nouncements of gatherings and events around town, some of which
I've gone to and enjoyed and would not have known about without
Facebook. This analogy to a newspaper is of interest for another reason: recall the study noted earlier of ten or so daily activities happy
people tended to do more than unhappy people. One was reading the
newspaper.

Facebook and similar sites have a pitfall that needs to be avoided,
and it's that virtual contact with others should supplement, but not
replace, actual interpersonal contact. In his book *Compulsive Acts,* psychiatrist Elias Aboujaoude documents an extreme form of this problem. A man and his fiancée approached the psychiatrist for treatment
for the man's obsessive use of a "second life" kind of website, one in
which people create virtual identities, with lives, families, and so forth,
and live a virtual life through the character. The fiancée was concerned
about the man's connection to his virtual life in general, and the attendant disconnection from actual life, and she was worried in particular
about the man's relationship with a virtual woman. Her concern was
very well founded; despite the psychiatrist's treatment efforts, the man
dropped out of treatment and separated from his actual wife-to-be in
favor of the virtual woman.

An increasing number of virtual friendships are available, and not
necessarily all have the dysfunctional qualities of the case just alluded
to. A smartphone app called "Honey, it's me!" calls the phone's owner
three or four times a day, and provides the owner with a pre-recorded
video conversation from a virtual girlfriend. The girlfriend is an actress,
who recorded over a hundred brief conversations for the app, such as
"I saw a horror movie today and I'm so scared. I miss you honey! Good
night, I will see you in my dreams." Hundreds of thousands of people
have downloaded the app. Teens and young adults can arrange for automated parental tweets from Twitter, along the lines of "Where are
you now? It's almost midnight. Mom is getting upset." These tweets are
not coming from the actual parents, but from a computer program. A
recent article ran with the following lead: "A ROBOT that can fall in
love with its owner could put an end to millions of lonely hearts across

the globe."[22] The robot looks like a large pillow, and is equipped with sensors that make it react to touch and to skin temperature. Its inventor stated, "People already bury themselves in possessions and shield themselves from real life with technology. So if robots and objects can fulfill all their emotional needs as well, why do they need other humans?"

As if in reply, an article was posted two days later, the headline of which read "Gadgets 'No Substitute for Talking.'"[23] The article quoted a psychologist who said, "Gadget to gadget is fine, provided it doesn't replace face to face." He continued, "In fact gadget to gadget comes into its own when it's used to arrange face to face. That way people get the best of both worlds—a digital fix followed by the rich rewards of human company."

The pope would agree, at least about the need for face-to-face human contact. In a 2010 conference at the Vatican, Pope Benedict XVI warned that the Internet is responsible for the "state of emergency regarding education," and that it can increase "feelings of loneliness and disorientation." In previous statements, the pope has expressed concern about the dangerous effects of new technologies because they blur the line between reality and fantasy. It is easy to imagine this latter notion being satirized in the *Onion* or some similar outlet, and I know my sons would find it hilarious, but the pope probably is on to something here, as illustrated by the case of the man who lost his real fiancée because of his virtual wife

As mentioned in chapter 3, over the last twenty or so years the number of people who report having no confidant has tripled. It is worth emphasizing that this same time period has witnessed an explosion in social media technology, suggesting that the latter is by no means a full solution to the problem of loneliness.

The inventor of the "affection robot" alluded to above posed a question: Why do we need other humans if the robots will suffice? The pope thinks they do not suffice. Who is right?

Even the most innovative of robot inventers is highly unlikely to outdo the results of eons of evolutionary progress. We have very complex and delicate circuitry when it comes to social things like face recognition and gazing into one another's eyes.

Researchers showed that two- to five-day-old babies are interested in mutual gaze, and that four-month-old babies' brains react differently to direct than to averted gaze. The researchers concluded that "The exceptionally early sensitivity to mutual gaze demonstrated in these studies is arguably the major foundation for the later development of social skills."[24] It is unlikely to be a coincidence that, in mental disorders such as autism and schizophrenia that profoundly affect social behavior, abnormalities in eye contact and gaze are very common.

Recognition of fear in others' faces is also of obvious evolutionary import. There is a brain structure called the superior colliculus that becomes active in monkeys when they look at snakes and in humans when they see fearful faces. "The ability to detect fear in others' faces has undoubtedly been helpful for survival and it may be mediated by so-called mirror, or empathy, neurons."[25] Problems with these very same neurons represent a prominent explanation of the causes of autism, a syndrome, alluded to in an earlier chapter, characterized by out-of-tune social sensors.

It is important not just to recognize fear in others' faces, but also to be able to quickly perceive the source of the danger. We and other primates are very skilled at this activity; we have automatic systems that allow us to track the direction of others' gazes. You can see this for yourself if a conversational partner suddenly looks away from you toward something else; it is extremely difficult to suppress your own urge to look at the thing, too. Attunement is essential for healthy social functioning, and problems in attunement characterize some groups more than others. One such group, as this book argues, is men.

These systems for fear detection and following gaze are, like most that are essential to functioning, hard to derail. For example, there are people who have a condition called prosopagnosia, sometimes referred to as "face blindness." Those who suffer from the condition are unable to recognize faces, even of people they know well like family and friends. They may even have difficulty recognizing themselves. Neurologist Oliver Sacks has the condition and related a story of wondering why a man on the other side of a café window was mimicking him, until, many seconds later, he realized it was his own reflection—he had trouble recognizing even his own face.[26] One might imagine that people who cannot recognize a face may have trouble with related activities such as detecting the emotion conveyed in facial expression. In many people with the condition, however, the ability to follow another's gaze or to read the emotion on someone's face is completely intact. Like circulation and respiration, following gaze and recognizing emotion are deep systems, difficult (though not impossible) to disrupt.

The underlying wiring is so complex, based as it is on millions of years of evolutionary tinkering, that robots or any such thing will be hard-pressed to match it. There are, however, alternatives that might also be called artificial but that may have more traction.

There is a website called "rentafriend," from which you can literally rent a friend. The site's creators are careful to distinguish it from dating or sex sites and claim that over three-hundred-thousand friends are available for rent worldwide. "Tele-talks" is a similar concept, geared toward regular, supportive phone calls from a trained, caring person. A call per day runs approximately $569 per year. One of the banners that pops up on its website reads, "You're not alone. No more loneliness."

I would certainly understand a skeptical or even dismissive reaction to such services, but I would not be quick to demean them. Our readiness to connect to others is, like our abilities to follow another's gaze and to read facial expression, deep. Just as the air we breathe has to be good enough but not perfect for survival and thriving, so relating has to be just good enough. And services like "rentafriend" might suffice.

A VERY COMMON RESPONSE from patients who are asked to engage in behavioral activation is "there's nothing to do around here." This reaction is analogous to that in response to the "call a friend" remedy, "there's no one to call." Yes, there is someone to call, and yes, there is something to do around here. I live in Tallahassee; you will not find a more loyal, pro-Tallahassee Tallahasseean, but even I acknowledge that it is not a huge metropolis. But it doesn't matter: there are dozens if not hundreds of things to do around town, and we keep a list of them handy in the clinic I direct, to combat the "there's nothing to do" malaise. And, to combat the "yeah, but I don't have any money to do things" malaise, we put a star next to all of the activities that are free (over half are).

Try this. Pick a university near you, and pull up its master calendar, the one that has all of the university's various activities compiled into one calendar. It is a challenge to find a single day on which there is nothing to do, usually free of charge. Master calendars are not unique to universities; cities, community organizations, and religious organizations, among others, all have them, too.

As shown by the "caring letters" study, small bits of socializing are important in and of themselves—as are minor interactions with the biosphere; in fact, they *are* minor interactions with the biosphere— they tend to add up, and, though I am not aware of scientific evidence on this point, it is my view that they add up more in an exponential than additive fashion. In her book *The Call of Solitude,* Ester Schaler Buchholz mentions the "odd and surprising relationships that form in prison from an exchange of a blink of an eye through cell windows or a prison guard's kindness."[27] Caring is to humans as a spark is to kindling; it does not take much of the one to light up the other. One of the "New Rules for Men" in a popular magazine reads "An elevator is the only place where a man should be aloof."[28] Many men confuse aloofness with a masculine laconicism; the former is mean whereas the latter is not.

Aloof men rarely apologize. Apology is, at least in our culture, an underappreciated art form—though at least one recent psychotherapy has incorporated a specific emphasis on apology. (Not coincidentally in my view, this therapy, called dialectical-behavior therapy, has been shown to be effective for people with marked interpersonal problems.) Consider the key ingredients of sincere apology (as opposed to apology in a begrudging form, or its opposite, the apology that is so ready that it loses its currency). First, apology requires perspective-taking: one can't really apologize well without understanding the effects of one's actions from the aggrieved person's viewpoint. Perspective-taking, and its close cousin empathy, set conditions for interpersonal connection. Second, apology sends the implicit message that maintaining a good relationship is valuable enough that it is worth any discomfort or awkwardness that apology may provoke; it is worth setting aside pride and anger (and that is saying something). Third, it implies trust—an apology says, "I can usually be trusted to do the right thing, and when I don't, to acknowledge it and make amends." Fourth, a sincere apology implies community—we are all the same in the sense that we are all imperfect, and therefore will occasionally need to apologize. And finally, apology implies an interpersonal atmosphere that tolerates imperfection but that adheres nevertheless to, as it were, "the rule of law."

Apology takes two to tango; that is to say, an apology proffered but not accepted does not as a rule yield the benefits enumerated above. As my friends and I were approaching our usual seats at a recent FSU football game, I was certain that a person—as it happens, a man of about fifty years of age and of a somewhat aloof nature, as I came to learn—was sitting in our seats. I told him so with an attitude that I think was friendly but fairly firm. He reacted very badly; he was evidently insulted and became insulting. I nevertheless insisted and asked that we all check our tickets. We did, and he was in the right seat, directly adjacent to ours. He was right; I was wrong . . . which I told him, apologetically. He fumed in response. We all took our seats, and a question arose in the minds of my friends and me: Who would sit directly next to our new, surly (and correct) neighbor? I rushed to do it myself because, though I really didn't want to, I especially didn't want my friends to have to. I had started the whole thing after all. And so I took the seat right next to him—these are bleacher seats, so he and I were sitting cheek to jowl— thigh to thigh would be more accurate—in the crowded stadium.

At this stage of the story, I had issued a sincere apology, but none of the benefits I listed above had accrued, because the apology had not yet been accepted. I resigned myself to the fact that this was how things were going to remain, and that I would watch the game trying to forget about the incident, but being unable to as the guy was right next to me. After a tense several minutes, he turned to me, extended his hand, and said "Sorry we got off to a bad start." I replied, "Me too. It was my fault to begin with," and with that, apology's benefits kicked in: understanding, trust, camaraderie.

Comedian Jim Belushi put out a 2006 book called *Real Men Don't Apologize*. Research has documented that, in fact, men do apologize less than women do—but, contrary to the message implicit in Belushi's title, this is to men's peril, because they lose out on apology's multiple dividends.

A major thesis of Thomas P. M. Barnett's *The Pentagon's New Map* is that "Eradicating disconnectedness" is "the defining security task of our age." He goes on, "by expanding the connectivity of globalization, we increase peace and prosperity planet-wide."[29] What, in Barnett's analysis, applies to the planet, applies, in my analysis, to the person, including, but not limited to, the planet's millions of lonely men.

SECTION IV

CONCLUSION

9

ON SEXISM, UNIVERSALITY, AND THE FUTURE

In his *Character and Opinion in the United States*, George Santayana wrote, "I speak of the American in the singular, as if there were not millions of them, north and south, east and west, of both sexes, of all ages, and of various races, professions, and religions. Of course the one American I speak of is mythical; but to speak in parables is inevitable in such a subject, and it is perhaps as well to do so frankly."[1] My book is a parable of the lonely man, a creature who is a mythical abstraction. Abstractions, however, can be true; in fact, the good ones, like $e = mc^2$, distill truth in to its purest form.

The lonely man depicted in this book is a true abstraction, not as pure as Einstein's equation, but pure enough. More than the individual man, I have described a set of tendencies that characterize men more than women, and some men more than other men. That these are true tendencies is corroborated by their appearance in domains as disparate as psychological scientific studies, the lives and deaths of financial analysts and Midwestern farmers, finger lengths, waist-to-hip ratios, writings of various people over the centuries, and the symbolism and imagery inherent in such American iconography as the Gadsden flag's rattlesnake.

There is a sense in which this book is sexist, in that it broadly stereotypes a group of people based on their gender. That group of people is men. In two other ways, however, the book is not sexist in the least. First, consider the nature of the book's broad stereotype. It hardly trumpets male virtues; on the contrary, it elucidates the character of male weakness and vulnerability. But neither is it derogatory toward men; it seeks to understand them and help them. Second, the processes and issues covered in the book—the consequences of loneliness, maladaptive and adaptive reactions, and so on—are universal in nature. As the book shows, they are more common in men. But they are not fully unique to them. It is therefore the case that anyone, of either gender, can suffer—and learn from—the plight of the lonely sex.

The book has focused on gender, but it might have also focused on the intersection of gender and ethnicity. An empirical touchstone for the work has been suicide rates; that is, the fact that men vastly outnumber women in the category of suicide decedents signals something of importance, something, I argue, heretofore given too little attention. That thing, of course, is accelerating male loneliness across the lifespan. But within the category of men, there is one ethnicity that is quite disproportionately represented among those who die by suicide, and that ethnicity is Caucasian. Regarding all of the book's claims—that men are lonelier than women; that this is fueled by phenomena like disharmony between emotional and social loneliness sensors, becoming spoiled, "don't tread on me" attitudes, overfixation on status and money, and "lonely at the top" experiences; that the consequences range from deteriorated health to an interest in NASCAR—it can be argued that the story is that of white men especially.

The comedian Louis C.K. (who is white) said he talked on the phone regularly with his friend and fellow comedian Chris Rock (who is African American), and Rock would often joke, "What's it like being white today, still great?" He responded, "Oh, it's great Chris, you have no idea, I mean, I can walk down the street and cops are friendly to me."[2] This is one of a sea of anecdotes that can be marshaled to show that, of all the combinations of gender and race, white men are subject to the "becoming spoiled" trajectory traced in chapter 2. And not just that trajectory; the other processes delineated in the book tend to apply more to men than to women, and more to white men than to men of color.

We need not rely on anecdote, however, to see this trend. In chapter 3, I mentioned extreme political groups whose only discernible principle is the notion of liberty overseen (if it can be called that) by a very minimal federal government. I noted that virtually 100 percent of the groups are male. I might also have noted that virtually 100 percent of the members of these groups are white males. To take a more hopeful example, African American men have been shown to be more likely than white men to visit/be visited by friends and to attend church/other group functions.[3] Additionally, both African Americans and Hispanic Americans are more likely to attend church than are European Americans, and church attendance has been shown to be a protective factor against suicide and a host of other problems, including loneliness.[4] More so than white men, non-white men have loneliness buffers built into their family networks and religious life, to their benefit.

There are still other demographic factors, besides gender and ethnicity, that may affect the trends and processes described in this book. Consider, in this context, birth order. In Frank Sulloway's book *Born to Rebel,* he shows that first-born males are particularly "instrumental," as distinct from "expressive." The instrumental traits, as described in chapter 2 on "Becoming Spoiled," are things like assertiveness, self-confidence, competitiveness, and aggression. The expressive ones are affection, cooperation, and flexibility. These distinctions should sound very familiar by now, and the upshot is that there is one lonely sex, but within that sex, those who are white and first-born are most likely to be affected.

The reasoning here, it should be emphasized, involves probabilities, not certainties. That is, there is a documented *likelihood* that the phenomena described in the book are more common in men than in women, more common in white men than in other men, and more common in first-born than in later-born men. The probabilistic nature of argument allows—in fact, predicts—that these processes will be applicable, to varying degrees, to other demographic groups, too.

For instance, at a few places in the narrative, I have referred to a male suicide decedent who was very dependent on his wife and who refused to seek health care, even though he was aware he needed help. He was suspicious of other people and grew very socially isolated in the years before his death by suicide. This lonely man, as it happens, was Hispanic.

As I write, I am serving as an expert witness regarding the case of a severely mentally ill man who, partly because of his untreated illness, became estranged from his family. Eight years after the last contact with his family, the man died by suicide. His death, like many by suicide, is being litigated. This lonely man, as it happens, was African American.

I have referred to another lonely man throughout the book, my own dad, who also died by his own hand. My dad's case conforms to some of the parameters noted above—he was male and white—but not to another: he was not a first-born, but rather a last-born, the fourth of four children.

A recent article reported on the growing earning power of young single women (though it should be noted that women overall still earn less, on average, than do men). The article states, "The trend was first identified several years ago in the country's biggest cities, but has broadened out to smaller locales and across more industries. . . . The greatest disparity is in Atlanta, where young, childless women were paid 121% the level of their male counterparts."[5]

The news here is mixed. It is hopeful to see income disparities decreasing, but there is much more progress needed, as overall, gender disparities in income favoring men remain the norm. More to the point of this book, loneliness disparities clearly exist, and currently, they are such that men have more loneliness. This has been an animating paradox of this book: that men have more of good things like status, money, preferential treatment, and so on, *and* they have more of bad things, too, like suicide and loneliness. It is conceivable that if women become, for example, more fixated on income and attendant status, that their levels of loneliness may start to inch up. This is one gender disparity,

I hope I have made clear, that women should hope decreases *not* by "catching up" to men, but rather, by men "falling back" to women.

AMONG THE LAST LINES of *The Future Is Unwritten,* a documentary about the life and times of the late Clash front man Joe Strummer, is a disarming and heartfelt remark by Strummer that "without people, you're nothing." This book has attempted to articulate the penetrating truth inherent in these words, to understand why and with what consequences they apply to men in particular, and to plead with men—to forewarn them—that the future is not unwritten; it is written, day in and day out, on the fibers of our relationships with wives, children, family, and friends. "Without people, you're nothing."

NOTES

CHAPTER 1

1. Kirp, 2000, p. 32.
2. Kirp, 2000, p. 32-33.
3. Kirp, 2000, p. 25.
4. Melville, *Moby Dick,* 1892, p. 531.
5. Dodson, 2007.
6. Kawachi, 1996.
7. Xu et al., 2010.
8. "Mars vs. Venus: The gender gap in health." *Harvard Men's Health Watch,* 2010, p. 1-5.
9. Wrangham, 2009, p. 135.
10. Eberstadt, 2009.
11. Judt, 2005, p. 331.
12. Kung, 2008.
13. Phillips et al., 2010, p. 125.
14. Ojeda & Bergstresser, 2008.
15. Author's personal papers.
16. Keel et al., 2010.
17. Keel et al., 2010.
18. *Men's Health,* November 2010, p. 179.
19. "Harper's index," March 2010, p. 11.
20. Data from the US Bureau of Labor Statistics.
21. Cauchon, September 14, 2010, *USA Today.*
22. McCloskey, 2010.
23. American Association of Suicidology, 2009.
24. Lawrence, 2010.
25. Tony Judt, *The Memory Chalet,* p. 189.
26. *Morning Edition,* 2010, November 16.
27. Burroughs, 2003, p. 91.
28. For example, Koenig & Abrams, 1999; Le Roux, 2009; Mahon et al., 2006.
29. For example, Borys & Perlman, 1985.
30. Kershaw, 1997.
31. Wilson, 2010, p. 39.
32. Joiner & Rudd, 1996; Joiner, 1997; Joiner et al., 1999, 2002.
33. Cohen & Wills, 1985.
34. Shneidman, 1996, p. 14-15.
35. Maris, Berman, Silverman, & Bongar, 2000, p. 266.
36. Kierkegaard, 1989, p. 75.
37. Orwell & Angus, 2000, p. 125.

38. Joiner et al., 2002.
39. Joiner, 2009.
40. Nesse, 1991.
41. For example, Baumeister et al., 2002.
42. Ephron, 2008.
43. James, 1890, p. 293.
44. Witvliet et al., 2010.
45. Burrough, 1998, p. 118.
46. Peplau & Perlman, 1982.
47. Hawkley, Thisted, Masi, & Cacioppo, 2010; House et al., 1988.
48. Collins et al., 1993.
49. Hawkley, Preacher, & Cacioppo, 2010.
50. Joiner, 1997.
51. Kiecolt-Glaser et al., 1984, 1987.
52. Goodwin et al., 1987.
53. Berkman & Syme, 1979.
54. Asarnow & Carlson, 1988.
55. Lewinsohn et al., 1994.
56. Joiner, 2005.
57. Stirman & Pennebaker, 2001.
58. Sym, 1637/1989.
59. Ertel, 2008.
60. Ertel, 2008, p. 1215.
61. Buckley, 2010
62. BBC News, 2009
63. Holt-Lunstad et al., 2010.
64. Epel et al., 2004.
65. Sapolsky, 2004, p. 17324.
66. Kimura et al., 2008.
67. Williams et al., 2009.
68. KSDK.com, 2010.
69. American College Health Association, 2010.
70. Romano & Dokoupil, 2010.

CHAPTER 2

1. Keijsers et al., 2010.
2. Bornstein et al., 2008.
3. DeLoache et al., 2007, p. 1579.
4. Hausman, 2000.
5. Kahlenberg & Wrangham, 2010.
6. Baumeister, 2010, p. 82.
7. Baumeister, 2010, p. 82.
8. Pierce et al., 2011.
9. Real, 1997.
10. Bedi, 2010.
11. Ely & Ryan, 2008.
12. Ericsson et al., 1993.
13. Sheets & Luger, 2005.
14. Poulin & Pederson, 2007.
15. For example, Tony Cassidy, presented at 2009 British Psychological Society meeting.
16. Solnit, 2009, p. 7.
17. "Harper's index," 2010, p. 11.
18. Baumeister, 2000.
19. Kroll-Zaidi, 2010, p. 88.
20. Dunbar, 2010.

21. McCarty et al., 2000.
22. See Lloyd, 1995.
23. Mill, 2001, p. 73.
24. *All Things Considered*, 2010.
25. Wrangham, 2010, p. 107.
26. Brody, 2010.
27. Baumeister, 2010.
28. Foster et al., 2003.
29. Taylor & Armor, 1996.
30. Viding, 2009.
31. Louis C. K., 2010.
32. Mencken, 1919, p. 141.
33. Seery et al., 2010.
34. Murakami, 2008, p. 19.
35. Murakami, 2008, p. 20.
36. Tennis, 2007.
37. Dalrymple, 2010, p. 37-38.
38. Judt, 2005, p. 83.
39. Exley, 1968/1988, p. 9.
40. Baumeister et al., 2003.
41. Dalrymple, 2009, p. 313.
42. Buchholz, 1997, p. 197.
43. Akst, 2010, p. 25.

CHAPTER 3

1. King, 1991, p. 630.
2. Chabon, 2009, p. 129.
3. Freud, 1917/1951, p. 247.
4. Joiner, 1999.
5. Joiner et al., 1997.
6. Joiner, 1995.
7. Cauchon, 2009.
8. Shen et al., 2011, p. 271.
9. Kitayama et al., 2010, p. 560.
10. Henrich et al., 2010, p. 76.
11. Akst, Summer 2010, p. 26.
12. Kitayama et al., 2010, p. 566.
13. *Fresh Air*, 2010.
14. Twenge et al., 2008.
15. Murray, 2009.
16. Kraus et al., 2010, p. 1716.
17. Broesch et al., in press.
18. OECD, 2007.
19. Turnbull, 1972, p. 101.
20. Eliot, 1948, p. 91.
21. Judt, 2006, p. 234.
22. Dalrymple, 2009, p. 116
23. Wolfe, 1976.
24. Lasch, 1979, p. 5.
25. Tocqueville, 1835/1862, p. 293.
26. Desai, 2010.
27. Judt, 2010, p. 154.
28. Zhou et al., 2008.
29. Roan, 2008.
30. Judt, 2010, p. 56.

31. *Fresh Air*, 2010, September 22.
32. Lasch, 1979, p. 128.
33. Chabon, 2009, p. 151.
34. Gilbert, 2006, p. 20.
35. Langer & Rodin, 1976.
36. Constantin, 2010.
37. SouthCoastToday.com, 2010.
38. McKibben, 2008, p. 45-46.
39. Goethe, 1906, p. 64.
40. Indiviglio, 2010.
41. McPherson, Smith-Lovin, & Brashears, 2006.
42. Keel et al., 2007.
43. Buchholz, 1997, p. 197.
44. Henrich et al., 2010, p. 79.
45. Vincent, 2006, p. 159.
46. Spencer, 2008.
47. Baumeister, 2010.
48. Cleckley, 1941, p. 29.

CHAPTER 4

1. Both studies described in Baumeister, 2010, p. 65.
2. Baumeister, 2010, p. 66.
3. For example, Burroughs & Rindfleisch, 2002; Kasser, 2002; Kasser & Ryan, 1993.
4. *Esquire*, 2010.
5. Kasser & Ryan, 1993.
6. Sullivan, 1953, p. 32.
7. Chabon, 2009, p. 138-139.
8. Akst, 2010, p. 25-26.
9. Peterson, 2005.
10. Westerlund et al., 2010, p. 6149.
11. Greene, 2007, p. 235.
12. Greene, 2007, p. 235.
13. Greene, 2007, p. 236.
14. Beauvoir, 1949/2009, p. 283.
15. Baumeister, 2010, p. 101.
16. Wilson, 2010, p. 43.
17. Zhou, Vohs, & Baumeister, 2009.
18. E!, 2009.
19. Zhou, Vohs, & Baumeister, 2009.
20. DeWall et al., 2010.

CHAPTER 5

1. Riesman, 1961, p. 151.
2. Ehrenreich, 2009, p. 189.
3. Osnos, 2010.
4. Tocqueville, 1840, p. 104.
5. Murray, 2009.
6. Jones, 2005.
7. DeWall et al., 2011, p. 61.
8. Danforth, 2010.
9. Maccoby, 1976, p. 100.
10. Maccoby, 1976, p. 110.
11. For example, Jorm, 1987.
12. Lasch, 1979, p. 66.

13. Vincent, 2006, p. 256.
14. Fredrickson, 1998.
15. Fredrickson & Joiner, 2002.
16. Burns et al., 2008.

CHAPTER 6

1. See Cacioppo & Patrick, 2009.
2. Wilson, 1999, p. 6.
3. Wallace, 1997, p. 23.
4. Vitello, 2008.
5. March 13, 2007.
6. Lasch, 1979, p. 100.
7. Lasch, 1979, p. 104.
8. Joiner et al., 2006.
9. Milgram & Sabini, 1978.
10. Van Vugt et al., 2007.
11. Darwin, 1871/2009, p. 110.
12. *Morning Edition,* 2010.
13. Rooney, 2010.
14. Robinson & Martin, 2008.
15. Rabin, 2008.
16. *Esquire,* 2010.
17. Lombardi, 2008.

CHAPTER 7

1. Faulkner, 1957.
2. Faulkner, 1950.
3. Jaffe, 2010.
4. Weinberg & Hajcak, 2010.
5. Ehrenreich, 2009, p. 104.
6. Kellert & Wilson, 1993, p. 31.
7. Roach, 2010, p. 57.
8. Roach, 2010, p 57.
9. Wilson, 2010, p. 95.
10. Department of Work and Pensions, 2010.
11. Lyubomirsky, 2008.
12. Beck, 2010.
13. Vincent, 2008, p. 282.
14. Curry, 2008.
15. Parker-Pope, 2009.
16. Conti et al., 2009.
17. De Botton, 2010, p. 7-9. Gravlax is a dish of raw, cured fish.
18. Marshall, 1976, p. 294.
19. Wrangham, 2009, p. 184.
20. Wrangham, 2009, p. 135.
21. Glenberg & Kaschak, 2002, p. 558.
22. Cacioppo et al., 1993.
23. Beilock & Holt, 2007.
24. Crain, 2008.
25. Boswell, 1791/2008, p. 747.
26. Dobson et al., 2008.
27. Louis C.K., 2010.
28. Cohen, 2010, p. 41.
29. Cohen, 2010, p. 74.

30. Dalrymple, 2009, p. 307.
31. President Obama relieved the general of his command in the wake of negative comments—made more by McChrystal's staff than by the general himself—about the president's policies and personnel. Nevertheless, it is hard to argue that McChrystal is anything but a paragon of human potential and achievement.
32. Osnos, 2010.
33. Gamaldo et al., 2010.
34. Gamaldo et al., 2010, p. 853.
35. Cukrowicz et al., 2006.
36. Krakow et al., 2001.
37. Raskind et al., 2003.
38. Troxel, 2010, p. 580.
39. Buchholz, 1997.
40. Wrangham, 2009, p. 30.
41. Zoroya, 2009.
42. Judt, 2010, p. 21.
43. Lasch, 1979, p. 4-5.
44. Burton, 1621/2010, p. 20.
45. Reported in 2008 in the *Journal of Consulting & Clinical Psychology.*
46. As a new version of the American Psychiatric Association's *Diagnostic and Statistical Manual of Mental Disorders* (DSM) is in preparation, critics have caused somewhat of an uproar by accusing the revision of pathologizing grief. The critics' point is that bereavement is natural and should not be viewed as a mental disorder. The architects of the DSM would agree with this point; they have no intention of viewing usual grief as a mental disorder. On the other hand, they insist, absolutely correctly in my judgment, that reactions like that of my patient—recurrent and severe depressive episodes accompanied by quite serious suicidality—*do* represent a mental disorder.
47. Judt, 2010, p. 164.
48. Rentfrow, Gosling, & Potter, 2008.
49. Witte, Smith, & Joiner, 2010.
50. Wilson, 2010, p. 91.
51. McKibben, 2008, November, p. 45-46.

CHAPTER 8

1. Foucault, 1990, p. 206.
2. Simmonds, 2010.
3. Dern, 2010, November 6.
4. Harounian, 2010.
5. Paz, 1961/1985, p. 195.
6. Buchholz, 1997, p. 278.
7. Dern, 2010.
8. Brooks, 2010.
9. Cohen, 2010, p. 73.
10. Buchholz, 1999, p. 121.
11. McKibben, 2008.
12. Murray, 2009.
13. Dewey, 2004, p. 141.
14. Dewey, 2004, p. 142.
15. Dewey, 2004, p. 145.
16. *Fresh Air,* 2010, October 14.
17. Motto & Bostrom, 2001.
18. Motto & Bostrom, 2001, p. 831.
19. Motto & Bostrom, 2001, p. 831.
20. Fleischmann et al., 2008.
21. Robinson et al., 2009.

22. Sales, 2010.
23. The Press Association, 2010.
24. Farroni et al., 2002.
25. Isbell, 2010.
26. *Fresh Air,* 2010, October 26.
27. Buchholz, 1997, p. 272.
28. *Esquire,* 2010.
29. Barnett, 2004, p. 8.

CHAPTER 9

1. Santayana, 1921, p. 167.
2. *Fresh Air,* 2010, July 7.
3. Snowden, 2001.
4. Dervic et al., 2004.
5. Dougherty, 2010.

REFERENCES

Aboujaoude, E. (2008). *Compulsive Acts*. Berkeley: University of California Press.

Akst, D. (2010, Summer). America: Land of loners? *The Wilson Quarterly*, 23-27.

American Association of Suicidology. (2009). AAS statement on the economy and suicide. Retrieved from http://www.suicidology.org/web/guest/current-research.

American College Health Association. (2010). National college health assessment: Reference group data report spring 2010. Retrieved from http://www.achancha.org/docs/ACHA -NCHA-II_ReferenceGroup_DataReport_Spring2010.pdf.

Asarnow, J. A., & Carlson, G. (1988). Suicide attempts in preadolescent child psychiatry inpatients. *Suicide & Life-Threatening Behavior, 18*, 129-136.

Barnett, T. P. M. (2004). *The Pentagon's New Map*. New York: Berkley Books.

Baumeister, R. (2000). Gender differences in erotic plasticity: The female sex drive as socially flexible and responsive. *Psychological Bulletin, 126*, 347-374.

Baumeister, R. (2010). *Is There Anything Good about Men?* Oxford, England: Oxford University Press.

Baumeister, R., Campbell, J., Krueger, J., & Vohs, K. (2003). Does high self-esteem cause better performance, interpersonal success, happiness, or healthier lifestyles? *Psychological Science in the Public Interest, 4*, 1-44.

Baumeister, R., Twenge, J., & Nuss, C. (2002). Effects of social exclusion on cognitive processes: Anticipated aloneness reduces intelligent thought. *Journal of Personality and Social Psychology, 83*, 817-827.

BBC News (2009, December 8). Loneliness makes cancer 'more likely and deadly. Retrieved from http://news.bbc.co.uk/2/hi/health/8398728.stm.

Beauvoir, S. (2009). *The Second Sex*. C. Borde & S. Malovany-Chevallier (Trans). New York: Alfred A. Knopf. Original published in 1949.

Beck, M. (2010, November 23). Thank you. No, thank you: Grateful people are happier, healthier long after leftovers are gobbled up. *Wall Street Journal*. Retrieved from http:// online.wsj.com/article/SB10001424052748704243904575630541486290052.html.

Bedi, R. S. (2010, November 28). Meet the real Patch Adams. Retrieved from: http://thestar .com.my/news/story.asp?file=/2010/11/28/nation/7516986&sec=nation.

Beilock, S. L., & Holt, L. E. (2007). Embodied preference judgments: Can likeability be driven by the motor system? *Psychological Science, 18*, 51-57.

Berkman, L., & Syme, S. (1979). Social networks, host resistance, and mortality: A nine-year follow-up study of Alameda County residents. *American Journal of Epidemiology, 109*, 186-204.

Bornstein, M., Putnick, D., Heslington, M., Gini, M., Suwalsky, J., Venuti, P., de Falco, S., Giusti, Z., & Zingman de Galperín, C. (2008). Mother-child emotional availability in ecological perspective: Three countries, two regions, two genders. *Developmental Psychology, 44*, 666-680.

Borys, S., & Perlman, D. (1985). Gender differences in loneliness. *Personality & Social Psychology Bulletin, 11*, 63-74.

Boswell, J. (1791/2008). *The Life of Samuel Johnson.* New York: Penguin Books.

Brody, J. E. (2010 , October 18). 100 candles on her next cake, and the three r's to get her there. *The New York Times.* Retrieved from www.nytimes.com/2010/10/19/health /19brody.html

Broesch, T., Callaghan, T., Henrich, J., Murphy, C., & Rochat, P. (in press). Cultural variations in children's mirror self-recognition. *Journal of Cross-Cultural Psychology.*

Brooks, L. (2010, November 21). The transfiguring qualities of silence and solitude. *The Guardian.* Retrieved from http://www.guardian.co.uk/commentisfree/2010/nov/11/trans figuring-qualities-of-silence-and-solitude.

Buchholz, E. (1997). *The Call of Solitude.* New York: Simon & Schuster.

Buckley, T., McKinley, S., Tofler, G., & Bartrop, R. (2010). Cardiovascular risk in early bereavement: A literature review and proposed mechanisms. *International Journal of Nursing Studies, 47*, 229-238.

Burns, A., Brown, J., Sachs-Ericsson, Plant, E., Curtis, T., Fredrickson, B., & Joiner, T. (2008). Upward spirals of positive emotion and coping: Replication, extension, and initial exploration of neurochemical substrates. *Personality & Individual Differences, 44*, 360-370.

Burrough, B. (1998). *Dragonfly.* New York: HarperCollins.

Burroughs, A. (2003). *Dry.* New York: St. Martin's Press.

Burroughs, J., & Rindfleisch, A. (2002). Materialism and well-being: A conflicting values perspective. *Journal of Consumer Research, 29*, 348-370.

Burton, R. (1621/2010). *The Anatomy of Melancholy.* New York: New York Review of Books.

Cacioppo, J., & Patrick, W. (2008). *Loneliness.* New York: W.W. Norton.

Cacioppo, J. T., Priester, J. R., & Berntson, G. G. (1993). Rudimentary determinants of attituees: II. Arm flexion and extension have differential effects on attitudes. *Journal of Personality and Social Psychology, 65*, 5-17.

Cauchon, D. (2010, September 14). Gender pay gap is smallest on record. *USA Today.*

Cauchon, D. (2009, July 30). Older white men hurt more by this recession. *USA Today.*

Chabon, M. (2009). *Manhood for Amateurs.* New York: HarperCollins.

Cleckley, H. (1941). *The Mask of Sanity.* St. Louis, MO: Mosby.

Cohen, S. (2010). *The Victims Return.* Exeter, NH: Publishing Works.

Cohen, S., & Wills, T. A. (1985). Stress, social support, and the buffering hypothesis. *Psychological Bulletin, 98*, 310-357.

Collins, N. L., Dunkel-Schetter, C., Lobel, M., & Scrimshaw, S. C. M. (1993). Social support in pregnancy: Psychosocial correlates of birth outcomes and postpartum depression. *Journal of Personality & Social Psychology, 65*, 1243-1258.

Constantin, B. (2010, November 28). Men's loneliness ends with purchase of potted plant. *The University of Calgary Gauntlet.*

Conti, G., Galeotti, A., Mueller, G., & Pudney, S. (2009). Popularity. *Institute for Social and Economic Research Report.*

Crain, C. (2008, October 30). Lonely together. *The* [United Arab Emirates] *National.* Retrieved from http://www.thenational.ae/arts-culture/books/lonely-together?pageCount=0.

Cukrowicz, K. C., Otamendi, A., Pinto, J. V., Bernert, R. A., Krakow, B. & Joiner, T. E. (2006). The impact of insomnia and sleep disturbances on depression and suicidality. *Dreaming, 16*, 1-10.

Curry, J. (2008, December 10). Baseball takes a back seat to Torre's guys' weekend. *The New York Times.* Retrieved from http://www.nytimes.com/2008/12/11/sports/baseball /11torre.html.

Dalrymple, T. (2009). *Second Opinion.* London: Monday Books.

Dalrymple, T. (2010). *The New Vichy Syndrome.* New York: Encounter Books.

Danforth, S. G. (2010, November 15). Social support at the top. *Milford* [Massachusetts] *Daily News.* Retrieved from http://www.milforddailynews.com/business/ x1615403788 /Social-support-at-the-top.

De Botton, A. (2010, August). Improvable feasts. *Harper's Magazine, 7-9.*

DeLoache, J., Simcock, G., & Macari, S. (2007). Planes, trains, automobiles—and tea sets: Extremely intense interests in very young children. *Developmental Psychology, 43*, 1579-1586.

Department of Work and Pensions (2010, November 23). Government gives £1to help people keep active at 60. Retrieved from http://www.dwp.gov.uk/newsroom/press-releases/2010 /nov-2010/dwp161-10-231110.shtml.

Dern, N. (2010, November 6). Solitude: Why do we fear it? *Huffington Post.* Retrieved from http://www.huffingtonpost.com/natasha-dern/solitude-why-do-we-fear-i_b_776884 .html.

Dervic, K., et al. (2004). Religious affiliation and suicide attempt. *American Journal of Psychiatry, 161*, 2303-2308.

DeWall, C. N., Baumeister, R. F., Mead, N. L., & Vohs, K. D. (2011). How leaders self-regulate their task performance: Evidence that power promotes diligence, depletion, and disdain. *Journal of Personality and Social Psychology, 100*, 47-65.

DeWall, C. N., MacDonald, G., Webster, G. D., Masten, C. L., Baumeister, R. F., Powell, C., Eisenberg, N. I. (2010). Acetaminophen reduces social pain: Behavioral and neural evidence. *Psychological Science, 21*, 931-937.

Dewey, L. (2004). *War and Redemption.* Burlington, VT: Ashgate.

Dobson, K., Hollon, S., Dimidjian, S., Schmaling, K., Kohlenberg, R., Gallop, R., Rizvi, S., Gollan, J., Dunner, D., & Jacobson, N. S. (2008). Randomized trial of behavioral activation, cognitive therapy, and antidepressant medication in the prevention of relapse and recurrence in major depression. *Journal of Consulting and Clinical Psychology, 76*, 468-477.

Dodson, D. C. (2007). Men's health compared with women's health in the 21st century USA. *Journal of Men's Health and Gender, 4*, 121-123.

Dougherty (2010, September 1). Young women's pay exceeds male peers'. *Wall Street Journal.* Retrieved from http://online.wsj.com/article/SB10001424052748704 4211045754 63790770831192.html.

Dunbar, R. (2010). *How Many Friends Does One Person Need?: Dunbar's Number and Other Evolutionary Quirks.* London: Faber & Faber.

E! (2009, September 16). Rich people do not need friends. *E! Science News.* Retrieved from http://esciencenews.com/articles/2009/09/16/rich.people.dont.need.friends.

Eberstadt, N. (2009). Drunken nation: Russia's depopulation bomb. *World Affairs Journal, 171*, http://www.worldaffairsjournal.org/articles/2009-Spring/full-Eberstadt.html.

Ehrenreich, B. (2009). *Bright-Sided.* New York: Metropolitan Books.

Eliot, T. S. (1948). *Christianity & Culture.* Orlando: Harcourt Inc.

Ely, R., & Ryan, E. (2008). Remembering talk: Individual and gender differences in reported speech. *Memory, 16*, 395-409.

Epel, E., Blackburn, E., Lin, J., Dhabhar, F., Adler, N., Morrow, J., & Cawthon, R. (2004). Accelerated telomere shortening in response to life stress. *Proceedings of the National Academy of Sciences, 101*, 17312-17315.

Ephron, N. (2008, April 20). White men. *Huffington Post.*

Ephron, N. (2010). *I Remember Nothing.* New York: Knopf.

Ericsson, K. A., Krampe, R. T., & Tesch-Römer, C. (1993). The role of deliberate practice in the acquisition of expert performance. *Psychological Review, 100*, 363-406.

Ertel, K. A., Glymour, M. M., & Berkman, L. F. (2008). Effects of social integration on preserving memory function in a nationally representative US elderly population. *American Journal of Public Health, 98*, 1215-1210.

Esquire (2010, October). New rules for men. *Esquire Magazine.*

Esquire (2010, October). Survey of American men. *Esquire Magazine.*

Exley, F. (1968/1988). *A Fan's Notes.* New York: Vintage.

Farroni, T., Csibra, G., Simon, F., & Johnson, M. H. (2002). Eye contact detection in humans from birth. *Proceedings from the National Academy of Science, 99*, 9602-9605.

Faulkner, W. (1950). Banquet speech. *Nobelprize.com.* Retrieved from http://nobelprize.org /nobel_prizes/literature/laureates/1949/faulkner-speech.html.

Faulkner, W. (Speaker). (1957). *William Faulkner audio collection* (Digital recording). Charlottesville, VA: University of Virginia Library.

Fleischmann, A., Bertotle, J., Wasserman, D., De Leo, D., Bolhari, J., Botega, N., et al. (2008). Effectiveness of brief intervention and contact for suicide attempters: A randomized control trial in five countries. *Bulletin of the World Health Organization, 86*, 703-709.

Foster, J. D., Campbell, W. K., & Twenge, J. M. (2003). Individual differences in narcissism: Inflated self-views across the lifespan and around the world. *Journal of Research in Personality, 37*, 469-486.

Foucault, M. (1990). *Politics, Philosophy, Culture: Interviews and Other Writings 1977-1984.* New York: Routledge, Chapman, & Hall, Inc.

Fredrickson, B. (1998). What good are positive emotions? *Review of General Psychology, 2*, 300-319.

Fredrickson, B., & Joiner, T. (2002). Positive emotions trigger upward spirals toward emotional well-being. *Psychological Science, 13*, 172-175.

Freud, S. (1951). Mourning and melancholia. In J. Strachey (Ed. & Trans.), *The Standard Edition of the Complete Psychological Works of Sigmund Freud.* (Vol. 14, pp. 237-260). London: Hogarth Press. (Original work published in 1917).

Gamaldo, A. A., Allaire, J. C., & Whitfield, K. E. (2010). Exploring the within-person coupling of sleep and cognition in older African Americans. *Psychology and Aging, 25*, 851-857.

Gilbert, D. (2006). *Stumbling on Happiness.* New York: Knopf.

Gladwell, M. (2000). *The Tipping Point.* New York: Little, Brown, and Company.

Goethe, J. W. (1906). *The Maxims and Reflections of Goethe.* B. Saunders (Trans.). New York: Macmillan.

Goodwin, J. S., Hunt, W. C., Key, C. R., & Samet, J. M. (1987). The effect of marital status on stage, treatment, and survival of cancer patients. *Journal of the American Medical Association, 258*, 3125-3130.

Greene, B. (2006). *And You Know You Should Be Glad.* New York: William Morrow.

Gross, T., & Miller, D. (Producers). (2010, July 7). *Fresh Air* [Radio Broadcast]. Washington D.C.: National Public Radio.

Gross, T., & Miller, D. (Producers). (2010, July 16). *Fresh Air* [Radio Broadcast]. Washington D.C.: National Public Radio.

Gross, T., & Miller, D. (Producers). (2010, September 22). *Fresh Air* [Radio Broadcast]. Washington D.C.: National Public Radio.

Gross, T., & Miller, D. (Producers). (2010, October 4). *Fresh Air* [Radio Broadcast]. Washington D.C.: National Public Radio.

Gross, T., & Miller, D. (Producers). (2010, October 14). *Fresh Air* [Radio Broadcast]. Washington D.C.: National Public Radio.

Gross, T., & Miller, D. (Producers). (2010, October 26). *Fresh Air* [Radio Broadcast]. Washington D.C.: National Public Radio.

Hall, E. (1966). *The Hidden Dimension.* Garden City, NY: Anchor Books.

Harounian, S. I. (2010, November 30). The case for loneliness. *Huffington Post.* Retrieved from http://www.huffingtonpost.com/s-isabelle-harounian/the-case-for-loneliness_b_783073.html.

Harper's index (2010, March). *Harper's Magazine.* 11.

Hausman, P. (2000, April). A tale of two hormones. Address presented at the National Academy of Engineering SE Regional Meeting, Atlanta.

Hawkley L., Preacher K., & Cacioppo J. (2010). Loneliness impairs daytime functioning but not sleep duration. *Health Psychology, 29*, 124-129.

Hawkley L., Thisted R., Masi, C., & Cacioppo J. (2010). Loneliness predicts increased blood pressure: 5-year cross-lagged analyses in middle-aged and older adults. *Psychology & Aging, 25*, 132-141.

Henrich, J. Heine, S. J., & Norenzayan, A. (2010). The weirdest people of the world? *Behavioral and Brain Sciences, 33*, 61-83.

Holt-Lunstad, J., Smith, T., & Layton, J. (2010). Social relationships and mortality risk: A meta-analytic review. *PLoS-Medicine, 7*, e1000316. doi:10.1371/journal.pmed.1000316.

House, J., Landis, K., & Umberton, D. (1988). Social relationships and health. *Science, 241*, 540-545.

Indiviglio, D. (2010, September 12). Profiling baby boomers' job stability. *The Atlantic*. Retrieved from http://www.theatlantic.com/business/archive/2010/09/profiling-baby -boomers-job-stability/62822/.

Isbell, L. (2010). *The Fruit, the Tree, and the Serpent*. Cambridge, MA: Harvard University Press.

Jaffe, E. (2010). Alan Kazdin: Reconsidering clinical psychology. *Observer, 23*. Retrieved from http://www.psychologicalscience.org/index.php/publications/observer/2010/september -10/alan-kazdin-reconsidering-clinical-psychology.html.

James, W. (1890/1950). *The Principles of Psychology*. Mineola, NY: Dover.

Joiner, T. (1995). The price of soliciting and receiving negative feedback: Self-verification theory as a vulnerability to depression theory. *Journal of Abnormal Psychology, 104*, 364-372.

Joiner, T. (1997). Shyness and low social support as interactive diatheses, and loneliness as mediator: Testing an interpersonal-personality view of depression. *Journal of Abnormal Psychology, 106*, 386-394.

Joiner, T. (1999). Self-verification and bulimic symptoms: Do bulimic women play a role in perpetuating their own dissatisfaction and symptoms? *International Journal of Eating Disorders, 26*, 145-151.

Joiner, T. (2005). *Why People Die by Suicide*. Cambridge, MA: Harvard University Press.

Joiner, T. (2009). *Reanalysis of existing loneliness data*. Unpublished manuscript.

Joiner, T. (2010). *Myths about Suicide*. Cambridge, MA: Harvard University Press.

Joiner, T., Catanzaro, S., Rudd, D., & Rajab, H. (1999). The case for a hierarchical, oblique, and bidimensional structure of loneliness. *Journal of Social & Clinical Psychology, 18*, 47-75.

Joiner, T., Katz, J., & Lew, A. (1997). Self-verification and depression in youth psychiatric inpatients. *Journal of Abnormal Psychology, 106*, 608-618.

Joiner, T., Lewinsohn, P. M., & Seeley, J. (2002). The core of loneliness: Lack of pleasurable engagement—more so than painful disconnection—predicts social impairment, depression onset, and recovery from depressive disorders among adolescents. *Journal of Personality Assessment, 79*, 482-501.

Joiner, Jr., T. E., & Rudd, M. D. (1996). Disentangling the inter-relations between hopelessness, loneliness, and suicidal ideation. *Suicide & Life-Threatening Behavior, 26*, 19-26.

Jones, D. (2005, June 20). It's not just lonely at the top: It can be 'disengaging' too. *USA Today*. Retrieved from: http://www.usatoday.com/money/companies/management/2005 -06-20-bummed-execs_x.htm.

Jorm, A. (1987). Sex and age differences in depression: a quantitative synthesis of published research. *Australia & New Zealand Journal of Psychiatry, 21*, 46-53.

Judt, T. (2005). *Postwar*. New York: Penguin Books.

Judt, T. (2010). *The Memory Chalet*. New York: Penguin Books.

Kahlenberg, S. M. & Wrangham, R. W. (2010, December). Sex differences in chimpanzees' use of sticks as play objects resemble those of children. *Current Biology, 20*(24). Retrieved from www.cell.com/current-biology/archive?year=2010.

Kasser, T. (2002). *The High Price of Materialism*. Cambridge, MA: MIT Press.

Kasser, T., & Ryan, R. (1993). A dark side of the American dream: Correlates of financial success as a central life aspiration. *Journal of Personality and Social Psychology, 65*, 410-422.

Kawachi, I., Colditz, G. A., Ascherio, A., Rimm, E. B., Giovannucci, E., Stampfer, M. J., & Willett, W. C. (1996). A prospective study of social networks in relation to total mortality in men in the USA. *Journal of Epidemiology and Community Health, 50*, 245-251.

Keel, P. K., Baxter, M. G., Heatherton, T. F., & Joiner, T. E., Jr. (2007). A 20-year longitudinal study of body weight, dieting, and eating disorder symptoms. *Journal of Abnormal Psychology, 116*, 422-432.

Keel, P., Gravener, J., Joiner, T., & Haedt, A. (2010). Twenty-year follow-up of Bulimia Nervosa and related Eating Disorders Not Otherwise Specified. *International Journal of Eating Disorders, 43*, 492-497.

Keijsers, L., Branje, S., Frijns, T., Finkenauer, C., & Meeus, W. (2010). Gender differences in keeping secrets from parents in adolescence. *Developmental Psychology, 46,* 293-298.

Kellert, S. R., & Wilson, E. O. (1993). *The Biophilia Hypothesis.* Washington D.C.: Island Press.

Kern, J. (Producer). (2010, November 16). *All Things Considered* [Radio Broadcast]. Washington D.C.: National Public Radio.

Kershaw, A. (1997). *Jack London: A Life.* New York: St. Martin's Press.

Kiecolt-Glaser, J. K., Fisher, L. D., Ogrocki, P., Stout, J. C., Speicher, C. E., & Glaser, R. (1987). Marital quality, marital disruption, and immune function. *Psychosomatic Medicine, 49,* 13-34.

Kiecolt-Glaser, J. K., Ricker, D., George, J., Messick, G., Speicher, C. E., Garner, W., & Glaser, R. (1984). Urinary cortisol levels, cellular immunocompetency, and loneliness in psychiatric inpatients. *Psychosomatic Medicine, 46,* 15-23.

Kierkegaard, S. (1989). *The Sickness unto Death.* New York: Penguin Putnam Inc.

Kimura, M., Hjelmborg, J., Gardner, J., Bathum, L., Brimacombe, M., Lu, X., Christiansen, L., Vaupel, J., Aviv, A, & Christensen, K. (2008). Telomere length and mortality: A study of leukocytes in elderly Danish twins. *American Journal of Epidemiology, 167,* 799-806.

King, M. L., Jr. (1991). *A Testament of Hope: The Essential Writings and Speeches of Martin Luther King Jr.* James M. Washington (Ed.). New York: HarperCollins.

Kirp, D. (2000). *Almost Home.* Princeton, NJ: Princeton University Press.

Kitayama, S., Conway, L. G., Pietromonaco, P. R., Park, H., & Plaut, V. C. (2010). Ethos of independence across regions in the United States. *American Psychologist, 65,* 559-574.

Koenig, L., & Abrams, R. (1999). Adolescent loneliness and adjustment: A focus on gender differences. In K. Rotenberg & S. Hymel (Eds.), *Loneliness in Childhood and Adolescence* (pp. 296-322). New York: Cambridge University Press.

Krakow, B., et al. (2001). Imagery Rehearsal Therapy for chronic nightmares in sexual assault survivors with Posttraumatic Stress Disorder. *JAMA, 286,* 537-545.

Kraus, M. W., Cote, S., & Keltner, D. (2010). Social class, contextualism, and empathic accuracy. *Psychological Science, 21,* 1716-1723.

Kroll-Zaidi, R. (2010, October). Findings. *Harper's Magazine,* 88.

KSDK.com (2010, October 27). Americans getting lonelier. http://www.ksdk.com/news/local/story.aspx?storyid=223867&catid=71.

Kung, H., Hoyert, D. L., Xu, J., & Murphy, S. L. (2008). Deaths: Final data for 2005. *National Vital Statistics Reports, 56,* 1-124.

Langer, E. J., & Rodin, J. (1976). The effects of choice and enhanced personal responsibility for the aged: A field experiment in an institutional setting. *Journal of Personality and Social Psychology, 34,* 191-198.

Lasch, C. (1979). *The Culture of Narcissism.* New York: W.W. Norton & Company.

Lawrence, C. (2010, November 28). "Stressed-out jobless tax helping professions." *The New Jersey Record.*

Le Roux, A. (2009). The relationship between adolescents' attitudes toward their fathers and loneliness: A cross-cultural study. *Journal of Child & Family Studies, 18,* 219-226.

Lewinsohn, P. M., Rohde, P., & Seeley, J. R. (1994). Psychosocial risk factors for future adolescent suicide attempts. *Journal of Consulting & Clinical Psychology, 62,* 297-305.

Lloyd, J. (1995). Raising lilies: Ruskin and women. *Journal of British Studies, 34,* 325-350.

Lombardi, L. (2008, January 17). 10 offbeat places to meet guys. *MSN.com.* Retrieved from http://www.match.com/msn/article.aspx?articleid=9121&ap=1.

Lyubomirsky, S. (2008). *The How of Happiness.* New York: Penguin.

Maccoby, M. (1976). *The Gamesman: The New Corporate Leaders.* New York: Simon & Schuster.

Mahon, N., Yarcheski, A., Yarcheski, T., Cannella, B., & Hanks, M. (2006). A meta-analytic study of predictors for loneliness during adolescence. *Nursing Research, 55,* 308-315.

McCarty, C., Kilworth, P., Bernard, H., Johnsen, E., & Shelley, G. (2000). Comparing two methods for estimating network size. *Human Organization, 60,* 28-39.

McCloskey, D. Needed: An economics for grownups. *National Review Online,* November 22, 2010.

McDonnell, E. (Producer). (2010, November 16). *Morning Edition* [Radio Broadcast]. Washington D.C.: National Public Radio.

McKibben, B. (2008, November). Localize. *Harper's Magazine.* 45-46.

McPherson, M., Smith-Lovin, L., & Brashears, M. (2006). Social isolation in America: Changes in core discussion networks over two decades. *American Sociological Review, 71,* 353-375.

Melville, H. (1892). *Moby Dick.* Boston: C. H. Simonds Company.

Mencken, H. L. (1919). *Prejudices: First Series.* New York: Alfred A. Knopf.

Men's Health (2010, November). 179.

Mill, J. S. (2001). *The subjection of women: A critical edition.* Edward Alexander (Ed.). New Brunswick, NJ: Transaction Publishers.

Minois, G. (1999). *History of Suicide.* Baltimore: Johns Hopkins University Press.

Motto, J. A., & Bostrom, A. (2001). A randomized controlled trial of postcrisis suicide prevention. *Psychiatric Services, 52,* 828-833.

Murakami, H. (2008). *What I Talk about When I Talk about Running.* New York: Vintage.

Murray, C. (2009, March 16). The Europe syndrome and the challenge to American exceptionalism. *The American.* Retrieved from http://www.american.com/archive/2009/march-2009/.

Nesse, R. (1991, November/December). What good is feeling bad? The evolutionary benefits of psychic pain. *The Sciences,* 30-37.

OECD (2007). *PISA 2006: Science Competencies for Tomorrow's World: Volume 1: Analysis,* PISA, OECD Publishing.

Ojeda, V. D., & Bergstresser, S. M. (2008). Gender, race-ethnicity, and psychosocial barriers to mental health care: An examination of perceptions and attitudes among adults reporting unmet need. *Journal of Health and Social Behavior, 49,* 317-334.

Okrent, D. (2010). *Last Call.* New York: Scribner.

Orwell, S, & Angus, I. (Eds.) (2000). *George Orwell: In Front of Your Nose.* Jaffrey, NH: Nonpareil.

Osnos, E. (2010, October 4). The next incarnation: As the Dalai Lama turns seventy-five, what is Tibet's future?. *The New Yorker.* Retrieved from http://www.newyorker.com/reporting/2010/10/04/101004fa_fact_osnos.

Parker-Pope, T. (2009, April 20). What are friends for? A longer life. *The New York Times.* Retrieved from http://www.nytimes.com/2009/04/21/health/21well.html.

Paz, O. (1961/1985). *The Labyrinth of Solitude.* New York: Grove Pres.

Peplau, L. A., & Perlman, D. (Eds.) (1982). *Loneliness: A Sourcebook of Current Theory, Research and Therapy.* New York: Wiley-Interscience.

Peterson, D. (2005). *Twelve Years of Correspondence with Paul Meehl.* Mahwah, NJ: Erlbaum.

Phillips, J. A., Robin, A. V., Nugent, C. N., & Idler, E. L. (2010, September-October). Understanding recent changes in suicide rates among the middle-aged: Period or cohort effects? *Public Health Reports,* 680-688.

Pierce, K., Conant, D., Hazin, R., Stoner, R., & Desmond, J. (2011). Preference for geometric patterns early in life as a risk factor for autism. *Archives of General Psychiatry, 68,* 101-109.

Poulin, F., & Pedersen, S. (2007). Developmental changes in gender composition of friendship networks in adolescent girls and boys. *Developmental Psychology, 43,* 1484-1496.

Raskind, M. A. et al. (2003). Reduction of nightmares and other PTSD symptoms in combat veterans by prazosin: A placebo-controlled study. *American Journal of Psychiatry, 160,* 371-373.

Real, T. (1997). *I Don't Want To Talk about It.* New York: Scribner.

Rentfrow, R., Gosling, S., & Potter, J. (2008). A theory of the emergence, persistence, and expression of geographic variation in personality traits. *Perspectives on Psychological Science, 3,* 339-369.

Riesman, D. (1961). *The Lonely Crowd.* New Haven, CT: Yale University Press.

Roach, M. (2010). *Packing for Mars.* New York: Vintage.

Roan, S. (2008, December 28). Maybe nostalgia's gotten a bad rap. *Los Angeles Times.*

Robinson, J., Hetrick, S., Gook, S., Cosgrave, E., Yuen, H. P., McGorry, P., & Yung, A. (2009). Study protocol: The development of a randomised controlled trial testing a postcard intervention designed to reduce suicide risk among young help-seekers. *BMC Psychiatry, 9.*

Romano, A. & Dokoupil, T. (2010, September 20). Men's lib. *Newsweek.*

Sales, D. (2010, November 19). Inventor makes real love machine. *The Sun.* Retrieved from http://www.thesun.co.uk/sol/homepage/news/3236725/Inventor-makes-real-love-machine.html.

Santayana, G. (1921). *Character and opinion in the United States.* New York: Charles Scribner's Sons.

Sapolsky, R. (2004). Organismal stress and telomeric aging: An unexpected connection. *Proceedings of the National Academy of Sciences, 101,* 17323-17324.

Sartre, J-P. (1938). *Nausea.* Paris, France: Editions Gallimard.

Sartre, J-P. (1944). *No Exit.* Paris, France: Librairie Gallimard.

Sartre, J-P. (1960). *Critique of Dialectical Reason.* Paris, France: Editions Gallimard.

Seery, M. D., Holman, E. A., & Silver, R. C. (2010). Whatever does not kill us: Cumulative lifetime adversity, vulnerability, and resilience. *Journal of Personality and Social Psychology, 99,* 1025-1041.

Sheets, V., & Lugar, R. (2005). Friendship and gender in Russia and in the United States. *Sex Roles, 52,* 131-141.

Shen, H., Wan, F., Wyer, R. S. Jr. (2011). Cross-cultural differences in the refusal to accept a small gift: The differential influence of reciprocity norms on Asians and North Americans. *Journal of Personality and Social Psychology, 100,* 271-281.

Shneidman, E. (1996). *The Suicidal Mind.* Oxford, England: Oxford University Press.

Simmonds, R. J. (2010, November 12). Loneliness is not a four-letter word. *Vail* [Colorado] *Daily.* Retrieved from http://www.vaildaily.com/article/20101112/NEWS/101119937.

Snowden, L. R. (2001). Barriers to effective mental health services for African Americans. *Mental Health Services Research, 3,* 181-187.

Solnit, R. (2009). *A Paradise Built in Hell.* New York: Viking Press.

Spencer, S. (2008, July). The toll of testosterone. *Oprah: The Magazine.* Retrieved from http://www.oprah.com/spirit/Men-Violence-and-Testosterone-by-Scott-Spencer.

Stirman, S.W., & Pennebaker, J.W. (2001). Word use in the poetry of suicidal and nonsuicidal poets. *Psychosomatic Medicine, 63,* 517-522.

Sullivan H. S. (1953). *The Interpersonal Theory of Psychiatry.* New York: W.W. Norton & Company.

Sulloway, F. (1996). *Born to Rebel.* New York: Vintage.

Sym, J. (1637/1989). *Lifes Preservative against Self-Killing.* Georgetown, ON, Canada: Routledge, Chapman & Hall.

Taylor, S. E., & Armor, D. A. (1996). Positive illusions and coping with adversity. *Journal of Personality, 64,* 873-898.

Tennis, C. (2007, August). Are men spoiled rotten? *Salon.*

The Press Association (2010, November 21). Gadgets 'no substitute for talking.' *London Glossy Magazine.* Retrieved from http://londonglossy.com/2010/11/gadgets-no-substitute-for-talking/.

Tocqueville, A. (1840). *Democracy in America: Part the Second.* H. Reeve (Trans.). New York: Thomas, Cooperwaite, & Co.

Tocqueville, A. (1862). *Democracy in America.* H. Reeve (Trans.). London: Longman, Green, Longman, & Roberts. Originally published in 1835.

Troxel, W. M. (2010). It's more than sex: Exploring the dyadic nature of sleep and implications for health. *Psychosom Med, 72,* 578-586.

Turnbull, C. (1972). *The Mountain People.* New York: Simon & Schuster.

Twenge, J. M., Konrath, S., Foster, J. D., Campbell, W. K., & Bushman, B. J. (2008). Egos inflating over time: A cross-temporal meta-analysis of the narcissistic personality inventory. *Journal of Personality, 76,* 875-901.

US Bureau of Labor Statistics. Record unemployment among older workers does not keep them out of the job market. *Issues in Labor Statistics, 10,* 1-3.

Viding, E., Simmonds, E., Petrides, K. V., & Frederickson, N. (2009). The contribution of callous-unemotional traits and conduct problems to bullying in early adolescence. *Journal of Child Psychology and Psychiatry, 50,* 471-481.

Vincent, N. (2006). *Self-Made Man.* New York: Viking Press.

Vincent, N. (2008). *Voluntary Madness.* New York: Viking Press.

Vitello, P. (2008, February 21). More Americans are giving up golf. *The New York Times.* Retrieved from http://www.nytimes.com/2008/02/21/nyregion/21golf.html.

Wallace, D. F. (1997). "E unibus pluram: television and U.S. fiction." In *A Supposedly Fun Thing I'll Never Do Again.* New York: Back Bay Books.

Weinberg, A., & Hajcak, G. (2010). Beyond good and evil: The time course of neural activity elicited by specific picture content. *Emotion, 10,* 767-782.

Weiner, E. (2008). *The Geography of Bliss.* New York: Twelve.

Westerlund, H., Vahtera, J., Ferrie, J. E., Singh-Manoux, A., Leineweber, C., Jokela, M., Siegrist, J., Goldberg, M., Zins, M., & Kivimaki, M. (2010). Effect of retirement on major chronic conditions and fatigue: French GAZEL occupational cohort study. *British Medical Journal, 341,* 6149.

Williams, J. B., Pang, D., Delgado, B., Kocheginsky, M., Tretiakova, M, Krausz, T. Conzen, S. D. (2009). A model of gene-environment interaction reveals altered mammary gland gene expression and increased tumor growth following social isolation. *Cancer Prevention Research, 2,* 850-861.

Wilson, E. (2010). *The Mercy of Eternity.* Evanston, IL: Northwestern University Press.

Witte, T. K., Smith, A. R., & Joiner, T. E. (2010). Reason for cautious optimism? Two studies suggesting reduced stigma against suicide. *Journal of Clinical Psychology, 66,* 611-626.

Witvliet M., Brendgen M., van Lier, P., Koot, H., & Vitaro F. (2010). Early adolescent depressive symptoms: prediction from clique isolation, loneliness, and perceived social acceptance. *Journal of Abnormal Child Psychology, 38,* 1045-1056.

Wolfe, T. (1976, August 23). The 'me' decade and the third great awakening. *New York Magazine.* Retrieved from http://nymag.com/news/features/45938/.

Wrangham, R. (2009). *Catching Fire.* New York: Basic Books.

Xu, J., Kochanek, K. D., Murphy, S. L., & Tejada-Vera, B. (2010). Deaths: Final data for 2007. *National Vital Statistics Reports, 58,* 1-136.

Zhou, X., Sedikides, C., Wildschut, T., & Gao, D. (2008). Counteracting loneliness: On the restorative function of nostalgia. *Psychological Science, 19,* 1023-1029.

Zhou, X., Vohs, K. D., & Baumeister, R. F. (2009). The symbolic power of money: Reminders of money alter social distress and physical pain. *Psychological Science, 20,* 700-706.

Zoroya, G. (2009, July 28). Program aims to curb Marine suicides. *USA Today.* Retrieved from http://www.usatoday.com/news/military/2009-07-27-marinesuicide_N.htm.

INDEX